GENERAL SIBLEY.

HISTORY

OF

THE SIOUX WAR

AND

Massacres of 1862 and 1863.

BY

ISAAC V. D. HEARD.

WITH PORTRAITS AND ILLUSTRATIONS.

NEW YORK:
HARPER & BROTHERS, PUBLISHERS,
FRANKLIN SQUARE.
1864.

PREFACE.

THE writer of the following pages has resided in the State of Minnesota twelve years, commencing at a time anterior to the removal of the Sioux from their ancient possessions to their reservations upon the Minnesota River. He was a member of General Sibley's expedition against the savages in 1862, from its arrival at St. Peter's in August until its return in November, and acted as the Recorder of the Military Commission which tried some four hundred of the participants in the outbreak. During that time and since, he devoted particular attention to obtaining from Indians, half-breeds, traders, white captives, fugitives from massacres, and others, particulars of the various outrages and the causes of the massacre. He has also carefully read the public treaties and other documents connected with Indian affairs, and the various newspaper articles pertinent thereto.

From the information thus derived, he has endeavored to form a connected and reliable history. He regrets that the haste required to place it before the public, while attention is directed to the subject, has militated against the symmetry of arrangement and finish of composition which should accompany such a work. It was his desire that portraits of Colonel Crooks, Colonel Miller, Major Brown, Major Forbes, the Rev. S. R. Riggs, and other noted men connected with the war, accompanied by personal notices, should have a place in the volume, but the publishers were not willing to incur the addititional expense.

He avails himself of this opportunity to acknowledge his great indebtedness to Mr. Antoine Frenier, the Sioux interpreter, for his patient interpretation of the many interviews he found it necessary to hold with the Indians. He now submits the result of his labors to the charitable perusal of the reader.

New York City, September 30, 1863.

CONTENTS.

CHAPTER I.

THE SCENE AND THE ACTORS.

The Actors.—Travelers and Traders.—Treaties.—Condition of the Indians.—Little Crow.—The Reservations....................Page 13

CHAPTER II.

CAUSES OF THE OUTBREAK.

Predisposition to Hostility.—Extortion of the Traders.—Corruptions in the Indian Department.—Red Iron and Governor Ramsey.—Lean Bear.—Sufferings of the Indians.—Intense Excitement.—Visit of the Sissetons and Wahpetons to the Upper Agency.—The Lower Agency.—The Lower Reservation.—The "Soldiers' Lodge." —Council at Rice Creek.. 31

CHAPTER III.

A SPARK OF FIRE.

A Quarrel.—A Murder.—The Alarm given............................ 52

CHAPTER IV.

COMMENCEMENT OF THE MASSACRES AND THE BATTLE OF RED-WOOD FERRY.

Council at Crow's House.—The "Signal-gun" and the Attack.—Escape of Rev. Mr. Hindman.—Burning of "the Agency."—Flight on all sides.—Captain Marsh and the Fifth Minnesota Volunteers. —Battle at the Ferry.—Council of Upper Indians.—Other Day 59

CHAPTER V.

THE ATTACKS UPON NEW ULM AND FORT RIDGELY.

The Alarm given at St. Peter's.—Re-enforcement of Fort Ridgely.—Fight at New Ulm.—Attack on Fort Ridgely by Little Crow.—Arrival of the Upper Indians.—General Engagement at New Ulm. —Repulse of the Indians.. 78

CHAPTER VI.

FARTHER OUTRAGES DURING THE FIRST WEEK OF THE OUTBREAK.

Murders at Yellow Medicine Agency.—Lean Bear, White Lodge, and Sleepy Eyes at Lake Shetek Settlement.—Horrible Outrage. —Lady Captives.—Story of Mrs. Hurd.—Tidings of the Massacre reach St. Paul.—Exciting Rumors................................Page 96

CHAPTER VII.

FORCES DISPATCHED TO THE FRONTIER.

Sibley moves up the Valley.—Arrival of Troops at New Ulm and Fort Ridgely.—No Indians found.................................... 117

CHAPTER VIII.

BIRCH COOLIE.

Major J. R. Brown dispatched to the Lower Agency.—Fate of the Expedition.—Battle of Birch Coolie................................ 131

CHAPTER IX.

THE WAR PARTY TO THE BIG WOODS.

Pursuit of Captain Strout's Force by Little Crow.—Fort Abercrombie besieged.. 138

CHAPTER X.

THE CAPTIVES.

Little Crow disposed to Peace.—Troubles between Upper and Lower Indians.—Paul's Speech to the Lower Indians.—Little Crow writes to Colonel Sibley.—Disputes as to Delivery of Prisoners....... 143

CHAPTER XI.

UPWARD MARCH AND BATTLE OF WOOD LAKE.

Breaking up of Camp at Fort Ridgely.—Battle of Wood Lake.—Other Day's Pledge.. 167

CHAPTER XII.

CAMP RELEASE.

Need of Cavalry.—Release of Captives.—Military Commission appointed.—Godfrey... 181

CHAPTER XIII.

GODFREY'S STORY.

Godfrey's personal History.—Painted by the Indians.—What Godfrey did and what he saw.. 191

CHAPTER XIV.

CAPTIVITY OF THE FAMILY OF JOSEPH R. BROWN.

Narrative of Samuel Brown.—The Warning.—Encounter with the Indians.—Cut-nose.—Little Crow's Protection ....Page 202

CHAPTER XV.

MRS. HUGGINS'S STORY.

A sad Birthday.—Alarm at Lac qui Parle.—The Flight.—Walking Spirit.—Sacred Nest.—Good Day's Proposition.—A Fright.—A long Journey 209

CHAPTER XVI.

HOMEWARD BOUND.

A Hurricane.—Homeward March.—Trials at the Lower Agency.—The Prairie Fire.—Attack on the Prisoners at New Ulm.—Estimate of Losses in 1862.—Incomplete Preparation.—Loss of the Indians 231

CHAPTER XVII.

TRIALS OF THE PRISONERS.

Trial of Godfrey.—Punishment commuted.—Manner of Proceeding.—Excuses of the Prisoners.—Humors of the Court-room.—Cut-nose.—Sentences given and their Justice.—Instances of New England "Barbarity" 251

CHAPTER XVIII.

EXECUTION.

Reading of the President's Order to the sentenced.—Regulations.—Statements of the Prisoners.—Death-dance and Song.—Ascent of the Scaffold.—The Execution and Burial 272

CHAPTER XIX.

DEATH OF LITTLE CROW.

Devil's Lake.—Little Crow at St. Joseph.—Renewed Massacres.—Little Crow shot by Mr. Lampson and "done up" for the Historical Society.—Son of Little Crow 296

CHAPTER XX.

THRILLING AND FATAL ADVENTURE OF MESSRS. BRACKETT AND FREEMAN.

Mr. Brackett's Narrative.—Encounter with the Indians.—Freeman shot.—Lone Prairie Grave 313

CHAPTER XXI.

THE BATTLES ON THE MISSOURI.

The Battle of Big Mound.—Battle of Dead Buffalo Lake.—Battle of Stony Lake.—Skirmish on the Missouri......................Page 321

CHAPTER XXII.

THE FUTURE.

Continuance of Hostilities.—Disaffection among the Tribes.—Danger of War with the Chippeways.—Cost of the Sioux War.—Some practical Suggestions... 337

APPENDIX.

AN APPEAL FOR THE RED MAN.

By Bishop Whipple, of Minnesota...................................... 343

LIST OF ILLUSTRATIONS.

	PAGE
Portrait of General Sibley	*Frontispiece.*
Indian Tepees	15
House of Chaska, a civilized Indian	19
Dr. Williamson's House	23
Squaws winnowing Wheat	29
Little Crow	60
The Captive saved	63
Other Day	75
Charles E. Flandreau	79
Escape of the Missionaries	87
Mrs. Estlick and Children	110
Hole-in-the-Day	114
Red Iron	155
Standing Buffalo	160
Little Paul	166
W. R. Marshall	174
Indian Camp taken by Colonel Sibley	180
Old Betz	182
Camp Release	183
Indian Boy	185
Cut-nose	204
Wild-Goose-Nest Lake	230
Indian Camp at Red-Wood	233
The Court-house of the Military Commission	238
Prairie on Fire	241
The Attack at New Ulm	245
Camp Lincoln	249
Interior of Indian Jail	273
One of the executed Indians	292
Devil's Lake	297
St. Joseph, from Pembina	301
Fort Garry	305
Lone Prairie Grave	320

THE SIOUX WAR AND MASSACRE.

CHAPTER I.

THE SCENE AND THE ACTORS.

IN the month of August, 1862, the Indians of the Upper Minnesota initiated a massacre which stands prominent in the bloody drama which attends the advance of the white race across the continent. The atrocities by which it was attended—the attempt of the actors to enlist other savage tribes on their behalf—the mysterious part enacted by the negro Godfrey, who received from the Indians the name of "Otakle," or "he who kills many"—the course of their great orator and chief, Little Crow, who was not second to Philip, Pontiac, or Tecumseh—the perilous condition of the captive whites, their shameful treatment, and the peculiar manner in which their deliverance was accomplished—the trial of over four hundred of the accused, and the simultaneous execution of thirty-eight of their number, are full of thrilling interest.

Those engaged in the massacre were, with but few exceptions, members of the M'dewakanton, Wahpekuta, Wahpeton, and Sisseton tribes of the great Sioux, or Dakota nation. They formerly occupied the north-eastern portion of Iowa, part of the western border of Wisconsin, the southwestern half of the State of Minnesota, and adjoining possessions in Dakota; a vast, fertile, and beautiful land, with great undulating plains, over which herds of buffalo roamed; with groves and woodlands in which the deer found a hiding-place; with countless lakes, and streams, and mighty rivers filled with choicest fish, and swarming with myriads of wild-fowl, the duck, the goose, the swan, and the brant; and their shores alive with the otter, the mink, and the beaver.

Their existence, customs, and manner of life have long been familiar to the whites. A hundred years before the American Revolution, the adventurous Hennepin, the first man who gave to the world a drawing of the cataract of Niagara, visited them, and on his return published a narrative of his adventures. Carver, Nicollet, Long, Schoolcraft, Cass, Frémont, Marryatt, and other travelers of repute, followed afterward. Catlin, the great Indian painter, has preserved the faces of their prominent chiefs on his immortal canvas, and Schiller and Longfellow have sung of them in their melodious verse.

As early as 1700 Dakotas visited Montreal, and Wabashaw, their head chief, was received at Mackinaw with greater honors than the Choctaws, Chickasaws, and Ojibeways, who were also present. The British officer in command wrote a song in honor of his coming, of which the following is the last refrain:

"Hail to great Wabashaw!
Soldiers! your triggers draw!
Guards! wave the colors, and give him the drum;
Choctaw and Chickasaw,
Whoop for great Wabashaw,
Raise the portcullis, the king's friend is come."

Quickly following the earliest traveler came the

INDIAN TEPEES.

traders, to exchange the commodities of civilization for furs, and, intoxicated with the wild and romantic life, and supplied by their principals at home with luxuries, intermarried with the natives, and established themselves permanently in the country.

At first they were received unwillingly, and occasional difficulties arose; but so necessary were they to supply the increased wants of the Indian, that when the English withdrew their traders from the country on account of the murder of one of their number, and refused to allow their return until the guilty parties were delivered for punishment, Wabashaw, the grandfather of the present chief of that name, to relieve the distress of his people, worked his toilsome way to Quebec, and gave himself up to be punished in the place of the murderer, who could not be found.

So, too, when the war of 1812 broke out, these tribes, although they had made a treaty of peace with the United States, and ceded a tract of land at the mouth of the Minnesota for the establishment of a military post, were easily induced by the traders, who were English subjects, to act as the allies of their government, and they composed a portion of the forces which compelled the surrender of the post at Mackinaw and besieged Fort Meigs.

Some time after peace was declared our own traders gained a foothold, and in 1825 a convention was entered into at Prairie du Chien between the tribes and the United States, by which it was agreed that every act of hostility committed by either of the contracting parties against the other should be mutually forgotten and forgiven, and that perpetual peace and amity should thereafter exist between them. In 1830 and

1836 they ceded part of their lands in Iowa, and in 1837 all that portion lying east of the Mississippi River. In 1849 Minnesota was organized as a territory, and the emigration rapidly settling upon the eastern shore of the Mississippi soon began to require and encroach upon the more fertile country opposite.

So in 1851 the Indians were induced to sign treaties by which they transferred to the United States over thirty millions of acres, embracing all their lands in Iowa, Dakota, and Minnesota, except a tract along the Upper Minnesota, which they reserved for their future occupancy and home. This commenced just below Fort Ridgely, and extended 150 miles to Lake Traverse, with a width of ten miles on each side of the river.

The Senate in 1852 approved the treaty, provided that the Indians would agree to an amendment by which the reservation should also be ceded, and they be located in such land as the President should select; and to this the Indians assented. The President never having made the selection contemplated, and the Indians having moved upon the reservation made in the first treaties, the government recognized their right to its possession, and in 1858, by treaties which were approved in 1860, purchased from them all that portion of the tract on the north side of the river. They continued to reside on the remainder until the outbreak, the M'dewakantons and Wahpekutas occupying in common all below the Yellow Medicine River, which was called the "Lower Reservation," and the other two tribes the part above the river, which was styled the "Upper Reservation."

Pursuant to the various treaties, large amounts of

HOUSE OF CHASKA, A CIVILIZED INDIAN.

money and goods were annually delivered to them, and labor performed for their benefit. For the superintendence of these matters, an agent resided among them, and two places for the transaction of business were established, one fourteen miles above Fort Ridgely, on the Minnesota River, and known as the "Lower" or "Redwood Agency," and the other at the mouth of the Yellow Medicine, and designated as the "Upper" or "Yellow Medicine Agency."

The habitations of the Indians were of a very comfortable character. Some lived in low circular houses, made by themselves from wood, and covered with bark; others in brick houses a story and a half high, constructed by the government; and others in tepees of canvas, resembling the Sibley tent now in use in our army, which was modeled after their tepees by the rebel General Sibley when stationed in Minnesota.

The different bands, under their hereditary chief, occupied separate villages, with the exception of some hundred families who had been induced by divers considerations to become "white men," and who lived together without distinction of bands. They had their hair cut short, wore coats and pantaloons, attended church and schools, cultivated the soil, elected their president or chief after the manner of a republic, were married by a clergyman, and buried their dead in the ground. The others remained *Indians*, left their hair unshorn, wore the breechcloth, blanket, and leggins, married as many wives as they pleased, after their own fashion, placed their dead on scaffoldings in the open air, made themselves brave with paint and with the feathers of the eagle, went upon the war-path against the Chippeways, and tortured, killed, scalped, and mutilated men, women, and children. In addition to the Indian population were many half-breeds or mixed-bloods, and a large number of whites, consisting of traders, employés of the government, and others. Around the agencies were churches, and schools, and warehouses, and stores, and residences, and shops, forming thriving villages. A few miles above the Yellow Medicine were the churches and schools of the Rev. S. R. Briggs and Dr. Williamson, long missionaries among the Sioux. At Lac qui Parle there was the dwelling-house and school of another missionary, the Rev. Mr. Huggins, and a store-house and blacksmith-shop belonging to the government; and on Big Stone Lake, at the upper extreme of the reservation, and at other points, trading-posts were established. The reservation was fertile and well adapted to farming purposes. There was an excellent road through it, upon which had recently been placed, over the sloughs and streams, eighteen well-constructed bridges, two of them fifty and one sixty-seven feet in length. About three thousand acres had been plowed, fenced, and planted, and which, as was afterward estimated, would have yielded, had the Indians remained and made a proper harvesting, over one hundred thousand bushels of corn, potatoes, and turnips, besides five hundred bushels of wheat, and large quantities of beans, peas, pumpkins, and other vegetables. At both agencies were saw-mills and corn-mills, and at the upper agency a brick-yard, where was manufactured a fine article similar to that made from the Milwaukee clay; also at both agencies were blacksmith and carpenter shops, where wagons, sleds, and farming utensils were made, and other ordinary work done. The

DR. WILLIAMSON'S HOUSE.

Indians had plows, hoes, scythes, cradles, ox-gearing, harness, carts, wagons, and the usual farming implements, and oxen, cows, calves, and sheep, and horses.* Large quantities of hay had been cut and partially cured, and the materials for the erection of some seventy or eighty new buildings prepared. The "Farmer" Indians had coats, pants, shirts, coffee, tea, salt, sugar, candles, soap, vinegar, molasses, rice, and lard, and tubs, buckets, churns, hardware, and queensware, and other household articles. New blacksmith shops were being put in operation at different points, and at the "Lower Agency" a bed of clay suitable for the manufacture of brick, and similar to the one at Yellow Medicine, had been discovered, and work commenced upon it for the purpose.

The agent, Mr. Galbraith, who was energetic and faithful, visited the whole reservation shortly before the outbreak, and congratulated himself on the thriving appearance of affairs. A conversation which he had with Little Crow, their head chief, three days before the fatal 18th of August, furnished no indication of what was about to transpire. Being aware of Crow's influence among the Blanket Indians, Mr. Galbraith had previously promised to build him a good house if he would aid in bringing around the idle young men to habits of industry and civilization, and would abandon the leadership of the Blanket Indians. Crow assented to this, and the carpenter-work had been ordered and nearly completed; and in the conversation before alluded to, Little Crow selected a location for it, and seemed to be well pleased with its position. He had shortly before been defeated for the

* See Agent Galbraith's Report.

speakership of the Lower Indians, but he said he cared nothing about this, for, if elected, the other Indians would be jealous of him. He stated he had a store, a yoke of oxen, a wagon, and plenty of corn and potatoes, and was now living more comfortably than ever before. He said he had just been grinding his scythe to cut hay, and that two or three of his young relatives were coming to help him, and that they would soon cure enough for winter. There was a young Indian of his band present who, Crow said, could make good gunstocks, and he showed a well-finished stock which he had made, and requested that he should have sent to him a set of tools with which to work. Crow had spoken of this before, and Galbraith told him he had sent for a complete set, and that they would soon arrive. These, he said, were all the requests he had to make, and believed they would be complied with. So far removed from the agent's thoughts was the terrible tragedy which afterward ensued, that the day before its occurrence, leaving his family at Yellow Medicine among the Indians, he started for Fort Snelling with some forty-five men whom he had recruited on the reservation, consisting of half-breeds, employés of the government, and went as far as St. Peter's.

Over the soil which Indians had sold civilization had made rapid strides. From Ireland, Germany, Norway, and Sweden, and many another country of the Old World, and from every part of the New, had come a quarter of a million of people, and made the land their home. Through the once quiet waters of Lake Pepin, past the tall cliff from which Winona had taken her death-leap, countless steam-boats puffed their way, and within earshot of the cave where Carver heard the Dakotas moaning and weeping for their departed, the locomotive uttered its harsh scream.

At St. Anthony's Falls, over which the canoe of Scarlet Dove dashed when she sung her last song, and to which the trembling Indian brought

"Belts of porcelain, pipes, and rings,
Tributes to be hung in air
To the fiend presiding there,"

prosperous villages had sprung up, and its mad waters whirled industry's vast machinery in obedience to the voice of man. Far and wide, where the buffalo roamed, herds of cattle and the quiet sheep-flock grazed, and the plowman turned the glebe. The scaffolding on which the Indian placed his dead passed away, and the cemetery, with its cross and whitened marbles, took its place. Almost within stone's-throw of the reservation was the prosperous town of New Ulm, and emigrants even crowded upon the land invacated by the treaty of 1858. Every where appeared those works by which the great Caucasian mind asserts itself supreme. Nor did the whites fear the Indians. It is true that Inkpaduta and eight of his band, in 1858, had killed some forty persons, but they were outlaws from their tribe, their acts were discountenanced by their nation, and one of them fell by the hand of Other Day, a native Dakota.

The weird religion of the savage, his mad dances, his antique traditions, his strange attire, attracted attention and interest, which were increased by the certainty of his not very distant extinction, and the fact that he would never be forgotten while river, and lake, and hill, and state, and county, and city, and town should owe to his language their beautiful and harmonious names. He passed unmolested on his hunting excursions through the settlements, and was entertained at the homes of the whites, and bartered with them the game which he killed. He battled with the Chippeways in view of the town of Shakopee, and danced his scalp-dance, and swung the reeking trophy of his victim within sound of the steam printing-press of St. Paul. The people of the state, and even strangers from abroad, crowded unarmed and fearless to the agencies when the payments were made, although a thousand armed warriors, in their plumes and paint, were present.

How many prophecies of danger there were the following chapter shall disclose.

SQUAWS WINNOWING WHEAT.

CHAPTER II.

CAUSES OF THE OUTBREAK.

THE Indians were predisposed to hostility toward the whites. They regarded them with that repugnance which God has implanted as an instinct in different races for the preservation of their national integrity, and to prevent the subjection of the inferior in industry and intelligence to the superior. When they first caught sight of Hennepin they saluted him with a discharge of arrows.

This inborn feeling was increased by the enormous prices charged by the traders for goods, by their debauchery of their women, and the sale of liquors, which were attended by drunken brawls that often resulted fatally to the participants. Death to the whites would have followed years ago had not commercial dealings with them, as before stated, become a matter of necessity.

The prohibition by our government of their sanguinary wars upon the Chippeways was another source of grievance. To them it appeared a tyrannical act. When upbraided during last summer for evading this command, they answered with this home thrust: "Our Great Father, we know, has always told us it was wrong to make war, yet now he himself is making war and killing a great many. Will you explain this to us? we don't understand it." This prohibition was not only distasteful on account of its imputed unreasonableness and tyranny, but because it also closed up the main avenue to distinction.

The imagination of the Indian can not exercise itself in painting, sculpture, and literature, or in any of the arts or sciences which gain renown in civilized climes. His crown comes from the red hand of war. As their agent correctly says, "The young Indian from childhood is taught to regard 'killing' as the highest of virtues. In the dance and at the feasts, the warriors recite their deeds of theft, pillage, and slaughter as precious things, and, indeed, the only ambition of the young Indian is to secure the '*feather*,' which is but the record of his having murdered, or participated in the murder of some humar being—whether man, woman, or child is immaterial; and after he has secured his first feather, his appetite is whetted to increase the number in his hair, as an Indian brave is estimated by the number of his feathers. Without the feather the young Indian is regarded as a *squaw*, and, as a general rule, can not get a wife, and is despised, derided, and treated with contumely by all. The head-dress filled with these feathers and other insignia of blood is regarded as '*wakan*' (sacred), and no unhallowed hand of man nor any woman dare touch it."

If you enter an Indian encampment you will notice the little boys engaged in shooting arrows, or in hurling miniature spears; and over the platform upon which bleaches the bones of one of their heroic dead you will find suspended the scalp of some slaughtered foe. Honorable wounds are considered a sure passport to "the happy hunting grounds," and the slaughter of an enemy by a friend of a dead warrior is regarded as a powerful propitiation to the Deity on his behalf. By his side, in his last resting-place, are laid the weapons of the fray, and friends periodically visit it to recite his gallant deeds.

The hostility arising from these causes was but trivial in comparison with that which arose out of the sale of their lands and the treaties therewith connected. The cession of their territory is necessarily enforced upon the Indians by the advance of the white race. Hunting and farming can not exist together, and the Indian can not and will not change his mode of life in a day, if ever. The whites cut down the trees; their steam-boats frighten the beaver and the wild-fowl, and their presence drives the deer and the buffalo far to the west. Were the treaties fairly obtained, and all their stipulations fully carried out, regrets for the homes they had lost, and the narrow limits, soon destitute of game, into which they are crowded, would soon bring repentance of their bargain, and force a bloody termination of the conflict of the races. But the treaties are born in fraud, and all their stipulations for the future are curtailed by iniquity.

The traders, knowing for years before that the whites will purchase the lands, sell the Indians goods on credit, expecting to realize their pay from the consideration to be paid by the government. They thus become interested instruments to obtain the consent of the Indians to the treaty; and by reason of their familiarity with their language, and the assistance of half-breed relatives, are possessed of great facilities to accomplish their object. The persons deputed by the government to effect a treaty are compelled to procure their co-operation, and this they do by providing that their debts shall be paid. The traders obtain the concurrence of the Indians by refusing to give them farther credit, and by representing to them that they will receive an immense amount of money if they sell their lands, and thenceforth will live at ease, with plenty to eat and plenty to wear, and plenty of powder and lead, and of whatever else they may request. After the treaty is agreed to, the amount of ready money is absorbed by the exorbitant demands of the traders and the expenses of the removal of the Indians to their reservation. After that, the trader no longer looks to the Indian for his pay; he gets it from their annuities. He therefore does not use the same means to conciliate their good will that he did when he was dependent on their honesty. Claims for depredations upon white settlers are also deducted out of their moneys before they leave Washington, on insufficient testimony; and these are always, when based on fact, double the actual loss, for the Indian Department is notoriously corrupt, and the hand manipulating the machinery must be crossed with gold. The "*expenses*" of obtaining a claim enter into the amount demanded and allowed. The demand is not only generally unjust, but, instead of its being deducted from the moneys of the wrong-doer, it is taken from the annuities of all. This course punishes the innocent and rewards the guilty, because the property taken by the depredator is of more value than the slight percentage he loses.

Many of the stipulations as to establishing schools, and furnishing them with farming utensils, are never carried out. Building and supply contracts are entered into at outrageous prices, and goods belonging to the Indians are put into the traders' stores, and sold to their owners, and the moneys realized shared by the trader and the agent. About four hundred thousand dollars of the cash payment due the Sioux under the treaties of 1851 and 1852 were paid to the traders on old indebtedness. So intense was the indignation of the Indians that there was serious apprehension that they would attack the government officials and traders. The opposition of Red Iron, the principal chief of the Sissetons, became so boisterous that he was broken of his chieftainship by Governor Ramsey, the Superintendent of Indian Affairs, and one of the commissioners who made the treaties.

An eye-witness has sketched the appearance of the chief on that occasion, and the interview between him and the governor, and what afterward transpired. It took place in December, 1852. The council was crowded with Indians and white men when Red Iron was brought in guarded by soldiers. He was about forty years old, tall and athletic; about six feet high in his moccasins, with a large, well-developed head, aquiline nose, thin, compressed lips, and physiognomy beaming with intelligence and resolution. He was clad in the half military, half Indian costume of the Dakota chiefs. He was seated in the council-room without greeting or salutation from any one. In a few minutes, the governor, turning to the chief in the midst of a breathless silence, by the aid of an interpreter opened the council.

Governor Ramsey asked, "What excuse have you for not coming to the council when I sent for you?"

The Dakota chief rose to his feet with native grace and dignity, his blanket falling from his shoulders, and purposely dropping the pipe of peace, he stood erect before the governŏr with his arms folded and right hand pressed upon the sheath of his scalping-knife. With the utmost coolness and prepossession, and a defiant smile playing upon his thin lips, and his eyes sternly fixed upon his excellency, with firm voice he replied,

"I started to come, but your braves drove me back."

GOVERNOR. "What excuse have you for not coming the second time I sent for you?"

RED IRON. "No other excuse than I have given you."

GOVERNOR. "At the treaty I thought you a good man; but since, you have acted badly, and I am disposed to break you—I *do* break you."

RED IRON. "*You break me!* My people made me a chief. My people love me. I will still be their chief. I have done nothing wrong."

GOVERNOR. "Red Iron, why did you get your braves together, and march around here for the purpose of intimidating other chiefs, and prevent their coming to the council?"

RED IRON. "I did not get my braves together; they got together themselves to prevent boys going to council to be made chiefs to sign papers, and to prevent single chiefs going to council at night to be bribed to sign papers for money we have never got. We have heard how the M'dewakantons were served at Mendota—that by secret councils you got their names on paper and took away their money. We don't want to be served so. My braves wanted to come to council in the daytime, when the sun shines, and we want no councils in the dark. We want all our people to go to council together, so that we can all know what is done."

GOVERNOR. "Why did you attempt to come to council with your braves when I had forbidden your braves coming to council?"

RED IRON. "You invited the chiefs only, and would not let the braves come too. This is not the way we have been treated before; this is not according to our customs, for, among Dakotas, chiefs and braves go to council together. When you first sent for us there were two or three chiefs here, and we wanted to wait till the rest would come, that we might all be in council together, and know what was done, and so that we might all understand the papers, and know what we were signing. When we signed the treaty the traders threw a blanket over our faces, and darkened our eyes, and made us sign papers which we did not understand, and which were not explained or read to us. We want our Great Father at Washington to know what has been done."

GOVERNOR. "Your Great Father has sent me to represent him, and what I say is what he says. He wants you to pay your old debts in accordance with the paper you signed when the treaty was made, and to leave that money in my hands to pay these debts. If you refuse to do that I will take the money back."

RED IRON. "You can take the money back. We sold our land to you, and you promised to pay us. If you don't give us the money I will be glad, and all our people will be glad, for we will have our land back if you don't give us the money. That paper was not interpreted or explained to us. We are told it gives about 300 ($300,000) boxes of our money to some of the traders. We don't think we owe them so much. We want to pay all our debts. We want our Great Father to send three good men here to tell us how much we do owe, and whatever they say we will pay, and (pointing to the Indians) that's what all these braves say. Our chiefs and all our people say this." All the Indians present responded "Ho, ho."

GOVERNOR. "That can't be done. You owe more than your money will pay, and I am ready now to pay your annuity and no more, and when you are ready to receive it the agent will pay you."

RED IRON. "We will receive our annuity, but we will sign no papers for any thing else. The snow is on the ground, and we have been waiting a long time to get our money. We are poor; you have plenty. Your fires are warm; your tepees keep out the cold. We have nothing to eat. We have been waiting a long time for our moneys. Our hunting season is past. A great many of our people are sick for being hungry. We may die because you won't pay us. We may die, but if we do, we will leave our bones on the ground, that our Great Father may see where his Dakota children died. We are very poor. We have sold our hunting-grounds and the graves of our fathers. We have sold our own graves. We have no place to bury our dead, and you will not pay us the money for our lands."

The council was broken up, and Red Iron was sent to the guard-house, where he was kept till next day. Between thirty and forty of the braves of Red Iron's band were present during this arrangement before the governor. When he was led away they departed in sullen silence, headed by Lean Bear, to a spot a quarter of a mile from the council-house, when they uttered a succession of yells, the gathering signal of the Dakota. Ere the echoes died away, Indians were hurrying from their tepees toward them prepared for battle. They proceeded to an eminence near the camp where mouldered the bones of many warriors. It was the memorable battle-ground where their ancestors had fought, in a Waterloo conflict, the warlike Sacs and Foxes, thereby preserving their lands and nationality.

Upon this field stood two hundred resolute warriors ready to do battle for their hereditary chief. Lean Bear, the principal brave of Red Iron's band, was a large, resolute man, about thirty-five years of age, and had great influence in his nation. The Dakotas gathered close to hear what he had to communicate. Throwing his blanket from his shoulders, he grasped his scalping-knife, and, brandishing it in his right hand, he recounted to his comrades the warlike deeds of their imprisoned chief, Red Iron (Maza-sha), to which they all responded "Ho, ho" many times, and in their most earnest tones. He then addressed them in a war-talk as follows:

"Dakotas, the big men are here; they have got Maza-sha in a pen like a wolf. They mean to kill him for not letting the big men cheat us out of our lands and the money our Great Father sent us."

"Ho, ho" frequently repeated the auditors. The orator continued:

"Dakotas, must we starve like buffaloes in the snow? Shall we let our blood freeze like the little streams? Or shall we make the snow red with the blood of the white braves?"

"Ho, ho," repeated by almost every voice with savage ferocity, and the war-whoop was yelled by the whole band.

"Dakotas, the blood of your fathers talk to you from the graves where we stand. Their spirits come up into your arms and make you strong. I am glad of it. To-night the blood of the white man shall run like water in the rain, and Maza-sha shall be with his people. ['Ho, ho.']

"Dakotas, when the moon goes down behind the hills, be ready ['Ho'], and I will lead you against the Long Knives and the big men who have come to cheat us, and take away our lands, and put us in a pen for not helping them to rob our women and children.

"Dakotas, be not afraid; we have many more braves than the whites. When the moon goes down, be ready, and I will lead you to their tepees." ["Ho, ho."]

The above talk was obtained from an educated half-breed, who was present during the scene described.

By the influence of the half-breeds and white men opposed to the payment, Lean Bear was induced to abandon his meditated attack. Other Indians were also deprived of their chieftainship. It was doubtful for a long time whether they would receive annuities and abandon the lands: and this was accomplished only through their distress, for many had come hundreds of miles, and were starving in the dead of winter; by the release of those imprisoned for making war upon the Chippeways; and by means of large presents, and the creation of chiefs to act in the place of those who had been deposed.

Even the chiefs did not reap the benefits they expected. $2900 were paid to the chiefs of the Lower

Indians, and placed before them on a table; and in two instances at least, those of Wabashaw and Wah-koo-ta, it was picked up from the table by a half-breed and given to a white man, and that was the last they ever saw of it. Little Crow afterward testified, on the investigation of the charges against Governor Ramsey in reference to the treaties,* that one of the traders promised that if he would sign a receipt for the moneys that were paid the traders he should have seventy horses, and double-barreled guns and pistols for many of his band, but that he never received them.

Over $55,000 of the moneys paid under this treaty for debts of the Indians went to one Hugh Tyler, a stranger in the country, for getting the treaties through the Senate, and for "*necessary disbursements*" in securing the assent of the chiefs.

In 1857, a trader, pretending that he was getting them to sign a power of attorney to get back the money which had gone to the traders under the treaty of 1851 and 1852, obtained their signatures to vouchers, by which he swindled them out of $12,000. Shortly afterward, this trader secured the payment of $4500 for goods which he claimed (falsely, it is said) to have been stolen. About the same time, a man in Sioux City was allowed a claim of $5000 for horses which he also alleged to have been stolen.

In 1858 the chiefs were taken to Washington, and agreed to the treaties before referred to for the cession of all their reservation north of the Minnesota

* The Senate decided unanimously that, whatever might have been done by traders and others, Governor Ramsey's conduct was not only free from blame, but highly commendable.

River, under which, as ratified by the Senate, they were to have $166,000; but of this amount they never received a penny until four years afterward, when $15,000 in goods were sent to the Lower Sioux, and these were deducted out of what was due them under former treaties.

The Indians, discovering the fraud, refused to receive them for several weeks, and only consented to take them after the government had agreed to rectify the matter. Most of the large amount due under these treaties went into the pockets of traders, government officials, and other swindlers.

The Indians were grievously disappointed with their bargains, and from that time the control of affairs passed from the chiefs, who it was believed had been bribed, to the young men. They had now nearly disposed of all their land, and received scarcely any thing for it. They were 6200 in number, and their annuities, when paid in full, were hardly fifteen dollars apiece.

Their sufferings from hunger were often severe, especially during the winter and spring previous to the massacre. This was owing to the lightness of the crops, for the cut-worms destroyed all the corn of the Sissetons, and greatly injured that of the other tribes; and also to an unprecedented fall of snow late in the season, which delayed the spring hunts. The Sissetons of Lac Traverse subsisted only by eating all their horses and dogs, and at least 1500 of the old men, women, and children had to be supported at an extra expense to the government, and this was so very parsimoniously done that some died from starvation.

Then the wild Indians were very much incensed at

the abandonment by the Farmer Indians of their ancient customs, their assumption of the white dress, and adhesion to the Christian religion. They styled them opprobriously "whitewashed Indians" and "Dutchmen," whom they designated as "ea seicha" (the bad language). These "Farmer" Indians did very little work, had their lands plowed for them by the whites, and were much better supplied with food and clothing than the others, and the extra expense was deducted out of the common fund. This the latter thought very unjust, especially as they engaged themselves in hunting, and did much more than the others toward earning their living. Every favor that was granted the "Farmers" they looked upon with jealous eyes, and accused the agent and the missionaries with gross injustice in making any distinction between them. This feeling was fanned by the medicine or wakan (supernatural) men. These combine in their individual persons the offices of priest, prophet, and physician.* They are invested with power to do good and evil. They can inflict diseases and heal them, and discover things which are hid from the eyes of others. They can tell the locality of enemies, and predict the result of battles. From the medicine-man the warrior receives the spear and tomahawk, carefully constructed after the model furnished from the armory of the gods, pointed after divine prescription, and charged with spirit and power; and by the medicine-men in a particular way must he be painted, so as to protect his body from wounds, and make him terrible to his foes. As a doctor, the medicine-man cures diseases by music or horrid chants, or by sucking them from the body,

* Rev. Mr. Pond.

and squirting them into a bowl of water to prevent their return. Their opposition to a system which was death to their profession was strenuous; and as their power over Indians was almost unlimited, the discontent which they fomented was great.

The dissatisfaction thus engendered was fearfully augmented by the failure of the government to make the annual payment, which had before taken place in June, and by the traders refusing them credit at a time when they needed it the most. They were informed by the traders, as a reason for their not trusting them, that it was doubtful, on account of the difficulties the government had to encounter to sustain itself, whether they would receive more than a half payment during that year, and that that would probably be the last.

Just before the massacre took place we had met with great reverses in Virginia, and half-breeds and others who could read* kept telling them all kinds of exaggerated stories about the war: some that the "niggers" had taken, or were about to take Washington; that the Great Father and the agent were friends to these "niggers;" that the Father was "whipped out;" that the Indians would get no more money; that the "niggers" would take it, or that it would be used up for the war.

They were fully aware of the magnitude of the contest. Little Crow often said to the agent, "When I arose this morning, and looked toward the south, it seemed to me that I could see the smoke of the big gun, and hear the war-whoop of the contending braves." The Indians who hunted toward the Big Woods, and

* Agent Galbraith's Report.

those who attended the payment from Faribault, said, as they passed along, they saw nothing but old men, women, and children, and that all that were fit to be soldiers had gone to the wars. This, together with the enlistment of half-breeds and employés of the government upon the reservation, strengthened the idea that the country had nearly exhausted its fighting material, and was going to ruin, and they would receive nothing more.

The Indians, having no diversion during the evening, naturally gather together around their fires and discuss subjects of interest, and among these subjects the action of the government and of the traders are freely canvassed, and the effect was to amplify that which was already bad enough. With the conviction of the weakness of the whites, the possibilities of a successful onslaught upon them were frequently discussed.

These tribes were well armed with double-barreled shot-guns, and could get plenty of powder and lead, and could call into the field 1300 warriors. The Yanktons, the Yanktonais, and the Tetawn Sioux, who would naturally sympathize with them on account of their relationship, and some of whom had recently been at war with the whites, could muster 4000 more.

The Winnebagoes, their near neighbors, were their frequent visitors, and most potent in mischief-making, and they promised their assistance in case a difficulty arose. The Chippeways were as dissatisfied as the Sioux from similar causes. Mysterious messages passed from tribe to tribe of that nation during the summer, and it was asserted that Little Crow corresponded with their great chief, Hole-in-the-day, in regard to their mutual grievances. These could furnish 4000 men, and, with such a force, it was believed they could regain their ancient possessions, if they made the attempt.

Hopes of assistance from the English were also entertained. They recollected that they had in former days been their allies and anxious for their trade, and that they hated the Americans, and that, on account of the Trent affair, a war would probably take place. Medals and flags presented by the British were still in existence among them, and some of the old men said that during the war of 1812 they had taken a cannon from one of our posts and presented it to the English; that they called it the "Little Dakota," and promised, if the Sioux were ever in trouble and wanted help, they would bring this cannon to them, with men to work it.

They despised our people, and believed they could not successfully contend with Indians, and instanced the Black Hawk War, on which occasion, they said, to be successful, we were compelled to ask their assistance.

The escape of Inkpaduta, with the loss of only one of his own men, who foolishly returned to Yellow Medicine, increased this feeling, and they boasted that it was not a white man, but an Indian, who killed this one. Little Crow openly said that if troubles should arise, Minnesota would be compelled to call on her sister states for assistance.

In June a number of chiefs and head men of the Sissetons and Wahpetons visited the Upper Agency, and inquired about the payment, whether they were going to get any money, saying that they had been told that they would not. When the agent informed them that it would take place, although he could not say when, or whether it would be a full payment, and that he would send them word when the money arrived, they returned to their homes; but on the 14th of July all came down again, to the number of 5000, and camped. They said they were afraid they would not get their money, and that they had been again told so by the whites. Here they remained for some time, all pinched for food, and several dying from starvation. They dug up roots to appease their hunger, and when corn was turned out to them, like animals, they devoured it uncooked.

With these Indians came a number of families of the Yanktonais, living near Big Stone Lake. This tribe claimed, and rightfully, an interest in the lands which the annuity Indians had sold, but none of them ever received any pay except those belonging to the Wanata's band, and this was unauthorized. Wanata was half Sisseton and Yanktonais, and his band was composed of Indians from both tribes. These Yanktonais were told that they should receive nothing in the future. When they became satisfied of this, they persuaded the other Indians, on the 4th of August, to break into the government warehouse, and take away the provisions there. This was done in the most boisterous manner, in the presence of one hundred soldiers with two twelve-pounder howitzers. The American flag was cut down, and the Indians stood around with their guns loaded, cocked, and leveled. Finally a council was held with them, and by the issuance of a large quantity of provisions they were induced to return to their homes.

On the Lower Reservation the excitement was likewise intense for a month before the outbreak. From longer intercourse with the whites they were more corrupt and disposed to mischief than the others, and more idle, because they had not, like them, buffalo to hunt.

About the first of July they formed the "Soldiers' Lodge." This is a secret organization of the young men to direct the action of the tribe when any thing of moment is to be undertaken. In this it was determined that they would get all the credit possible, and when their annuities arrived, not permit the traders to receive them; and if they insisted, rob the stores, drive their owners from the reservation, or take their lives, as might seem expedient. The chiefs did not dare express dissent to this plan, for they were accused by the young Indians with bribery to the interests of the whites. The old chief Wabashaw even went so far as to say in council that he should not oppose this action, as the traders and government had cheated them long enough, and as the whites twenty years before had killed four of his relatives, and pitched them over the bluff near St. Paul.

The traders knew from the organization of the lodge that it boded no good for a collection of their demands, and when an Indian would ask for credit they would retort, "Go to the Soldiers' Lodge and get credit," and the Indian would angrily reply, "Yes, if I was your kept squaw I could get all the credit I wanted; but as I am a man, I can not."

They supposed that three certain Indians had disclosed the secrets of the lodge to the traders. They started after one who was riding on horseback; he jumped off and ran into the woods. Then those who had guns shot a hundred balls into the horse, and the others stabbed him with their knives. The other two they caught in the street, and cut every piece of clothes from their backs before all the people.

On another occasion they appeared in large numbers before Myrick's store, and one made a speech, saying, "You have told us that you will give us no more credit, and that we might starve this winter, or eat hay or dirt. Now, since you will not give us credit, when you want wood or water don't get it on our reservation." To this Myrick replied, "Ho! all right! When you are cold this winter, and want to warm yourselves by my stove, I will put you out of doors." Then they made the same speech to the other traders, and received about the same reply.

Some of the more violent were ready for a general war. Jack Frazier, the celebrated friendly half-breed, heard one of them say, months before, that blood would be shed at the payment; and Indian members of Mr. Hindman's church at the agency told him frequently that the Sioux were "wo-hi-ti-ka," *i. e.*, furious for a fight. Other half-breeds said that if war took place with England, which was then imminent on account of the Trent affair, there would be a war along the whole frontier.

Shortly after the organization of the Soldiers' Lodge, 150 of its members took an interpreter living off of the reservation, and who was not in the interest of the traders, and went to Fort Ridgely, where they counciled with Captain Marsh, the commander of the post. They asked him, if they refused to pay their traders at payment, if he would assist the traders, and he assured them that he would not. It was usual to have a company of soldiers at payment, and they endeavored to dissuade Marsh from sending any, as they said they had their own soldiers, who would see that every thing was conducted orderly. They visited him several times afterward on a like errand.

The night before the outbreak a large council was held at Rice Creek, fifteen miles above the agency, at which a number of Winnebagoes were present; and here it was determined that on the next day they would go down to the Lower Agency, camp there that night, then go to Fort Ridgely, and to St. Paul if necessary, to urge the making of the payment, and if they did not succeed more violent measures should be adopted.

Thus, on the 17th day of August, 1862, we find the instinctive hatred of this savage and ferocious people, who are able to bring into the field 1300 well-armed warriors, the most expert and daring skirmishers in the world, fanned to a burning heat by many years of actual and of fancied wrong, and intensified by fears of hunger and of cold. We find this feeling belligerent, and manifesting itself in acts through the possibilities of success. We see the authority of the chiefs and older men set aside, and the energetic and turbulent spirit of youth assuming the direction of affairs. We see violence determined upon if a certain contingency should happen, and the more violent declaring for a general war. We find on the reservation the stores of the hated traders filled with goods which they have long sought to obtain, and within easy access the unarmed people upon whom rage and mania for the "*feather*" may wreak itself in slaughter.

What happens among a civilized people when one class oppresses another of the same color and nation? Why, the archangel of revolution unsheathes his flaming sword. What shall happen now when the wronged are fiendish and cruel by nature, and the hated ones are of another race and within their power? What shall happen when, besides, despair stares them in the face, and the gaunt wolf starvation waits for them with open jaws? The agent, who left the reservation with many of its young men two days before, heard not the question, though philosophy uttered it in thunder tones "with most miraculous organ." Much less did the peaceful people, who were quietly pursuing their toils, and gathering into their garners for the coming winter the summer's bounteous harvest.

All seemed alike to be ignorant of the existence of the magazine whose explosion awaited but the spark —ignorant of the dark and lowering storm which threatened to burst with malign fury over their happy homes.

CHAPTER III.

A SPARK OF FIRE.

On the 10th of August, a party of twenty Indians from the Lower Reservation went to the Big Woods,* near Forest City, for the purpose of hunting deer and obtaining a wagon which the chief Mak-pe-yah-we-tah, one of their number, had left the previous autumn with Captain Whitcomb as security for the purchase-money of a sleigh. This chief, and four others of the party, separated from their companions and went to Whitcomb's. The remaining fifteen lingered in the neighborhood of Acton. Four of these were Upper Indians by birth, but had intermarried with the M'de-wakantons, and were living with Shakopee's band at the mouth of Rice Creek. This band was the worst disposed upon the reservation, and the most violent in its complaints against the whites. The others resided around the Lower Agency.

On Sunday, the 17th of August, when within about six miles of Acton, one of the latter picked up some hen's eggs on the prairie, and proposed to eat them. "No," said one of the four, "they are the eggs of a tame fowl; they are the property of a white man. You must not touch them." "Nonsense," replied

* A large and remarkable forest, commencing about eighty miles above the Falls of St. Anthony, and extending south at a right angle across the Minnesota River to the branches of the Mankato, or Blue Earth River.

the first speaker; "they are worth nothing, and we are hungry, and might as well eat them." "No," still insisted the other; "they are not ours. It is wrong to take them, and we will get into trouble with the whites if we do so." "Oh!" angrily retorted the first, "you are putting on very virtuous airs. You Rice Creek Indians talk a great deal against the whites, and yet you dare not take a few paltry eggs. I am not afraid of the miserable fools." "Don't abuse the white man," said the other; "he is absent. Abuse me. I am here, and am not frightened at your loud talk." "To the devil with you and the eggs," exclaimed the first, and he dashed them to the ground. "That's a very bold act," said the other, sneeringly, "to destroy a few hen's eggs! You are a coward."

The dispute waxed hotter and hotter as they proceeded on their way. Presently they saw an ox, and the one who had broken the eggs cried out, "I am a coward, am I? I am so brave, and so little afraid of the whites as to dare to kill one of their oxen. There!" and he drew up his gun and shot the ox. "You call that brave too, do you?" said his former disputant; "I call it the act of a coward. You break eggs and kill an ox. You are a woman. I am a brave man, and know what is brave. I have been on war parties against Chippeways, and have taken scalps."

And so the quarrel progressed in bitterness, and the whole party became embroiled in it, the four Rice Creek Indians being arrayed in opposition to the others, and each side accusing the other of cowardice. The difficulty bid fair to result in blows, when the larger number said, "Since we can't agree we will take different trails, and you will find out whether we are brave or not, for we are going to kill a white man." And so they left the four to themselves.

Some little time afterward the four heard the others firing off their guns, and erroneously supposed they were killing whites, as they had threatened, and two insisted that they must do the same, or they would be charged with being cowards. The other two reasoned against it, and so debating they continued on their way to Acton.

The first house they came to was untenanted. The next was that of Mr. Robinson Jones, whom they found at home with his wife and a young lady, a Miss Clara D. Wilson. This house they reached about eleven o'clock in the morning. Here they got into a contention with Jones about his refusal to give them liquor, and about the failure of one of them to return a gun which he had borrowed of Jones the previous winter, in consequence of which Jones compelled them to leave the house.

From there they went to Mr. Howard Baker's, a quarter of a mile distant, where they found Mr. Baker, and a Mr. Webster and his wife. Baker was a son of Mrs. Jones by a former husband. Webster and his wife were emigrants from Michigan, and had just arrived that day. They intended going to a different part of the country, but had on the road fallen in with Baker, and were by him induced to come to Acton.

When the Indians came to Baker's they asked for water, which was given them. They then wanted tobacco, and Mr. Webster handed them some tobacco, and they filled their pipes and sat down and smoked. They acted perfectly friendly until Jones came over with his wife and began talking with them. Jones again accused the Indian of having taken his gun to shoot deer, and having never returned it, and again the Indian denied it. Mrs. Baker asked Mrs. Jones if she had given them any whisky, and she said "No, we don't keep whisky for such black devils as they." The Indians appeared to understand what she was saying, for they became very savage in their appearance, and Mrs. Webster begged Mrs. Jones to desist.

The Indians, irritated by Jones, had now determined on murder. Presently Jones traded Mr. Baker's double-barreled gun with one of the Indians for his, and the Indians proposed that they should go out and shoot at a mark for the purpose of having the white men discharge their guns. Jones accepted the banter, saying "that he wasn't afraid to shoot against any damned Redskin that ever lived," and they went out and fired at a mark. Webster had a gun, but did not go out with the party, and one of the Indians said the lock of his own gun was defective, and persuaded Webster to take the lock off, and to loan him his own. After they had discharged their pieces they carefully loaded them again, which Jones and Baker omitted to do.

Then one of the Indians started in the direction of Forest City for the purpose of ascertaining if there were any whites near. On his return the four counseled together, and acted as if they were going away, when they suddenly turned and fired, the shots taking effect upon Jones and his wife, and Baker and Webster. Jones started for the woods, but a second shot brought him to the ground. The others were mortally wounded at the first fire. Mrs. Baker and Mrs. Jones were in the house. Mr. Webster was hit while going toward his covered wagon to bring some things which his wife was handing him from it. The Indians went immediately to Jones's house, broke it open, shot Miss Wilson, and departed. Mrs. Baker, who had a child in her arms, in her fright fell down cellar, and was not noticed; nor was Mrs. Webster, who was in the covered wagon.

When the Indians left, Mrs. Baker came up from the cellar, and she and Mrs. Webster put pillows under the heads of the wounded. Jones was a man of powerful and athletic frame, six feet and an inch in height, straight as an arrow, with dark complexion, jet black hair and whiskers, and fiery eye—the beau ideal of a cavalry officer, as Whitcomb often told him. His fine physique offered great resistance to death. So terrible were his sufferings that he crammed handfuls of dirt into his mouth in his agony, and dug great holes with his heels in the hard ground. He ordered his wife to fly and save her child, but she insisted on remaining until he died, and then went into the woods.

To add to the terrors of these helpless women in this lonely place, while they were listening to the groans of their husbands a white man passed along, and on his assistance being requested, looked at the bodies and laughed, and said that they now only had "the nose-bleed," and that the Indians would soon come again and finish them.

When the wounded were dead, Mrs. Baker and Mrs. Webster hastened to the house of a Norwegian a few miles distant, and, half dead with fright, narrated what had occurred. There was no man at home, and a boy was dispatched to give the alarm at Ripley, twelve miles distant, where a meeting was then being held to raise volunteers for the war. So incredulous were the people of any hostility on the part of the Indians, that they did not credit what the boy said for some little time, but finally they sent a messenger with the news to Forest City, twelve miles distant, where Captain Whitcomb had a number of recruits; and twelve or fifteen horsemen rode to Acton, which they reached at dusk. They placed a wagon-box over Jones, but did not disturb the bodies until next morning, after an inquest was held.

While the inquest was progressing, the eleven Indians before referred to, not knowing what their companions had done, appeared on horseback, and some of the whites who were mounted gave chase. They crossed a slough, and all the whites checked their horses at the edge except a daring fellow from Forest City, who followed over and fired. One of the Indians dismounted and returned the fire, and then mounted his horse again and fled with the others.

There were seventy-five persons at the inquest. The surrounding country was thrown at once into the greatest alarm. The danger to be apprehended from the dissatisfied condition of the Indians upon the reservation was now fully appreciated. A total uncertainty as to their designs and their numbers prevailed.

Mak-pe-yah-we-tah and his four companions had been to Captain Whitcomb's on Saturday and Sunday, and had demanded the delivery of the former's wagon without paying the amount for which it had been pledged, and, on Whitcomb's refusal to deliver it, had threatened to cut the wagon to pieces, and had flourished their axes over his head—and these still remained in the neighborhood.

Then thirteen had been at a house five miles from Acton on Sunday and cleaned their guns and ground their knives; and fourteen of Little Crow's band were in the adjoining county of Monongalea. Messengers were dispatched at once to the governor at Saint Paul for assistance.

The four Indians who committed the murders immediately proceeded to the house of a Mr. Eckland, near Lake Elizabeth, and stole two horses, one of them engaging the owner in conversation while it was done, and then mounting, two on each horse, rode at a rapid pace to Shakopee's village, at the mouth of Rice Creek, which they reached before daylight, and stated what had occurred.

CHAPTER IV.

COMMENCEMENT OF THE MASSACRE AND THE BATTLE OF RED-WOOD FERRY.

When the relatives of the murderers heard their story, they determined at once to commence the massacre, knowing that, unless they did so, the guilty parties would be caught and delivered up to justice.

The more cautious of the band were opposed to this; but it was finally understood that, as it was agreed in the council of the previous evening to camp at the agency that night on their way to Fort Ridgely and Saint Paul, they would start for there as soon as it was light, and consult with Crow and the other Indians about the best course to pursue.

So down they came in the early morning, their numbers increasing rapidly with accessions from the different villages, and when they reached Crow's house, two miles above the agency, they mustered one hundred and fifty men, most of them armed and well mounted, and all shouting and mad with enthusiasm, and anxious and eager for the fray.

Crow had not yet arisen. He was awakened by their noise, and sat up with his blanket around him; and they told him what had transpired, and asked what they had better do. The exigency of the occasion was startling; and so fully alive was he to the perils to which a decision either way would expose him, that, as he afterward stated, the perspiration came

LITTLE CROW.

out in great beads upon his forehead. It was evident that the minds of those before him were made up, and that they would be joined by all the young men of the tribes. Suspicion of bribery by the whites had already attached to him and defeated his election for speakership, and his influence was fast waning. This nettled his scheming, ambitious spirit, and he knew that if he fell in with this movement his eloquence and superior intellect would secure him the leadership of the nation.

On the other hand, in his various trips to Washington, he had acquired a knowledge of the immense forces of the whites and the danger of a hostile collision with them. But the fear of imminent personal danger which his refusal might then incite—the dream of possible success—the ties and affinities of kindred —the mad excitement of the hour, decided him, and he said, "Trouble with the whites is inevitable sooner or later. It may as well take place now as at any other time. I am with you. Let us go to the agency, and kill the traders and take their goods."

Then sending the news down by swift messengers to the bands of Wabashaw, Waconta, and Red Legs, the Indians hastened with Crow to the agency, breaking up, as they entered the village, into small parties, and surrounding the different houses and stores. It was agreed that the attack upon the houses and stores should be as nearly simultaneous as possible, and that upon the discharge of the first gun the massacre should commence.

Nothing save the presence of an overawing force of armed men could now have restrained their purpose. Such there was not. On the contrary, as before stated, many of the men at the agency were on the way to Fort Snelling to be mustered into one of the new regiments for the Southern war, and those who were left were unprepared for defense and unsuspicious of danger. The doom of the people was sealed; the signal gun sounded, and "suddenly, as from the woods and the fields—suddenly, as from the chambers of the air opening in revelations—suddenly, as from the ground yawning at their feet, leaped upon them, with the flashings of cataracts, Death, the crowned phantom, with all the equipage of his terrors, and the tragic roar of his voice."

The first shot was fired at Myrick's store, in the upper part of the town, between six and seven o'clock in the morning. James Lynde was the first victim. He was standing in the door and saw them coming. One of the murderers cried out just before he shot, "Now I will kill the dog who wouldn't give me credit." Mr. Lynde was a clerk in the store, but had been a member of the State Senate, and was possessed of fine literary attainments. Then they killed in the same store, almost immediately, Divall, a clerk, and Fritz, the cook.

Young Myrick was up stairs, and when the first gun was fired he concealed himself under a dry-goods box. The Indians, fearful that he would shoot at them, dared not ascend the stairs, and after some little time hit upon a plan of routing him by proposing to burn the building. When Myrick heard this he clambered up through the scuttle, slipped down the lightning-rod to the roof of a low addition used as a warehouse, and jumped to the ground, and ran toward the brush covering the steep bank of the Minnesota River, which was near, and promised possible safety. As he ran, some Winnebagoes discharged their arrows at him without effect; but just as he reached the thicket a Sioux shot him with his gun and brought him to the ground, where he was found days afterward with a scythe and many arrows sticking in his body.

At Forbes's store they killed Jo. Belland and Antoine Young; at Roberts's store, Brusson; and at La Batte's, old La Batte and his clerk. The superintendent of farms was shot, and the workman who was digging the well for a brick-yard for his destroyers' benefit. Many others perished at the same time. At Forbes's store they wounded George Spencer in the arms and side, but he was saved by an Indian friend.

THE CAPTIVE SAVED.

Bourat, a clerk, ran up stairs. Presently he heard one say, "Let us go up and kill him, and get him out of the way," and he determined to make a rush for his life. He dashed down the stairs, and succeeded in getting about two hundred yards from the store, when he received a heavy charge of duck-shot in the side, which brought him down. Another shot was fired, which took effect in his left leg. Then the Indians came up, stripped him of his clothing and shoes, and piled some logs over him to prevent his escape, promising to come back soon and cut him up. He succeeded in extricating himself from the logs and making his escape after the most excruciating torture.

The Indians being much engaged in plundering the stores, many escaped uninjured. Among these was the Rev. Mr. Hindman, who lived in the lower part of the town. He thus stated to the writer his experience on that eventful morning:

"I arose early, expecting to go to Faribault; had just finished breakfast, and was sitting outside smoking a pipe and talking with a mason about a job which he had just finished upon the new church which I was building. Presently I saw a number of Indians passing down, nearly naked and armed with guns. The mason exclaimed, 'I guess they are going to have a dance.' 'No,' said Dr. Humphreys's son, who was standing near us, 'they have guns, and are not going to dance.' Then I noticed that, instead of going by, they commenced sitting down on the steps of various buildings.

"About this time I heard the guns in the upper town. A man by the name of Whipple said he guess ed the Chippeways had come over, and they were having a battle. He then crossed the road to his boarding-house. I soon noticed that the people at the boarding-house who could see the upper stores were running down the bluff. Then four Indians came down the street. One of them left the others, and went into the Indian farmer Prescott's house, and came immediately out. Frank Robertson, a young clerk in the employ of the government, followed him out, looking very pale. I asked him what was the matter. He said he didn't know, but that the Indian told them all to stay in the house. He told me he thought there was going to be trouble, and started for Beaver Creek, a few miles above, where his mother lived.

"Soon White Dog, formerly president of the 'Farmer' Indians, ran past very much frightened. I asked him what the matter was, and he said that there was awful work, and that he was going to see Wabashaw about it. Then Crow, in company with another Indian, went by the gate, and I asked Crow what was the matter. He was usually very polite, but now he made no answer, and, regarding me with a savage look, went on toward the stable, the next building below.

"Just before Wagner ran by, and I asked him also what the trouble was. He said the Indians were going to the stable to steal horses, and that he was going there to stop them. I told him that he had better not, as I was afraid there was trouble. He paid no attention to what I said. The next I saw was the Indians leading away the horses, and Wagner, John Lamb, and another person trying to prevent them. By this time Crow had reached them, and I heard him say to the Indians, 'What are you doing? Why don't you shoot these men? What are you waiting for?' Immediately the Indians fired, wounding Wagner, who escaped across the river to die, and killing Lamb and the other man.

"Then I found Mrs. West, and we started for the ferry. After we got about half way she ran into a house, and I lost sight of her.

"Just as I got to Dickerson's house I came across a German who was wounded. I managed to get him down the hill and put him into a skiff, and we passed safely over, and arrived at Fort Ridgely about three o'clock. The people were crossing the ferry rapidly, and flying in every direction." The bands of Wabashaw and of the other chiefs below the agency soon came up and joined in the plundering and murdering. When the work was completed at the agency, the savages rapidly betook themselves to the surrounding country. The ferryman, Mauley, who resolutely ferried across the river at the agency all who desired to cross, was killed on the other side just as he had passed the last man over. He was disemboweled; his head, hands, and feet cut off, and thrust into the cavity. Obscure Frenchman though he was, the blood of no nobler hero dyed the battle-fields of Thermopylæ or Marathon. William Taylor, a colored man, flying from the agency, was also shot on the opposite side of the river, two miles below. A few days before he had dressed himself in the Indian fashion, and had his daguerreotype taken, and given it to Crow, and if he had been present Taylor would probably not have been killed. He was a barber, and an old resident of St. Paul—a fat, jolly, good-natured, kindly fellow, who never did an ungentlemanly act. With his tonsorial accomplishments he was possessed of fine musical taste, and his twanging violin was always in demand at the balls and parties of the city.

Dr. Humphreys, the physician to the Lower Indians, fled with his wife and three children, two boys and a girl, the eldest aged twelve years, and reached the house of one Magner, two miles from the river. The doctor sent one of the boys down a little hill to bring some water, as they were very thirsty. While the child was gone the Indians killed his father, and burned his mother and the other two children in the house. Hearing the report of the fatal gun, and seeing the Indians, the child remained concealed until they left. When he emerged from his hiding-place he went and looked at his father, and found that the miscreants had cut his throat. Then he retired to a hiding-place again, and presently some more Indians came along and chopped off his father's head with an axe. All the buildings at the agency but two were committed to the flames.

Down the river, on each side, below the fort, and within six miles of New Ulm, and up the river to Yellow Medicine, the massacres that day extended. At Beaver Creek, and at the Sacred Heart Creek, large numbers perished. Parties gathering together for flight with their teams and movables, and partially armed, would be suddenly met by large bands of Indians, and, seeing the futility of resistance, would give up every thing, thinking that thereby they would appease the wrath of their opponents, and be allowed to escape, but all in vain. Quick and barbarous destruction was their portion. Occasionally some would be allowed to indulge in a hope of escape, and to pass a little distance on their way, but soon a gunshot would bring them to the ground, and death would teach them that their foes were only toying with them as the cat toys with the mouse.

The naked forms of the savages, hideous with paint, their mad shouts and wild merriment, increased the horrors of the victim. Former friendship and kindness availed nothing. On the contrary, the Indians started off at first to the neighborhood where they had camped on their hunting excursions, and been hospitably treated by the murdered. Helplessness, innocence, tender age, prayers, tears—these were not calculated to induce mercy. They served but to furnish embellishments for the tale to be told for the plaudits of the camp, where narratives of common slaughter had become stale, and excess in cruelty received the palm. Continually discussing and puzzling their minds as to how they should outvie one another in the next outrage, by adding some new element of atrocity, nothing which devilish ingenuity could suggest was omitted.

A gentleman living near New Ulm with his family went to the town without apprehending any danger. While he was gone the Indians came and killed two of his children before their mother's eyes, and were quickly dispatching her infant son, when she seized it and fled to her mother's house, a few yards distant. They pursued her and shot at her a number of times, but without success. They killed her mother, her sister, and servant-girl, but she escaped with her infant. When the father returned, he found one of his boys, aged twelve years, who had been left for dead, still living, and he dragged him from the field. While doing so five bullets whizzed about his ears. He brought him safely to St. Peter's, though cut and bruised in every limb, his face horribly mangled, and his skull fractured. An eye-witness of his sufferings says, "He was asleep, but occasionally a low, heart-piercing moan would escape his lips. At times he would attempt to turn over, and then, in the agony occasioned by the effort, he would groan most piteously. At length he awoke, his lips quivered with pain, and the meaningless expression of his eyes added new horrors to the dreadful scene, until, sickened to my soul, I left the room."

Another little boy, whom they left for dead, was brought into the settlements badly wounded. They had driven a knife into his right eye, and it had fallen from its socket and decayed upon his cheek.

A farmer and his two sons were engaged in stacking wheat. Twelve Indians approached unseen to a fence, and from behind it shot the three. Then they entered the farmer's house and killed two of his young children in the presence of their mother, who was ill with consumption, and dragged the mother and a daughter aged thirteen years miles away to their camp. There, in the presence of her dying mother, they stripped off her clothes, fastened her upon her back to the ground, and one by one violated her person until death came to her relief.

One Indian went into a house where a woman was making bread. Her small child was in the cradle. He split the mother's head open with his tomahawk, and then placed the babe in the hot oven, where he kept it until it was almost dead, when he took it out and beat out its brains against the wall.

Children were nailed living to tables and doors, and

knives and tomahawks thrown at them until they perished from fright and physical pain. The womb of the pregnant mother was ripped open, the palpitating infant torn forth, cut into bits, and thrown into the face of the dying woman. The hands and heads of the victims were cut off, their hearts ripped out, and other disgusting mutilations inflicted. Whole families were burned alive in their homes.

Before noon the news of the outbreak reached the fort, and Captain Marsh, of the 5th regiment of Minnesota Volunteers, started at once for the agency with forty-eight men. He was mounted on a mule, and his men were in wagons.

Mr. Hindman, with ten fugitives from the agency, met him at two o'clock a mile from the fort. Mr. Hindman asked him if he was going to the ferry at the agency. He said he was, and the former cautioned him against it, telling him if he went there he would be sure to get into trouble; that the Indians were killing every body, and that he had better go no farther than the bluff opposite the ferry, and there collect what women and children he could, and bring them into the fort. He replied that he had plenty of powder and lead, and enough men to whip all the Indians between there and the Pacific Ocean, and that he was not only going *to* the ferry, but *across* the ferry.

Hindman told him that it was none of his business, but that the Indians outnumbered him three to one, and that certain death awaited him. The other fugitives with Hindman coincided in his admonitions; but Marsh, naturally a brave, daring fellow, and experienced in war by his service in a Wisconsin regiment during the Virginia campaign, and sharing in the common contempt of Indian valor, thanked them for their suggestions and rode on.

Five miles from the ferry they met John Magner, a member of Marsh's company, who had been visiting his home near the agency on furlough. It was in his house that Dr. Humphreys's wife and children were burned. He had lain secreted in a cornfield, and had witnessed the flames of his house, and had seen many of the people slain. Marsh ascertained from him what had happened, but, nothing daunted, boldly advanced to the ferry.

On the road they saw many dead bodies. Dr. Humphreys's little boy, who had remained concealed until now, joined them, as also did another fugitive, and accompanied them to the ferry. When they reached the ferry, which was at sundown, the Indians came to the opposite bank, and a conversation ensued between them and Marsh, through his interpreter Quinn.

Marsh told them he was coming over to look into things, and ascertain what the trouble was. Some said he must not, and that they would shoot any one who tried it. White Dog advised him to cross. While this parley was going on, many Indians had secretly crossed over and surrounded Marsh. It was a long distance across the bottom to the bluff. Both banks were wooded, and thick with tall grass and bushes. On the opposite shore, around the saw-mill, were many logs, behind which Indians lay concealed.

Marsh saw nothing of the Indians on his side of the river, and sent Magner a little distance below to where he could get a good view to ascertain the numbers on the other side, and sent another man into the water to bring in the ferry-boat, which was a few feet from shore. Magner soon returned, and told him it was certain death to cross. Others sided with Magner, and Marsh said he would this time yield his own judgment to that of others, and ordered his men who were fronting the ferry to an about face. The Indians evidently desired all the soldiers to get upon the boat and partly across the river before they fired, as then all could be killed.

As soon as it became manifest that the idea of crossing was abandoned, Little Crow gave the signal to White Dog to fire. White Dog passed it to others, and from every side, amid hideous yells, burst on the terror-stricken whites the storm of bullets. Nearly half of their number fell at the first fire, and those who were not killed outright perished by the tomahawk.

Quinn, the interpreter, who was standing with his band on the corner of the ferry-house, received twenty balls in his body, and, at the same time, an Indian standing close by shot him with arrows. The survivors sought safety in flight, discharging, however, before they left, several volleys at their enemies, by which one was killed and five wounded.

Captain Marsh was uninjured, although he stood close beside Quinn, and had his mule killed under him. Gathering nine of his men together, among whom was Magner, he succeeded in getting two miles down the river, but, discovering that the Indians were cutting off his way to the fort, he ordered his men to cross the stream at a point where it was supposed to be fordable, and bravely led the way himself, holding over his head his revolver in one hand, and his sword in the other. He was soon beyond his depth, and it was perceived that he was drowning. Magner and another man went to his assistance, but too late. He sank from their sight, and his corpse was found in the river miles below some days afterward. He must have suddenly been taken with cramp, as he was an expert swimmer.

His nine companions safely made their way into the fort. Others also escaped; among them was Dr. Humphreys's son. Twenty-four of the number perished.

Nine Winnebagoes were present, and participated in the battle. Little Priest, one of their most distinguished chiefs, was seen to fire upon the whites. The Indians were highly jubilant over this success. Whatever of doubt there was before among some as to the propriety of embarking in the massacres disappeared, and the Lower Indians became a unit upon the question. Their dead enemies were lying all around them, and their camp was filled with captives. They had taken plenty of arms, and powder, and lead, and provisions, and clothing. The "Farmer" Indians and members of the Church, fearing, like all other renegades, that suspicion of want of zeal in the cause would rest upon them, to avoid it became more bloody and brutal in their language and conduct than the others.

During the day three messengers were dispatched with the news to the Upper Indians at Yellow Medicine. The first messenger was not believed. When his report was confirmed by the second messenger, the Indians assembled together in council to the number of one hundred or more. Among them were thirty of the young Yanktonais. They were divided in sentiment as to what action should be taken. Some advised the killing of all the whites, and the taking of their goods, as they would all be considered by the whites as embroiled in the difficulties which had already taken place. The others insisted that the whites should be sent to the settlement, with their horses and what they could carry away.

Other Day, a civilized Indian, addressed the coun-

OTHER DAY.

cil, telling them that they might easily kill a few unarmed whites—five, ten, or a hundred—but the consequence would be that their whole country would be soon filled with soldiers of the United States, and all of the Indians would be killed or driven away. "Some of you," he said, "say you have horses, and can escape to the plains; but what, I ask you, will become of those who have no horses?"

Their reply was that they would have to suffer for

what the others had done in any event. Then came the other messenger with news of Marsh's disaster, and the council broke up in a row, and the Yanktonais, Sissetons, and a few of the Wahpetons moved toward the houses of the whites for an attack.

Then Other Day seized his wife, who was a white woman, by the arm, took his gun, and went to the houses of the whites, who knew nothing of the assembling of the council, to warn them of their danger, and they assembled in the warehouse to the number of fifty, with the determination to defend themselves to the last extremity. Other Day and four of his relatives stood on the outside of the building all night, to watch for and give notice of any attack. While there, squads of Indians hovered around, watching an opportunity to catch them unawares. At ten o'clock they went to Garvie's store, and found him there, as he supposed they were only bent upon pillage. They fired seven shots at him, two of which took effect. He ran up stairs, got his gun, jumped out of the second story window, and made his way into the warehouse. Two others were killed on the bottom lands near the agency buildings.

About daybreak they heard a gun go off near a warehouse a mile away, followed by others in rapid succession, and then a general yell as the Indians broke into the building. Then those who were watching the whites ran for this warehouse, and the whites, under the guidance of Other Day, crossed the river and made their way to the settlements. The party consisted of forty-two women and children, and twenty men. Among the former was the wife and children of the agent, Mr. Galbraith. Garvie was left at

Hutchinson, and died soon after from the effects of his wounds.

On the same Monday night, at nine o'clock, the people at Mr. Riggs's place, six miles above the Upper Agency, were informed of the danger by friendly Indians, and forty-two, including the missionaries, Riggs and Williamson, made their escape.

Messengers were dispatched by the Indians at once to all the Indians to notify them of what was being enacted. Fort Ridgely and New Ulm were filled with fugitives that night, many bleeding from ghastly wounds, and all trembling with affright. Blazing houses were to be seen in every direction as the incendiaries plied their hellish work. The frightened inmates prepared themselves for battle as well as they might, and dispatched messengers for relief to the settlements, and after Lieutenant Shehan, who had started on the 16th for Fort Ripley, to accompany Commissioner Dole, who was about to make a treaty with the Red Lake Chippeways. The messenger overtook Shehan forty miles away that night, and also carried the news to St. Peter's and other towns.

CHAPTER V.

THE ATTACKS UPON NEW ULM AND FORT RIDGELY.

AGENT GALBRAITH, with his company of forty-five men, who were known as the "Renville Rangers," were in St. Peter's when the news arrived. That night was spent in running bullets, and getting ready for the relief of the fort and New Ulm.

Early in the morning the bells were rung, and the alarm generally given. The people assembled between seven and eight o'clock to determine upon a course of action. The Renville Rangers had started between six and seven o'clock for the fort, and it was determined to send a detachment to the succor of New Ulm.

The meeting adopted a resolution that every man who had any character of fire-arms or ammunition should produce them, and notify his neighbors to do the same, at the Court-house, within the next hour, for which time the meeting adjourned.

At the expiration of the hour the people reassembled, bringing with them every description of fire-arms that could be obtained. Then a committee was appointed who collected lead, powder, and caps, and an organization had by the election of the Hon. Charles E. Flandreau, associate justice of the Supreme Court, as captain, William B. Dodd as first lieutenant, and Mr. Meyer as second lieutenant. Every body busied himself in getting wagons, horses, ammunition, blank-

CHARLES E. FLANDREAU.

ets, cooking utensils, and provisions, and by eleven o'clock sixteen men, mounted and tolerably well armed, reported themselves for duty. Ex-Sheriff Boardman was placed in charge of this squad, and directed to scout toward New Ulm. He started off at once.

Little Crow, with three hundred and twenty warriors, left the agency for the fort during the morning, pursuant to an understanding had the previous evening, but on the way dissensions arose, which resulted in a division of the force. One hundred and twenty, under Little Crow, went to the vicinity of the fort, but made no attack that day. While they were concealed in the neighborhood, Shehan and Galbraith, with their men, made their way into the fort unmolested. Had the design of attacking the fort, which was proposed by Crow, been carried out, it could easily have been taken, as the garrison only numbered about thirty effective men before the arrival of the re-enforcements.

The remainder of the party, intent upon plunder, scattered themselves through the settlements around New Ulm and on the Cotton-Wood.

At four o'clock one hundred of them gathered together, and made an attack upon the town, burning the buildings on the outskirts, and killing several persons in the street. This town contained a population of some 1500 souls, principally Germans, and this number was now largely increased by the fugitives. It is situate on the Minnesota River, twenty-eight miles above St. Peter's. The houses were scattered over a long extent of ground, and this rendered the place difficult of defense. While the attack was progressing, Boardman, with his fifteen mounted men, arrived at the ferry, and dashed into the town at full gallop.

The people were in a state of utter frenzy, and there was no organization for defense. The interior of the town was barricaded, making a large square, surrounded by wagons, barrels, and all kinds of trumpery, within which the people were huddled together like a flock of frightened sheep. As soon as Boardman's men arrived, they went outside of the barricades, and, by vigorous firing, drove the Indians away at dark with a loss of several killed and wounded. It is conceded that these men saved the town.

During this attack, Samuel Coffin, from Nicollet County, who had gone to New Ulm to inquire about the massacre, and the Rev. Charles A. Stein, from Judson, and Messrs. Buel, Swift,* and Boardman, of St. Peter's, were conspicuous for their gallantry. While the fight was progressing, the latter volunteered to return toward St. Peter's and inform Judge Flandreau of the situation of affairs. On his way from town he was attacked and fired upon by the Indians, but succeeded in crossing the ferry and making his way into St. Peter's, although he took a different road from Flandreau, and missed seeing him. Flandreau left St. Peter's at one o'clock, with one hundred men from that place and Le Sueur, and arrived at the ferry about nine that evening. The buildings in the town were still blazing.

They made their way safely into the town, and were heartily welcomed by the people. Nor were they less pleased, for they were drenched to the skin and shivering with cold. Guards were kept out during the whole night in expectation of an attack. The next day was passed in strengthening the barricades and organizing the men generally for defense. Judge Flandreau was selected as commander-in-chief, and he appointed Captain Dodd provost marshal, and S. A. Buell deputy. Dr. Daniels, of St. Peter's, Dr. M'Mahan, of Mankato, Drs. Ayer and Mayo, of Le Sueur, and the resident German physicians of the town, were placed in charge of the sick and wounded. A public butcher was also appointed, and foraging and scouting parties selected. A theodolyte was placed on one of the principal buildings, by which the country for three miles around could be swept, and persons stationed there to keep a sharp look-out. During the

* Now Governor of Minnesota.

day fifty men from Mankato, under Captain Bierbaur, arrived, and about the same number from Le Sueur.

No Indians appearing, the men commenced roaming about the prairie. A mile and a half from town they found nine men, some dead and others nearly so —all horribly mutilated. These were a portion of a party of sixteen who had started for their homes at Leavenworth, on the Cotton-Wood, and, being beset by Indians, endeavored to make their way back during the attack on the previous day. Three of the party were seated upon a buck-board on a wagon. Two were killed. The horses were hit and ran, and the wagon struck a clod and knocked the board off. The survivor managed to suspend himself to the reach with his feet and hands, and was so carried untouched into the town, the horses on the full gallop, and one of them dropping dead as soon as they arrived. Another, who had been fearfully cut with hatchets, crawled up a cow and sucked her milk, and was afterward picked up. Many dead bodies were found and buried. There were no farther signs of Indians for several days.

At a quarter past three o'clock P.M. on Wednesday, Little Crow, being re-enforced by those who had been at New Ulm on the previous day, made an attack upon Fort Ridgely. The garrison were not expecting any thing of the kind, and were at once thrown into the utmost confusion. The first announcement that the Indians were in the neighborhood was a volley fired through one of the openings, which was attended with fatal effect. Sergeant Jones, the ordinance sergeant, attempted to use the cannon, but found, to his surprise, that they could not be discharged. On removing the charges, they were found to be stuffed with rags, the work of some half-breeds, who had left the fort under pretense of going to cut kin-ne-kin-nic,* and had deserted to the enemy. They were reloaded, and a brisk fire kept up. At half past six o'clock in the evening the attack ceased, with a loss to the garrison of three killed and eight wounded, and to the Indians of several killed and wounded. Among the latter was Little Crow, who was grazed across the breast by a cannon ball.

On Thursday morning, at half past nine o'clock, the attack was renewed, and lasted for about half an hour. At ten minutes before six o'clock P.M. the attack was again renewed, and continued about the same length of time. The assailants were by no means as numerous as before, as many had left upon marauding excursions through the surrounding neighborhood.

Little Crow returned that night with his men to the agency, and found that the Upper Indians, whom he had sent for by Little Six, had arrived; and next morning, enthusiastic with the hope of success, 450 warriors, Little Crow among the number, started for the fort with a long train of wagons in which to carry their plunder. Leaving these on the reservation side of the river, they crossed over and concealed themselves in the ravines around the fort. The first intimation to the garrison of the presence of the Indians was the appearance of about twenty warriors on the prairie, who began waving their blankets and uttering shouts of derision and defiance. This was done for the purpose of luring the whites from the fort, when

* A species of willow, the bark of which the Indians mix with tobacco and use for smoking.

a rush was to be made to the inside. In this they failed; and as soon as it became apparent that this stratagem would not succeed, a shower of bullets rained upon the fort from every direction. The ravines were alive with men, and the firing was accompanied by hideous shouts and yells. The attack continued until a quarter before seven o'clock P.M., nearly five hours, and was most determined, bitter, and persistent.

During the fight the Indians went into the government stables and let loose all the horses and mules. All the buildings around the fort, except the magazine, were fired by the assailants or the besieged. Fire-arrows were shot upon the roof of the fort, but went out without accomplishing their design. A number of Indians posted themselves in one of the stables and opened fire. Sergeant Jones skillfully exploded a shell within it, and set the building on fire. Just as the shell exploded, Thomas Robertson, a half-breed, by direction of the Indians, was engaged in firing upon a man on one of the porches of the fort. He escaped miraculously without injury. During the fight one white was killed and seven slightly wounded. At one time a charging party was placed near the fort, and Little Crow was heard urging them to charge, but without avail. Lieutenants Shehan, Gorman, and Whipple, and Sergeants Jones and M'Grew, did good service in these actions.

Among those in the fort were the Sioux agent, Mr. Galbraith, and Messrs. Ramsey, Hatch, and Wykoff, who had with them some $72,000 in coin to make the payment. They had reached the fort with it on Monday, the first day of the outbreak.

Fort Ridgely was ill adapted for defense, and a determined charge upon it would have resulted in its fall. There are two stone buildings placed at right angles, in the shape of the letter "L," and on each side of this are arranged rows of wooden buildings, so as to form two squares. It is situated upon the spur of a bluff, and commanded on two sides by ravines. The ends of the buildings were pierced with bullets, which fell into the rooms in showers.

A little while before the first fight Henry Balland left the fort to obtain a horse to go to the settlements. Before he could return the Indians had surrounded the place and made it impossible. He sprang into the bushes, where he remained concealed for several hours, the Indians being close enough to him for their words and motions to be noted. Several times they nearly stumbled over him. While the attack was progressing a heavy storm sprung up, and Balland saw some one hundred Indians come close up to where he was lying. There they remained some time, ranged along in a single line, with their guns under their blankets to keep them dry.

As the dusk came on, guided by the flashes of lightning, he wormed his way cautiously toward the river and effected his escape. When about thirty miles on his journey, he met a soldier who said he was going to the fort. Balland cautioned him against it, and told him how it was surrounded by hundreds of Indians; but the other said he didn't care, that he would look for himself, and should not return until he could say he had seen the fort. Balland told him he might see it, but that he would never live to tell of it. He rode laughingly on, and was shot close to the fort by Little Crow's brother. Antoine Frenier, on his return from Yellow Medicine, passed near while the fight was progressing, and, finding it impossible to enter, went on toward Henderson. He also met at Cummings's Place, below, a soldier, who also continued on to the fort contrary to his warning, and met with the fate of the other.

On the night of the last attack, the party of the missionaries Riggs and Williamson arrived in the vicinity, and Mr. Hunter, one of their number, crawled in to ascertain the condition of the garrison. He was told that the place was already filled with fugitives, and that they had better make their way to Henderson. He crept cautiously back, and communicated the news to his wearied friends, who had expected here, without doubt, to find relief. Bracing up their courage as well as they could, they camped until morning, and, strange to say, passed through the carnival of blood that was raging in safety.

Early on Saturday, the 23d instant, the Indians made their way to New Ulm. Since Tuesday no attack had been made upon that place, and the time had been passed in strengthening their works, burying their dead, and in scouting through the surrounding country. Many fugitives were thus rescued. At nine o'clock in the morning a series of fires were seen along the Fort Ridgely side of the river, commencing from the direction of the fort, and rapidly nearing New Ulm. The anxious inmates of the town knew that these arose from the houses along the road, and indicated the approach of their foes. As the fires reached opposite the town, long lines of Indians were seen coming down the gullies in the bluff, near the middle ferry, and taking positions.

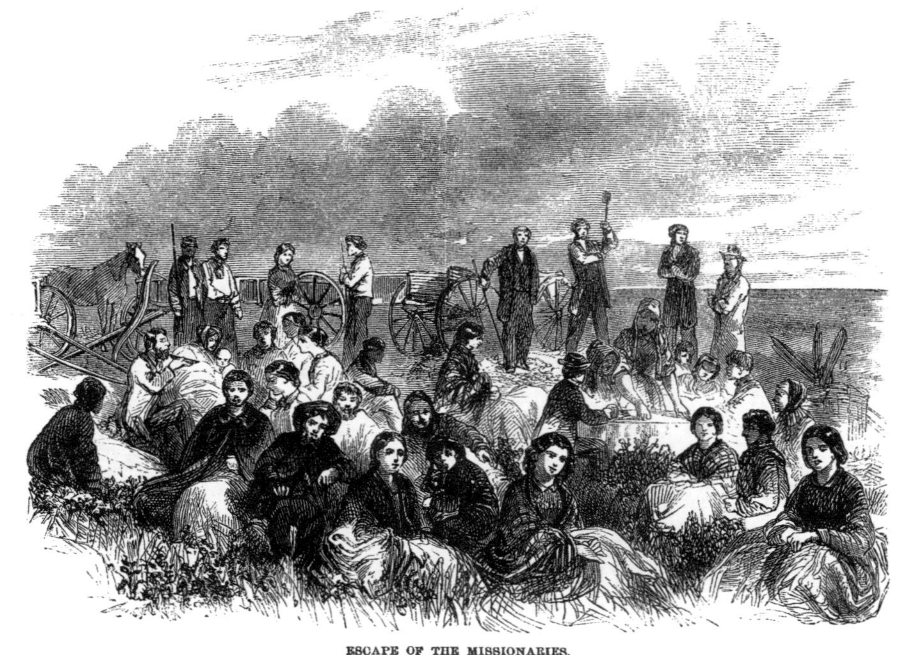

ESCAPE OF THE MISSIONARIES.

About seventy-five men under Captain Huey, of St. Peter's, at the request of citizens who owned property on the other shore, had volunteered, before the Indians appeared, to check their depredations. They crossed at the upper ferry just before the Indians came in sight. They soon got into a brisk fight, and lost two of their men. Being outnumbered and unable to return, they retreated toward St. Peter's, and at Nicollet, fourteen miles from New Ulm, joined Captain Cox's command of 150 men, who were on their way to New Ulm from St. Peter's.

Simultaneous with this attack, a large body of Indians, variously estimated from 350 to 500, made their appearance two miles and a half above the town. Then those at the middle ferry, as a signal for the attack, built a fire which gave out a large smoke, which the others answered in like manner, and then they came down upon the town.

Judge Flandreau, conceiving that a battle on the open prairie would be more advantageous to the whites, posted all his available force, numbering some two hundred and fifty men, on the open field outside the town, about half a mile distant at some points, and at a greater distance in the direction toward the place where he conceived the first attack would be made.

He thus describes what subsequently occurred: "At nearly 10 o'clock A.M. the body of Indians began to move toward us, first slowly, and then with considerable rapidity. Their advance upon the sloping prairie in the bright sunlight was a very fine spectacle, and to such inexperienced soldiers as we all were, intensely exciting. When within about one mile and a half of us the mass began to expand like a fan, and increase in the velocity of its approach, and continued this movement until within about double rifle shot, when it had covered our entire front.

"Then the savages uttered a terrific yell, and came down upon us like the wind. I had stationed myself at a point in the rear where communications could be had with me easily, and waited the first discharge with great anxiety, as it seemed to me that to yield was certain destruction, as the enemy would rush into the town and drive all before them. The yell unsettled the men a little, and just as the rifles began to crack they fell back along the whole line, and committed the error of passing the outer houses without taking possession of them—a mistake which the Indians immediately took advantage of by themselves occupying them in squads of two and three, and up to ten. They poured into us a sharp and rapid fire as we fell back, and opened from houses in every direction. Several of us rode up the hill, endeavoring to rally the men, and with good effect, as they gave three cheers, and sallied out of various houses they had retreated to, and checked the advance effectually. The firing from both sides then became general, sharp, and rapid; and it got to be a regular Indian skirmish, in which every man did his own work after his own fashion.

"The Indians had spread out until they had got into our rear and on all sides, having the very decided advantage of the houses on the bluff, which commanded the interior of the town with the exception of the wind-mill, which was occupied by about twenty of the Le Sueur Tigers, who held them at long range.

"The wind was from the lower part of the town; and this fact directed the larger part of the enemy to that point, where they promptly commenced firing the houses and advancing behind the smoke. The conflagration became general in the lower part of the town on both sides of the street, and the bullets flew very thickly both from the bluff and up the street. I thought it prudent to dismount and conduct the defense on foot. Just at this point Captain Dodd, of St. Peter's, and some one else whose name I do not know, charged down the street to ascertain whether some horsemen seen in the extreme lower town were not our friends coming in, and were met about three blocks down with a heavy volley from behind a house, five bullets passing through Captain Dodd's body, and several through that of his horse. The horsemen both turned, and the captain got sufficiently near to be received by his friends before he fell. He died about five hours after being hit. Too much can not be said of his personal bravery and general desire to perform his duty manfully. Captain Saunders, of the Le Sueur company, was shot through his body shortly after, and retired, placing his rifle in effective hands, and encouraging the men. The fight was going on all around the town during the whole forenoon and part of the afternoon, sometimes with slight advantage to us and again to the Indians; but the difficulty which stared us in the face was their gradual but certain approach up the main street behind the burning buildings, which promised our destruction.

"We frequently sallied out and took buildings in advance; but the risk of being picked off from the bluff was unequal to the advantage gained, and the duty was performed with some reluctance by the men. In the lower part of the town I had some of the best men in the state, both as shots and for coolness and determination. It will be sufficient to mention two as types of the class of the best fighting men—Asa White and Newell Horton, known to all old settlers.

"They did very effective service in checking the advance, both by their unerring rifles and the good example their steadiness placed before the younger men. We discovered a concentration of Indians on the side of the street toward the river and at the rear of the buildings, and expected a rush upon the town from that position, the result of which I feared more than any thing else, as the boys had proved unequal to it in the morning; and we were not disappointed; for in a few moments they came on, on ponies and on foot, furiously, about sixty in number, charging around the point of a little grove of oaks.

"This was the critical point of the day; but four or five hours under fire had brought the boys up to the fighting temperature, and they stood firmly, and advanced with a cheer, routing the rascals like sheep. They received us with a very hot fire, killing Houghton and the elderly gentleman, whose name I did not know. As they fled in a crowd, at a very short range, we gave them a volley that was very effective, and settled the fortunes of the day in our favor, for they did not dare to try it over. I think, after once repulsing them in a fair fight, we could have successfully resisted them had they returned a second time, as the necessary confidence had been gained. White men fight under a great disadvantage the first time they engage. There is something so fiendish in their yells, and terrifying in their appearance when in battle, that it takes a good deal of time to overcome the unpleasant sensation it inspires. There is a snake-like stealth in all their movements that excites distrust and uncertainty, and which unsteadies the nerves at first.

"After this repulse the battle raged until dark, without sufficient advantage on one side or the other to merit mention in detail, when the savages drew off, firing only an occasional shot from under close cover. After dark we decreased the extent of our lines of barricades; and I deemed it prudent to order all the buildings outside to be burned, in order to prevent them from affording protection to the savages while they advanced to annoy us. We were compelled to consume about forty valuable buildings; but, as it was a *military necessity*, the inhabitants did not demur, but themselves applied the torch cheerfully. In a short time we had a fair field before us of open prairie, with the exception of a large brick building, which we held, and had loopholed in all the stories on all sides, and which commanded a large portion of our front toward the bluff. We also dug a system of rifle-pits on that front outside the barricades, about four rods apart, which completed our defenses.

"That night we slept very little, every man being at the barricades all night, each third man being allowed to sleep at intervals. In the morning the attack was renewed, but not with much vigor, and subsided about noon."*

* Judge Charles E. Flandreau, the gallant defender of New Ulm, is aged about thirty-five years. He is tall of stature, and as lithe, sinewy, and active as an Indian. His father, who is now deceased, was an eminent lawyer of the State of New York, and once a partner of the celebrated Aaron Burr. Judge Flandreau was once a midshipman in the United States Navy, but abandoned that profession for

During the morning Captain E. St. Julien Cox, with one hundred and forty-five volunteers from Sibley and Nicollet counties, arrived. The whites lost about ten killed and fifty wounded. The loss of the Indians in killed and wounded was also considerable.

During the fight heavy firing was kept up on the whites from a wood-pile, and an Indian observed standing upon it. The whites fired upon him until the Indians left, but he kept his position undisturbed. On approaching, he was found to be dead and pierced with bullets. He had been propped up there to draw our fire. A half-breed named Le Blanc lay in the grass as our men advanced, and fired and wounded one of them. He rose and ran partially bent over, but a bullet sped after him, and cut the great artery on the shoulder, from which the blood spirted in a large stream. He was soon finished, his head cut off and scalped. He had been one of the most desperate of the foe. The savages used the hill for their hospital, and from this they had a white flag flying during the fight. On Sunday morning one of their number was secreted in one of the houses close to the whites, and escaped by throwing a feather bed over his back, so as to hide his body, and walking leisurely away. A dozen shots could have been fired with fatal effect,

the study of law, in which he has achieved signal success. His quick apprehension, his ready application of principles to the case before him, and untiring activity, early attracted the attention of the public. He has been Indian Agent, judge of the Territorial District Court of Minnesota, member of the State Constitutional Convention and of the Senate, and now holds the position of associate justice of the Supreme Court. At the first intimation of the outbreak he left his family and repaired to the defense of the frontier, where he remained until relieved by the regular forces several weeks afterward.

but all supposed he was a white man, and several remarked, "What a fool that man is, to expose himself in that way." When he got out of range he threw the bed down, and danced and shouted in triumph.

CHAPTER VI.

FARTHER OUTRAGES DURING THE FIRST WEEK OF THE OUTBREAK.

SOME of the individual outrages which occurred on Monday were detailed in the fourth chapter; but while New Ulm and Fort Ridgely were attacked, the depredations extended throughout the whole western frontier of Minnesota, and into Iowa and Dakota. During this week over seven hundred people perished, and about two hundred were made captive. On Tuesday two Indians killed Mr. Amos W. Huggins at Lac qui Parle. He was there engaged in conducting a school for their children, and was born and bred among them. Mr. Galbraith thus speaks of him: "Mr. Huggins exercised nothing but kindness toward the Indians. He fed them when hungry, clothed them when naked, attended them when sick, and advised and cheered them in all their difficulties. He was intelligent, industrious, energetic, and good, and yet he was one of the first victims of the outbreak, shot down like a dog by the very Indians whom he had so long and so well served." His wife and child, and a Miss Julia La Fromboise, also a teacher, were dragged into captivity.

Early on Wednesday, Antoine Freniere, the Sioux interpreter, who had been dispatched from Fort Ridgely on Tuesday, by the agent Galbraith, to ascertain the condition of affairs at the Yellow Medicine Agency, where he had left his family, went into a house a few miles below the agency to get a match to light his pipe. There he saw seven little children, the eldest not over eight years of age, Germans. One of them, a girl, was wounded in the hand. They appeared to be stupid and unconscious of their condition. Freniere asked the eldest where her mother was, and she pointed out of doors in a particular direction. He went out, and, passing down a little path toward the spot indicated, suddenly came upon a sight which froze his veins with horror. There, closely grouped together, were twenty-seven dead bodies, pierced with bullets, and hacked with knives and hatchets, pale and ghastly, and clotted with blood. The only living creature was a little child on the breast of a woman, probably its mother, vainly seeking for nourishment. Terrified by the sight, knowing that the savages were close around him, and that he could not save the children, he hastened away, leaving them to their fate.

On the same day they began murdering at Lake Shetek and Spirit Lake, in Iowa, and also in the neighborhood of Forest City, one hundred and twenty miles apart.

About seven o'clock four Indians came to the house of a farmer named Anderson, residing with his family thirty miles west of Forest City, on Eagle Lake. They had often visited there before, were well acquainted with the family, and had received many favors from them. One was called John, and could talk English a little. They were all dressed in white men's clothes, wore hats, and had their hair cut short. Each one carried a double-barreled shot-gun. When they came to the door they shook hands with Anderson, and asked for some milk to drink, which he brought them in a pan. They drank it and handed the pan back, and he set it down and passed out the door. Then two of the Indians fired and killed him instantly. A son of Anderson had gone into the garden to dig potatoes for the Indians at their request, and they fired and killed him. Another son, standing in the door, was wounded in the shoulder and left for dead. The mother, with her little child, rushed down cellar and escaped notice. A daughter, named Julia, ran into the high grass with a little sister aged ten years. The Indians, after a long search, discovered them, and, placing them on a pony, carried them west a mile and a half, where they camped, one of their number keeping watch upon the captives during the night. Early in the morning their ponies ran away, and the Indians started in pursuit. Julia and her sister ran into the bush, and reached Forest City two days afterward, "camping," to use her own words, on the open prairie at night, and sucking the cows for sustenance.

Four other Indians on the way pursued and discharged their guns at them, but without effect. They escaped these by again getting into the brush. They saw lying dead along the road two acquaintances named Buckland and Peterson. Both had their heads cut off. All the skin was torn from Peterson's face, and many long gashes, running lengthwise, were cut into his body, and two knives inserted in his stomach. When the Indians left the house, the mother, carrying her child, went to Green Lake, ten miles distant, expecting to find assistance, but the Indians had preceded her. Two days afterward she returned to her house, and found the wounded son, whom she had left for dead, composedly baking bread.

Attaching the ox-team to their wagon, the three got in, and went to a Mr. Foote's house, several miles distant. There they found Foote and a Norwegian, named Erickson, both severely wounded. Placing these in their wagon, they all started for Forest City, and arrived in safety on Sunday evening. The daughter, Julia, had left before, and did not know of their safety for a week afterward.

The Lake Shetek settlement was about seventy miles west of Mankato, and numbered about forty-five persons, men, women, and children. They were attacked by Lean Bear and eight of his men, and by the bands of White Lodge and Sleepy Eyes. Ten or eleven of the party were taken captives, about twenty escaped, mostly severely wounded, and about fifteen were killed. Three women and six children were shot by one man, who was the recipient of frequent charities from the hands of the whites whom he killed. Among the persons killed was a child of Mr. Duly, four and a half years old, who was pounded to death by a squaw. Among those who escaped was the father, Mr. Duly; but, before he did so, he managed to put an end to the mortal career of one of his assailants —Lean Bear.

The prisoners were carried to the Missouri River, and were afterward ransomed. Among the number was the wife and two children of Mr. Duly, Mrs. Wright and child, and two children of Mr. Ireland, and a daughter of Mr. Everett. The distance is estimated to be seven hundred and fifty miles by the route which they traveled. The women were compelled to witness the murder of most of their children. The children who accompanied them are believed to be the only survivors of their respective families, with one exception.

One of the lady captives was severely wounded in the foot by a gunshot, from which she suffered excruciatingly. She was *enceinte* at the time; but, notwithstanding her delicate condition, had the dreadful alternative presented to her of submitting to the vile embraces of her captors, or seeing her only surviving child brutally murdered. This brutality produced premature labor; but even this did not relieve her from the foul treatment to which she was continually subjected. From the time of her captivity to her release she was five times sold to different Indians, and has often been compelled to submit to the gratification of their brutal passions.

The other lady, a very intelligent and respectable woman, who, at the time of her capture, had an infant several months old, after having been compelled to submit to the same heartless indignities for the sake of saving the life of her infant, had it wrested from her arms and its brains dashed out against the wagon she was driving. She, too, was changed from owner to owner in the same manner as the other, and forced to submit to the same treatment.

One little girl, ten years old, who had received several wounds at the hands of the savages, was held prostrate on the ground by four of her captors, and violated by more than twenty young men of the tribe at a time. This treatment was kept up from day to day, until her system became completely prostrate, and herself well-nigh lifeless.

Another little girl, nine years of age, was subject to treatment still more brutal. In consequence of her tender years, the savages resorted to horrid mutilations of her person to enable them to gratify their lustful desires. It is improper to detail publicly all the cruelties to which they were subjected. Imagination can hardly depict the enormities perpetrated upon these poor women. While suffering these barbarities, their cries are represented to have been of the most heart-rending character.

At the time the little girl last mentioned was subject to these inhumanities, she was suffering from the effects of a compound fracture of the bones both above and below the elbow, produced by a gunshot wound, from which she has not yet recovered. During the massacre in Minnesota, and while on their journey to the Missouri, the savage practices of the younger Indians far surpassed in atrocity that of the older members of the tribe. Neither age, condition, nor sex among them were exempt from participation in these cruelties. The practice of shooting arrows into defenseless women and children constituted their favorite amusement.*

The meeting between Mr. Everett and his little daughter, many weary months afterward, was most affecting. His wife had been murdered, a son four years old had been killed before his eyes, and another, still younger, was alive when last seen. He himself was then suffering from his wounds. Out of this once happy family father and child alone remained. An eye-witness of their reunion says: "The child took the hand of her father, and he pressed her to his bo-

* See "Mankato Record" and "Washington Republican."

som, but not a word was spoken by either. The joy of meeting the sole remnant of his family was so saddened by the recollection—so vividly forced upon his mind by the presence of his child—of the fate of his dearly-loved wife and darling boys, that the strong man was overcome with emotion. He wept like a child. He asked his daughter about her little brother two years old, of whom the father had heard no tidings. She replied that when she saw him last he was crawling into the bushes to hide himself from the savages. He probably escaped the tomahawk of the Indian only to die of starvation in the thickets of Lake Shetek."

At the Lake Shetek settlement also lived Mrs. Phineas B. Hurd. She was born in Western New York, passed her childhood in Steuben County in that state, where she was married in 1857, and emigrated to La Crosse, Wisconsin. Here she and her husband remained about two years, and from there removed to the neighborhood of St. Peter's with the intention of settlement, but finally joined in the emigration still farther westward, and settled at Lake Shetek, where she resided three years.

On the 2d of June last, Mr. Hurd, with another man, left home on a trip to Dacota Territory, to be absent a month, taking a span of horses and wagon, and such other outfit as would be required upon such an expedition, thus leaving Mrs. Hurd alone with her two children and a Mr. Voigt, who had charge of the farm. On the morning of the 20th of August, about five o'clock, while Mrs. Hurd was milking, some twenty Indians rode up to the house and dismounted. She discovered among the horses one of their own that was taken away by Mr. Hurd. She got into the house before the Indians, who entered and began smoking, as was their custom. Five of these men she knew, one being a half-breed that could speak English. Her children were in bed, and at the time of the entrance of the Indians asleep. The youngest, about a year old, awoke and cried, when Mr. Voigt took it up and carried it into the front yard, when one of the Indians stepped to the door and shot him through the body. He fell dead with the child in his arms. At this signal some ten or fifteen more Indians and squaws rushed into the house, they having been concealed near by, and commenced an indiscriminate destruction of every thing in the house, breaking open trunks, destroying furniture, cutting open feather-beds, and scattering the contents about the house and yard. Mrs. Hurd, in her uncommon energy and industry as a pioneer housewife, had, with a good stock of cows, begun to make butter and cheese even in this new country, and had on hand at the time two hundred pounds of butter and twenty-three cheeses. These the Indians threw out into the yard and destroyed. While this destruction was going on, Mrs. Hurd was told that her life would be spared on condition that she would give no alarm, and leave the settlement by an unfrequented path or trail leading directly east across the prairie, in the direction of New Ulm, and was ordered to take her children and commence her march. Upon pleading for her children's clothes, she was hurried off, being refused even her sun-bonnet or shawl. She took her youngest in her arms and led the other, a little boy of about three years, by the hand, and, being escorted by seven Indians on horseback, she turned her back on her once prosperous and happy home. The distance across the prairie in the direction which she was sent was sixty or seventy miles to a habitation. The Indians went with her three miles, and before taking leave of her repeated the condition of her release, and she was told that the whites were all to be killed, but that she might go to her mother. Thus she was left with her two children almost naked, herself bareheaded, without food or raiment, not even a blanket to shelter her and her children from the cold dews of the night or the storm.

After the Indians left her, three miles from her home, on the prairie, "we took our way," said Mrs. Hurd, "through the unfrequented road or trail into which the Indians had conducted us. It was clear, and the sun shone with more than usual brightness. The dew on the grass was heavy. My little boy, William Henry, being barefooted and thinly clad, shivered with the cold, and, pressing close to me, entreated me to return to our home. He did not know of the death of Mr. Voigt, as I kept him from the sight of the corpse. He could not understand why I insisted upon going on, enduring the pain and cold of so cheerless a morning. He cried pitifully at first, but, after a time, pressing my hand, he trudged manfully along by my side. The little one rested in my arms unconscious of our situation. Two guns were fired when I was a short distance out, which told the death of my neighbor, Mr. Cook. I well knew its fearful meaning. There was death behind, and all the horrors of starvation before me. But there was no alternative. For my children, any thing but death at the hands of the merciless savage; even starvation on the prairies seemed preferable to this.

"About ten o'clock in the forenoon a thunder-storm suddenly arose. It was of unusual violence; the wind was not high, but the lightning, thunder, and rain were most terrible. The violence of the storm was expended in about three hours, but the rain continued to fall slowly until night, and at intervals continued until morning. During the storm I lost the trail, and walked on, not knowing whether I was right or wrong. Water covered the lower portions of the prairie, and it was with difficulty I could find a place to rest when night came on. At last I came to a sand-hill or knoll; on the top of this I sat down to rest for the night. I laid my children down, and leaned over them to protect them from the rain and chilling blast. Hungry, weary, and wet, William fell asleep, and continued so until morning. The younger one worried much; the night wore away slowly, and the morning at last came, inviting us to renewed efforts. As soon as I could see, I took my little ones and moved on. About seven o'clock I heard guns, and for the first time became conscious that I had lost my way and was still in the vicinity of the lake. I changed my course, avoiding the direction in which I heard the guns, and pressed on with increased energy. No trail was visible. As for myself, I was not conscious of hunger; but it was harassing to a mother's heart to listen to the cries of my precious boy for his usual beverage of milk, and his constant complaints of hunger; but there was no remedy. The entire day was misty and the grass wet. Our clothes were not dry during the day. Toward night William grew sick, and vomited until it seemed impossible for him longer to keep up. The youngest still nursed, and did not seem to suffer materially. About dark on the second day I struck a road, and knew at once where I was, and to my horror found I was only four miles from home. Thus had two days and one night been passed, traveling, probably, in a circle. I felt almost exhausted, and my journey but just began; but, discouraging as this misfortune might be, as the shades of night again closed around me, the sight of a known object was a pleasure to me. I was no longer lost upon the vast prairie.

"It was now that I felt for the first time it would be better to die at once; that it would be a satisfaction to die here, and end our weary journey on this traveled road over which we had passed in our happier days. I could not bear to lie down with my little ones on the unknown and trackless waste over which we had been wandering. But this feeling was but for a moment. I took courage and started on the road to New Ulm. When it became quite dark I halted for the night; that night I passed as before, without sleep. In the morning early I started on. It was foggy and the grass wet; the road, being but little traveled, was grown up with grass. William was so sick this morning that he could not walk much of the time, so I was obliged to carry both. I was now sensibly reduced in strength, and felt approaching hunger. My boy no longer asked for food, but was thirsty, and drank frequently from the pools by the wayside. I could no longer carry both my children at the same time, but took one at a distance of a quarter or half a mile, laid it in the grass, and returned for the other; in this way I traveled *twelve* miles, to a place called Dutch Charlie's, sixteen miles from

Lake Shetek. I arrived there about sunset, having been sustained in my weary journey by the sweet hope of relief. My toils seemed about at an end; but what was my consternation and despair when I found it empty! Every article of food or clothing removed! My heart seemed to die within me, and I sunk down in despair. The cries of my child aroused me from my almost unconscious state, and I began my search for food. The house had not been plundered by the Indians, but abandoned by its owner. I had promised my boy food when we arrived here, and when none could be found he cried most bitterly. But I did not shed a tear, nor am I conscious of having done so during all this journey. I found some carrots and onions growing in the garden, which I ate raw, having no fire. My eldest child continued vomiting. I offered him some carrot, but he could not eat it. That night we staid in a cornfield, and the next morning at daylight I renewed my search for food. To my great joy, I found the remains of a spoiled ham. Here, I may say, my good fortune began. There was not more than a pound of it, and that much decayed. This I saved for my boy, feeding it to him in very small quantities; his vomiting ceased, and he revived rapidly. I gathered more carrots and onions, and with this store of provisions, at about eight o'clock on the morning of the third day, I again set forth on my weary road for the residence of Mr. Brown, twenty-five miles distant. This distance I reached in two days. Under the effects of the food I was able to give my boy, he gained strength, and was able to walk all of the last day. When within about three miles of the residence of Mr. Brown, two of our neighbors from

Lake Shetek settlement overtook us, under the escort of the mail-carrier. Both of them had been wounded by the Indians and left for dead in the attack on the settlement. Thomas Ireland, one of the party, had been hit with eight balls, and, strange to say, was still able to walk, and had done so most of the way. Mrs. Estlick, the other person under escort, was utterly unable to walk, having been shot in the foot, once in the side, and once in the arm. Her husband had been killed, and her son, about ten years old, wounded. The mail-carrier had overtaken this party after the fight with the Indians at the lake, and, placing Mrs. Estlick in his sulky, he was leading his horse.

"As the little party came in sight I took them to be Indians, and felt that after all my toil and suffering I must die, with my children, by the hand of the savage. I feared to look around, but kept on my way until overtaken. This was a little before sunset, and we all arrived at the residence of Mr. Brown that night. This house was also deserted and empty, but, being fastened up, we thought they might come back. Our company being too weak and destitute to proceed, we took possession of the house and remained ten days. There we found potatoes and green corn. The mail-carrier, accompanied by Mr. Ireland, lame as he was, proceeded on the next morning to New Ulm, where they found there had been a battle with the Indians, and one hundred and ninety-two houses burned. A party of twelve men were immediately sent with a wagon to our relief. It was now that we learned the fate of Mr. Brown and family—all had been murdered! We also learned of the general outbreak and massacre of all the more remote settlements; and the sad, sickening thought was now fully confirmed in my mind that my husband was dead—my fatherless children and myself made beggars."

She has been dealt kindly with, and will probably be paid for loss of property; but what can bring back to her the murdered husband, the beauty, loveliness, and enjoyment that surrounded her on the morning of the 20th of August, 1862, or blot from her memory those awful dreary nights of watching alone upon the broad prairie, in the storm and in the tempest, amid thunderings and lightnings? Or who can comtemplate that mother's feelings as her sick and helpless child cried for bread, and there was none to give, or as she bore the one along the almost trackless waste and laid it down amid the prairie grass, and then returned for her other offspring?

The Mantuan bard has touched a universal chord of human sympathy in his deep-toned description of the flight of his hero from the burning city of Troy, bearing his "good father" Anchises on his back, and leading "the little Ascanius" by the hand, who, ever and anon falling in the rear, would "follow with unequal step." The heroine of Lake Shetek bore her two Ascanii in her arms; but, unequal to the double burden, was compelled to deposit half her precious cargo in the prairie grass, and, returning for the other, to repeat for the third time her painful steps over the same. This process, repeated at the end of each half or quarter of a mile, extended the fearful duration of her terrible flight through the lonely and uninhabited prairie.

The force of nature could go no farther, and maternal love has no stronger exemplification. But for the plentiful showers of refreshing rain, sent by a merciful Providence, these poor wanderers would have fainted by the way, and the touching story of the heroine of Shetek would have been forever shrouded in mystery.*

Mrs. Estlick's son Burton, not ten years of age, and his little brother, aged five years, having become sep-

MRS. ESTLICK AND CHILDREN.

arated from their mother, arrived safely at the settlements days after the attack. Burton alternately led and carried the little fellow a distance of eighty miles.

* Correspondence of the Davenport Gazette.

Such instances of heroic fortitude were not common. Many strong, burly men basely deserted their friends to save their own lives. Many were armed and did not fire a shot, so paralyzed were they by terror. Not over three Indians fell except in battle.

Five persons were burning charcoal for the department on Big Stone Lake, at the upper extremity of the reservation, on Thursday. They had their tents pitched on the edge of a ravine near some woods. Toward morning they heard several war-whoops, and rushed out to see what was the matter, when fifty or sixty Indians, some on foot and some on horseback, surrounded them, and when they got within ten paces fired and killed all but one—Anthony Menderfield. He plunged in the ravine and made his escape amid a shower of bullets. He saw Mrs. Huggins and Miss La Framboise at Lac qui Parle.

On Saturday they massacred settlers and committed depredations in the Norwegian Grove settlements back of Henderson. There they committed one of their grossest outrages. Stripping a captive naked, they fastened her arms and legs to the ground by tying them to stakes. Then a dozen of them ravished her; and while she was almost fainting with exhaustion, they sharpened a rail and drove it into her person. This soon ended her life with the most horrible of tortures. On the same day, while the second battle at New Ulm was progressing, the Upper Sissetons commenced their ravages in the valley of the Red River of the North, murdering several persons at Breckinridge, and threatening Fort Abercrombie.

Tens of thousands of acres of crops, the fruits of hardy labor, into which the sickle had just been put, were abandoned to destruction. Cattle, wantonly shot down, lay rotting upon the prairies beside their owners; others roamed, scared and wild, through the cultivated fields. From Fort Abercrombie to the Iowa line, a frontage of two hundred miles, and extending inwardly from Big Stone Lake to Forest City, an area of over twenty thousand square miles, the torch and the tomahawk asserted themselves supreme. Here and there armed parties from the interior settlements ventured a little distance forth for the burial of the dead, and to watch the movements of the foe; but, with this exception, in this vast district there was no white person save the flying fugitive, hiding himself by day, and shivering with affright at every sound and at every shadow that fell upon the grass.

The news of the first murders at Acton, on Sunday, and of the outbreak at Red-Wood, on Monday, reached St. Paul on Tuesday, the messengers notifying all the settlements through which they passed. It spread quickly throughout the country. Not credited at first, fearful confirmation was received in every passing hour. The frightened fugitives poured into the towns by thousands; large numbers of them crowding even to St. Paul, Hastings, and Winona, and many of them not stopping until they had left the state far behind them.

St. Peter's, Mankato, Henderson, St. Cloud, Forest City, and Glencoe, and all the towns along the immediate frontier, were jammed with the sufferers. On every street corner they bared their wounds and told their piteous tales.

The uncertainty of the number of the hostile Sioux, and the probability that the Winnebagoes and the

Chippeways were involved with them, increased the public excitement. A number of the Winnebagoes, it will be recollected, were at Red-Wood when the outbreak commenced; and several of these were arrested on Tuesday on their way to their own reservation, who said their guns were loaded with shot, but which proved to be balls. The Chippeways on the same day commenced plundering the government property at their agency on the Upper Mississippi, and taking captives, and assembling their warriors at Gull Lake, twenty miles north of Fort Ripley, and sending their families to points remote from danger. Mysterious messages had been passing between their reservations in Wisconsin, Minnesota, and Michigan during the previous year, and it was known that they complained of the same class of grievances as the Sioux. Hole-in-the-Day, a wise, brave, and distinguished chief, openly advocated a junction with the Sioux, and he himself had a personal encounter with the whites, in which shots were exchanged. He urged an exterminating war in the councils of his people, and only waited for the arrival of warriors from Leech Lake to attack Fort Ripley. Commissioner Dole, who had progressed as far as St. Cloud on his way to the Red River of the North to form a treaty with the Red Lake Chippeways, returned, and Walker, the agent for the Chippeways at Crow-Wing, fled from the agency, and, the troubles so weighing upon his mind as to produce insanity, committed suicide near Monticello on the day of the second attack on New Ulm.

Rumor magnified the danger; but the reasonableness of apprehension will be apparent when it is considered that the Winnebagoes, who had four hundred

HOLE-IN-THE-DAY.

warriors, were within a few miles of the large town of Mankato, which was surrounded by woods, from which an attack with impunity could be made; and that the Chippeways, who muster four thousand warriors, were many of them within two days' march of

St. Paul, and that their country abounded in morasses and swamps as inaccessible as those into which the Seminoles retreated during the Florida war.

Thus but faintly seen in the outline were the first week's ravages of that fierce hurricane that strode forth with the suddenness of thought from the deep, luxuriant peace of the glorious August, desolating the happy fields, and filling the broad land with louder lamentations than were heard in Bethlehem "when Herod's sword swept its nurseries of innocents."

No tongue touched with fire—no master hand with tragic colorings of black and of red, could adequately portray the horrid sublimities of the sorrow-stricken plains—the smoking ruins of happy homes planted in the wilds with laborious care, and blossoming round with carefully-tended flowers—the perishing harvests, the reaper lying dead in the swath, with his sickle in his hand—the wild and startled ox trampling out the fruit of his labors, and inquiring, with raised head and staring eyes, the meaning of this midnight that had rushed upon the realm of noon—the dogs "moaning for vanished faces" around deserted roof-trees, some gone mad with despair—the swollen bodies of the dead cattle, huge and strange as those of some antediluvian world—the heaps of the untimely slain, their headless corpses festering and rotting in the heat, the hogs rooting in the clustering hair and feeding on the gentle cheek, and all deserted by the retreating, palpitating border "where the fierce hurry of flight and pursuit ceases not by day or by night."

Only the sufferer—only he who has been stricken with as hopeless a despair as that which blanched the face of the last survivor of the Deluge, as he stood on some lone mountain peak, and the hungry waters mounted to his lip; only he whose home has been consumed, his wife dishonored before his eyes, and the arms of his child unlinked forever from his neck, and heard the dull thud of the tomahawk as it sunk into their brains; only he who has been wounded unto death, and in his concealment felt upon his cheek the hot breath of his foe—only he can adequately appreciate the horrors of the fiendish protest of the savage Sioux against Civilization's irresistible march.

CHAPTER VII.

FORCES DISPATCHED TO THE FRONTIER.

WHILE the effect of the sorrows and troubles caused by these raids were increased by their supervening upon those growing out of the gigantic civil war in which the country was plunged, yet in the existence of that war there was compensation. Had the difficulty arisen in a time of peace, weeks would have elapsed before troops could have been raised, or ammunition and arms furnished; and the absence of opposition would have widened the area of devastation, and have added the Winnebagoes and the Chippeways to the ranks of the destroyers. But now, under the recent call of the President for volunteers, there were in the state several thousand men organized into regiments, and partially armed. These were at once hurried toward the frontier. Mounted volunteers were also called out by proclamation of the governor to join in pursuit of the foe. Officers in command, and the sheriffs of different counties, were authorized to impress horses and teams, and whatever else was judged necessary in the emergency.

Upon the receipt of the news on Tuesday, Governor Ramsey hastened to Mendota, and requested the Hon. H. H. Sibley to take command, with the rank of colonel, of an expedition to move up the Minnesota Valley. He at once accepted the position, to which he was peculiarly fitted by reason of his long residence among the Indians and his sound judgment, and the next morning started with four companies of the 6th regiment for St. Peter's, where he arrived on Friday, the day of the last battle at the fort. On Sunday this force was increased by the arrival of some two hundred mounted men, called the Cullen Guard, under the command of W. J. Cullen. These, with about one hundred more mounted men, were placed under the command of Colonel Samuel M'Phaill.

On the same day arrived six more companies of the 6th regiment, of which Wm. R. Crooks was colonel. Several companies of volunteer militia had also congregated here, which swelled Sibley's command to some 1400 men.

Large as this force was, a total ignorance of the whereabouts, number, and designs of the enemy, and the vast importance of not suffering a defeat, rendered their movements slower than the fiery impatience of the people demanded. Besides, though arms and ammunition were more accessible than in time of peace, they were not such as the magnitude of the occasion required. The mounted men had no experience in war and were only partially armed, and that only with pistols and sabres, about whose use they knew nothing. A portion of the guns of the infantry were worthless, and for the good guns there were no cartridges that would fit. The foe was experienced in war, well armed, confident of victory, and wrought up to desperation by the necessity of success. Colonel Sibley's upward march was through scenes calculated to impress him with the importance of caution. The stream of fugitives down the valley far outnumbered those who marched up for their relief.

Shakopee, Belle Plaine, and Henderson were filled with fugitives. Guards patroled the outskirts, and attacks were constantly apprehended.

Henderson was in the midst of woods, and the people expected every moment that the enemy, whose work could be seen from the village in their blazing fires, would suddenly emerge from the woods and commence their depredations. St. Peter's, where he now was, a large, straggling town of several thousand inhabitants, and swelled to double its true number, presented a picture of excitement not easily forgotten. Oxen were killed in the streets, and the meat, hastily prepared, cooked over fires made on the ground. The grist-mills were surrendered by their owners to the use of the public, and kept in constant motion to allay the demand for food. All thought of property was abandoned. Safety of life prevailed over every other consideration. Poverty stared those who had been affluent in the face, but they thought little of that. Women were to be seen in the street hanging on each other's necks, telling of their mutual losses, and the little terror-stricken children, surviving remnants of once happy homes, crying piteously around their knees. The houses and stables were all occupied, and hundreds of the fugitives had no covering or shelter but the canopy of heaven.

Were the town attacked great destruction must necessarily ensue, as it was scattered over such a vast extent of country and difficult to be defended. People had been killed within ten miles of the place, and Antoine Frenier had been shot at within six miles.

On the 26th Lieutenant Governor Donnelly wrote to the executive from St. Peter's: "You can hardly conceive the panic existing along the valley. In Belle Plaine I found six hundred people crowded. In this place the leading citizens assure me there are between three and four thousand refugees. On the road between New Ulm and Mankato are over two thousand. Mankato also is crowded. The people here are in a state of panic. They fear to see our forces leave. Although we may agree that much of this dread is without foundation, nevertheless it is producing disastrous consequences to the state. The people will continue to pour down the valley, carrying consternation wherever they go, their property in the mean time abandoned and going to ruin."

The safety of these towns and the panic-stricken people depended entirely upon Colonel Sibley's success, and he could not risk every thing to march, until prepared, to the relief of New Ulm and Fort Ridgely. The men under Captain Cox, who reached New Ulm on Sunday morning, were dispatched by Colonel Sibley on Saturday. On Monday he sent there also Captain Anderson, with forty mounted men of the Cullen Guard, and twenty foot soldiers in wagons.

The prospect to these was by no means agreeable. The last report from New Ulm was that the town was entirely surrounded by Indians, and that an attempt to penetrate their lines was perilous in the extreme. Not over half of the mounted men were armed with any thing but pistols and swords, and at the first fire the inexperienced riders would probably be placed *hors du combat.* The scenes through which they had already passed had been of a character to excite the imagination, and the stories which had been told magnified the apprehension. They had stood guard in the woods of Henderson the previous night, and had seen a boy brought in there bleeding from wounds he had just received; and on their ride from that point to St. Peter's they found that the settlers had all fled; the only whites they met were some scouts from Le Sueur, heavily armed, and a fugitive flying toward St. Peter's to obtain relief for a family who had just been chased in the woods by the Indians. In these they were just about to ride when the Indians made their appearance on the outskirts. While they were debating on the mode of attack, William Quinn, a half-breed, rode up at full speed with a note from Colonel Sibley, telling them not to go into the woods, as they were filled with Indians, but to hurry to St. Peter's. It was noon before the command was ready to start for New Ulm, as wagons, ammunition, provisions, cooking utensils, axes, ropes to assist in crossing the river at the town if the ferry was destroyed, and many other things, had to be obtained.

When three miles out, all the men discharged their pieces and reloaded them. At the same time they saw a man in the distance who ran for the woods. They had ridden about four miles farther when they were overtaken by Colonel Hewitt, of St. Paul, a member of the company, who informed them that the man they had seen had heard the discharge of the fire-arms, and had rushed into St. Peter's and told them the command had been attacked by the Indians, a number killed on each side, and that the battle was still progressing. All was excitement; the long roll was beaten; soldiers assembled and marched out a good distance before it was found to be a false alarm. This was the only man seen on the route. Far in advance of the troop rode the guide, the brave, stalwart Scotchman, George M'Leod, unarmed save with a knife and an old sabre which he had swung when an officer in the Canadian war.

Fifteen miles out of St. Peter's they came to a belt of woods. Here M'Leod halted them and made a short address, in which he said that in those woods they should probably be attacked by Indians; that they must not be discouraged by seeing their comrades fall around them; that there was no such thing as a retreat if a contest took place; and that the only possible chance of safety was to stand their ground. The horsemen who were armed with guns were then ordered to dismount and leave their horses in charge of their companions, and then, with the twenty infantry men, they scoured the woods.

The possibility of speedy death enforced itself upon the minds of all, and the imagination was busy in conjecturing what would be one's sensations as the fatal knife advanced to the throat, cut through the flesh, and severed the head from the body, and how one would look after it was done. Not an Indian, though, was to be seen. The same course was taken in passing through all the groves on the route.

That night they camped on an eminence within eight miles of New Ulm, having made twenty miles. Just below was a deserted farm-house. Its inmates were evidently persons of taste. Pictures hung upon the walls. There were flowers in pots on the porch, and vines clambering over it. The table was set, apparently for the evening meal; the dishes were still upon it, and the half-tasted food, and the chairs pushed back, as if the occupants had suddenly jumped up on hearing the news, and rushed at once away. Near by was a garden, from which the men supplied themselves with vegetables, and at a distance beyond an oat-field, on which the crop lay bound in sheaves. These furnished food for the wearied horses.

Barricading themselves as well as possible with rails from neighboring fences, they passed an anxious night. Every man was on guard, lying flat upon the ground. Jaded by four days continuous riding, and destitute of proper clothing and blankets to protect themselves against the cool night air—apprehensive at every moment of an attack from the stealthy foe, and drenched with heavy rain, they longed impatiently for the morning light.

Far out in the tall, wet grass were a number of pickets, who were instructed to shoot at the first man who approached, and then rush into camp, when all were to make the best defense possible. Their excited imaginations construed every noise as coming from the enemy. To one going the rounds a picket whispered, "There! don't you hear that signal cry? they will soon attack us." It was nothing but the melancholy tuwhit of an owl in a neighboring tree.

"Be still," said another, drawing him upon the ground, where he was lying with his gun cocked; "I have heard for some time the tramping of an Indian pony over there, and am just waiting to catch a glimpse of him before I shoot." It was the picket on the next beat walking to keep himself warm. Excited as most of the pickets were, there were two or three so dead to all sense of danger, through the fatigue they had endured, that they went soundly to sleep, and snored so loud that they could be heard all over the camp.

Just before dawn the bark of a dog was heard. Every one was then on the *qui vive*, as the Indians attack in the gray of the morning, and the dog was supposed to belong to them. Soon came the crowing of cocks from the deserted farm-houses—joyful sounds, as indicative of the coming morning; melancholy sounds, as indicative of civilization which had fled far away. Presently the dog came into camp, wagging his tail with joy. He belonged to one of the settlers, and was glad to see white men once more.

The dawn came without an attack, and hurriedly feeding the horses, and taking a few morsels to satisfy their hunger, they proceeded hastily, but with caution, on their way. The clouds had passed away; the sun soon rode up bright in the blue sky; the vegetation, "washed by the rain, and wiped with the sunbeam," glittered exuberant in the clear light, and

> "All the bugle breezes blew
> Reveille to the breaking morn."

An hour and a half's brisk gallop brought them to the ferry, two miles below the town. This they expected to find guarded by Indians; but not a person was to be seen. A pair of oxen, yoked together, were struggling in the river. The boat, half filled with water, lay in the centre of the stream. Two men swam out and brought her to the shore. She was quickly bailed out and the troops ferried across. Cautiously they approached the town, expecting to cut their way through the beleaguering Indians, and to be received with the cheers and hospitality of the people; but no sound greeted their ears. Soon they saw thickly scattered around vast swollen carcasses of cows, and oxen, and horses, perforated with balls. These were fast approaching decomposition. They lay on their sides and backs, their legs pointing out stiff and straight in the air. Swarms of large black flies were settled on them, which started buzzing up at the approach of man, and the most sickening stench pervaded the atmosphere. Presently they came to the blackened remains of the burned buildings, where the fire had not yet died out, and from which there flickered a faint yellow, unearthly smoke. Across the principal street lay the naked, headless body of a man, swollen like the cattle and blackened with the sun—the head cut off and scalped, and tumbled some distance from the trunk. Just off the street were many new-made graves, with boards fixed at the head, with the names of the dead upon them. The doors of the unburned houses were standing wide ajar. Goods from the stores, and household utensils, and bedding, and furniture were littered over the ground in endless confusion. Buildings were loopholed for musketry, and the marks of bullets every where visible.

The day had now become intensely hot; no breath of air was stirring; the sky was brazen, and over the devastated town, where the beauty of the winding river, and the riotous luxuriance of the foliage contrasted so with the ruin around, there seemed to the awe-stricken beholder to rest an atmosphere peculiarly its own, such as one would fancy over a city devastated by the plague, or over the frightful spot where an earthquake had ingulfed a people. The loud voice of the captain broke the awful silence. "Go up yonder street," he said to the twenty foot soldiers. They hesitated, for they were many of them residents of the place, and expected to find their friends dead in the houses. "Forward," again cried the captain, drawing his pistol; "the first man who falters I will shoot him dead." Striking up a wild German war-song, they rushed forward. Then the order was given the horsemen to draw their sabres and charge up another street. This they did, yelling like demons, and startling the echoes with their infuriated shouts, until their progress was checked by the barricades. But there was no living thing there except a few dogs, which came out yelping at their approach. Some thought they saw Indian tepees on an adjoining eminence, and the company rode briskly over, but found they were deceived. The place was deserted by friend and foe.

Helping themselves to blankets and cooking utensils, the men retraced their course to St. Peter's, as their orders were positive to return at once. Before they left they buried the body they saw on their entrance alongside of the street. In crossing the ferry, one of the teams attached to the wagon loaded with the eatables backed off the boat. They struggled madly in the stream, and all efforts to save them proved unavailing. They were impressed from a poor fellow, who stood watching them with tears in his eyes. He had to wait many weary months before he received his pay.

The hard service which the horses had endured made it necessary to walk them most of the distance, and darkness came on before they were half way to St. Peter's. Many went to sleep on their horses, and dreamed horrid dreams of the ghastly town they had just seen, and of perils around, and of anxious mourning relatives if death should meet them. From these they would be aroused, at every grove in which there might be a lurking foe, by the sharp order "Forward, double-quick," and away they would dash through the silent, solemn woods, their sabres rattling, and the loud rumble of the wagons, and the quick clatter of the horses' feet sounding painfully afar.

At midnight they reached St. Peter's, and found that Colonel Sibley had left that morning for Fort Ridgely with his command, and had ordered them to follow immediately on their return. Here they learned what had become of the people of New Ulm. On Monday, the 25th of August, and the day before they entered the place, the people, numbering about two thousand persons, comprising the women and children, the sick and the wounded, with a train of one hundred and fifty-three wagons, had abandoned the town and gone to Mankato. The exhaustion of their ammunition; the ravages of disease, arising from the decomposition of the dead animals and the close quarters into which they were penned; the uncertainty of relief from below, and the fate of Fort Ridgely and neighboring towns, with the consequent isolation of the place, seemed, in the judgment of a council of the officers and soldiers, to necessitate this course.

During Monday night one of their sentinels saw some one approaching the camp, who, to the challenge "Who goes there?" responded "A Winnebago." The sentinel aimed his gun at the person, and snapped two caps upon it without being able to effect a discharge, which was singular, as the piece was a Springfield musket—a gun that hardly ever misses fire. It was a lucky incident, for the person was a white woman, a fugitive from Lake Shetek. She answered that she was a Winnebago because she feared that it was an encampment of the Sioux. She had traveled seventy miles without tasting a morsel of food, and carried her baby on her back. The Indians had fired at her, and a ball had passed through her shoulder and carried away the child's finger. The remainder of her family had been killed. She said that the child was very fretful, and would often cry when its wound commenced to pain; but that, whenever she saw Indians and crouched in the grass for concealment, the baby, as if by instinct, would keep perfectly quiet.

Most of the fugitives had arrived at St. Peter's. Some forty of the wounded were placed in a large room, and the surgeons were at their work. The cries and groaning from the writhing forms were piteous to hear. The Rev. Henry B. Whipple, the Episcopal Bishop of Minnesota, active in every good work, and whose heart is as kind and tender as that of a woman, had hastened hither, and was busily engaged in alleviating their sufferings.

On Wednesday the troop which had visited New Ulm started for the fort, forty-five miles distant. On their way they met a man in a wagon who had just been shot at by an Indian, who was probably a scout, and desirous of getting the man's horse to convey the news of Sibley's movement. He pointed out the marsh in which the Indian had concealed himself. They found where he had lain, and presently routed him out, but he made his way into the woods and escaped pursuit. The next day they reached the fort, having ridden two hundred miles since Friday. Colonel Sibley had arrived that morning, Colonel M'Phaill, with a body of horsemen, having preceded him the previous night. On his way Colonel Sibley had buried a man whose scalp Anderson's troop found. He had been killed on Monday or Tuesday. Duncan Kennedy, a messenger from the fort to St. Peter's, while groping his way in the night, had stumbled upon this body. There was a low mist over the ground, which prevented its being seen. The horrible stench, and the sensation received from contact with the corpse, caused him almost to faint with dizziness; but, cocking both barrels of his gun, he staggered on, and reached St. Peter's in safety. Nathan Myrick and Charles Mix, volunteer scouts from St. Peter's to the fort, had also seen this body days before, and shudderingly told of its appearance. The corpses of the two soldiers before spoken of were found near the fort and buried.

Intrenchments were thrown up around the fort, and upon a neighboring elevation which commanded the camp. Cannon were placed in enfilading positions, and a strong guard continually kept up. The first two nights after the arrival of the forces shots were fired into the camp, and a general attack expected, but none came. It could never satisfactorily be determined whether the shots were from Indians or from our own frightened outposts.

The soldiers now rambled freely through the woods, which a few days before would have been attended with certain death. The numerous tents, the armed host and frowning cannon, were welcome to those who had been so long besieged.

"The drum
Beat; merrily-blowing shrilled the martial fife;
And in the blast and bray of the long horn
And serpent-throated bugle undulated
The banner."

Some of the men amused themselves by digging up a dead Indian, and using him as a mark for their rifles. One of his ribs was cut out and preserved by an officer possessed of a morbid desire for a relic. Most of the mounted men had enlisted for no particular time; they had left their business unattended to—the merchant had closed his doors, and the farmer had abandoned his crops on the field; they had accomplished what they started for—the relief of Fort Ridgely and New Ulm; there was no prospect of a speedy conflict, and they insisted on returning home. Ninety men, however, of the Cullen Guard, under Captain Anderson, still remained, and these were soon increased by the arrival of forty-seven men under Captain Sterritt. On the 1st of September, Lieutenant Colonel Marshall, with a portion of the 7th regiment, joined the expedition. All that was now needed for a forward movement were ammunition and provisions, but these did not arrive in sufficient quantity for many days afterward. Excitement soon came in most woful shape.

CHAPTER VIII.

BIRCH COOLIE.

On Sunday, the last day of August, Captain Grant's company of infantry, seventy men of the Cullen Guard under Captain Anderson, and a detail of citizens and other soldiers, together with seventeen teamsters with teams, numbering in all about one hundred and fifty men, were dispatched, under command of Major Joseph R. Brown, to the Lower Agency, for the purpose of burying the dead, and ascertaining, if possible, the whereabouts of the enemy.

The next evening, several of the citizens who had accompanied them returned, and informed Colonel Sibley that on that morning the cavalry and a small portion of the infantry had crossed the river at the agency, buried the dead, and had gone some little distance above, and that there were no indications of the Indians having been there for several days. Captain Grant, with the infantry, had interred the dead on the Fort Ridgely side, including those at Beaver Creek, and had encamped during the afternoon on the same side of the river, where they were joined in the evening by Major Brown and his detachment.

The report that Major Brown, whose long residence among the Indians had made him a competent judge, could discover no indications of their presence in the neighborhood, caused the commander of the expedition to rest easy as to the safety of the detachment;

but on the morning of Wednesday the sentries sent word that they could hear the report of guns in the direction of the agency. The eminences around the camp were quickly crowded with anxious listeners. The wind was blowing strongly toward the direction from which the sound was stated to have proceeded, but by throwing one's self upon the ground, the rapid discharge of fire-arms could be distinctly heard. Colonel M'Phaill, with fifty horsemen, Major M'Laren, with one hundred and five infantry, and Captain Mark Hendricks, with a mountain howitzer, were at once sent forward to their relief. The musketry still continued to be heard, and in a few hours the sullen boom of the howitzer indicated that the second detachment had become engaged. The tents were ordered to be struck and taken into the fort, and the entire command to put themselves at once in readiness for marching. Just as the sun was setting, and in an incredibly short time after the order was given, the whole force was in motion. Accompanying it was Sergeant Jones, with two pieces of cannon.

After a slow, weary march of thirteen miles, the darkness, which had now become intense, was lit up by a bright flash, followed by the quick roar of the howitzer; and guided by its repeated discharges, to which our cannon answered, we found ourselves at the camp of the second detachment. During the afternoon they had advanced within three miles of where Major Brown was supposed to be; had been attacked by a large force of Indians, and had thought it better to choose a position and wait for re-enforcements. At early dawn the entire force was in motion. As we neared the head of Birch Coolie tents could be seen through the trees, and speculations were rife as to whether it was Brown's camp or that of the Indians, as they have tents very similar to our own.

The Indians were soon seen swarming through a belt of woods toward our column from the direction of the tents, and quickly scattering along the line, waving their blankets and shouting defiance, as if to entice us into the woods in pursuit. Some were mounted, and one on a white horse was especially conspicuous, riding up and down the line, and encouraging his comrades. Failing to draw the forces into the wood, they advanced nearer, and, throwing themselves down behind eminences which would afford protection, poured a rapid fire into the column. Nearly all the balls flew too high or were spent, and only one of our men was wounded. Skirmishers were at once thrown out, who, with quick discharges, drove them back, and the bursting shells from the cannon soon put them to rout. They retreated rapidly down Birch Coolie, and crossed the river at the agency.

The tents proved to be those of Major Brown, and the scene presented was most horrible. The camp was surrounded by the dead bodies of the horses, over ninety in number, perforated with balls. The tents were riddled with bullets, as many as one hundred and four being found in a single one. Ditches were dug between the tents, and the horses and the dirt piled on them so as to form a breastwork. Within this circuit lay thirteen of the soldiers dead, and a number wounded, many of them mortally, and a few feet distant were more dead bodies. Among the wounded were Major Brown, Captain Anderson, Agent Galbraith, and Captain Redfield, of Colonel

Sibley's staff. The groanings of the wounded could be heard a long distance off. William Irvine, of west St. Paul, presented a terrible spectacle. He had been shot in the head, and his brains were oozing over his face; and yet he lived for a number of hours, his breathing heavy and painfully distinct.

I have already stated that they had camped here on Monday evening. The spot was chosen because of its accessibility to wood and water, and but little reference to an attack had in view, as it was supposed that no Indians were in the neighborhood. In fact, a worse spot to repel an attack could not have been found. It was within gunshot of the head of the wooded ravine on one side, and of an elevation on the other, from behind which an attacking party could command the camp with safety to themselves. In the afternoon, just after the camp was pitched, some one thought he heard several guns fired, but little attention was paid to the statement. Ten sentinels were placed around the camp, with orders to keep a strict look-out, and to give the alarm at once in case of any suspicious appearance. The remainder, fatigued with the hard marching which they had endured for the past week, and with the labors of the day, for they had buried fifty-four victims of the outbreak, were soon wrapped in profound slumber, little dreaming of being prematurely aroused from it.

Just as it began to grow a little gray in the east, one of the sentinels thought he saw something creeping toward him in the grass. He fired at it, and before the echoes of the report had died away, a volley from three hundred guns, within a hundred yards of the slumbering camp, raked the tents "fore and aft." For more than three hours this firing was kept up with scarcely an intermission, and in that fatal three hours some twenty men were killed or mortally wounded, some sixty severely wounded, and over ninety horses killed. The Indian guns were mostly double-barreled, and there was a perfect rain of lead upon the little camp; the tents were riddled with balls, and the scene beggared description. After the effect of the first fire was partially over the men commenced to "dig," and dig they did with one pick, three spades, a couple of old axes, knives, bayonets, and sticks, and by four o'clock P.M. they had holes enough in the ground to protect them from shooting at a distance. When they were relieved by Colonel Sibley they had been thirty-one hours without food or water, with but thirty rounds of ammunition to the man when they commenced, and with less than five when relieved.* This was the most severe battle of the war in proportion to the number engaged. Twenty-three men were killed or mortally wounded, forty-five more severely wounded, and the remainder had been hit or received bullet-holes in their garments. One horse alone survived—a powerful stallion, who had been impressed at Henderson, and he was wounded.

Captain Grant had found a woman the day before near Beaver Creek, who, though badly wounded by a discharge of buckshot, had made her escape from the massacre near Patterson's Rapids. She had been fourteen days without seeing a human being, and had eaten nothing during this time but a few berries, obtained by dragging herself through the briers. When found she was nearly dead, and in such an exhausted

* Agent Galbraith's Report.

state as to be almost unable to speak, and could give but little account of herself or her sufferings. She was lying in a high wagon in the centre of the camp during the attack, and, strange to say, received no injury, though a number of balls passed through the wagon from different directions. God would not break the bruised reed.

Major Brown was correct in his conclusion that the Indians had left the Lower Agency several days before. On Thursday, four days after the last attack on New Ulm, hearing of Sibley's march to the fort, and anxious to place their families in safety, they had moved up above the Yellow Medicine River. Shortly after, an Indian, who had been getting in his traps back of New Ulm, told them that he had been within view of the town, and that it appeared to him to be deserted. On hearing this, a war party was at once organized to proceed to New Ulm and get what plunder they wanted, and then to attack St. Peter's and Mankato.

Early on Monday morning three hundred and forty-nine warriors, with a long train of wagons to carry their plunder, started down the river on the reservation side, under Gray Bird, of Crow's band, a Farmer Indian, and speaker of the Soldiers' Lodge. One hundred and ten more, under Crow, followed in an hour, with the intention of joining them, but crossed over the river at Yellow Medicine to meet any troops who might be coming up on that side to attack their families. They changed their minds after they had marched five or six miles, and went toward the Big Woods, in the neighborhood of Acton.

When Gray Bird's force arrived at the Lower Agency they caught sight of Major Brown's horsemen winding up the ravine to Grant's camp. Runners were sent over to watch their movements, and ascertain whether they were moving toward Yellow Medicine or the fort. When these returned and informed them that the whites had encamped, their joy knew no bounds, and they at once resolved on the attack which followed.

Had we sent out spies upon the movements of the Indians at Yellow Medicine, the result would have been different, for we might have surprised both parties, perhaps, with great slaughter. Colonel Sibley, in his report of the battle, says: "That the command was not destroyed before I arrived to rescue them from their perilous situation may be ascribed chiefly to the coolness of nerve displayed by Major Brown and Captain Anderson, both of whom were severely wounded." Captains Grant and Redfield, and Lieutenants Turnbull, Gillam, and Baldwin, behaved with great gallantry, as did all the men during the trying ordeal. After the dead were buried the command returned to the fort, carrying the wounded with them.

Disastrous as this affair was, it saved New Ulm from total destruction, and Mankato and St. Peter's, which were now left almost defenseless, from attacks which would necessarily have been attended with great loss of life and property.

CHAPTER IX.

THE WAR PARTY TO THE BIG WOODS.

LITTLE CROW'S party to the Big Woods traveled thirty miles on Monday, and camped near Acton. Twenty of them were mounted, and Little Crow rode in his own wagon with Jo. Campbell, a mixed blood, who acted as his driver and private secretary. Baptiste Campbell, Jo.'s brother, Louis la Belle, and Mágá (the Swan), all half-breeds, were also with the party. They traveled together until noon of the next day, when a quarrel arose. Little Crow, with thirty-four Indians and the half-breeds, started for Cedar Mills to get flour, after which they were to return to Yellow Medicine. They camped a mile and a half from Acton. The other party determined to make a raid through the country to St. Cloud, and camped within half a mile of Crow, without either being aware that night of the presence of the other, or of their proximity to any white men.

There was a party of white men, equally ignorant of the presence of these Indians, encamped at Acton, about a mile distant, in the yard of Howard Baker, one of the victims of the outrage which preceded the massacre. They were enlisted men and volunteer militia from Hennepin County, numbering in all about seventy-five men, under the command of Captain Richard Strout, of company B of the 9th Minnesota regiment. In the night several scouts came through from Forest City, informing them that on the preceding morning Captain Whitcomb had been attacked near that place by Indians (who belonged to another party than that just referred to), and to be on the lookout for them, and to hurry to the defense of the town. Early in the morning they started toward Hutchinson, intending to go from there to Forest City, as the direct road was more dangerous.

They passed by the larger body of Indians unperceived. As they approached Crow's camp, one of his Indians caught sight of them, and told the others there were three hundred whites coming. Then the Indians sent the half-breeds with the horses into the woods, and stripped themselves for battle. Just then the other party of Indians discovered the white men, and followed them up, whooping and firing. Crow's party appeared in their front, and the whites charged through them, firing as they advanced, and made their way to Hutchinson, closely followed by the Indians for four or five miles, losing nine horses, and several wagons containing arms, ammunition, cooking utensils, tents, etc., together with three killed and fifteen wounded.

Among the killed was Edwin Stone, a respectable merchant of Minneapolis. He was on foot when wounded, and endeavored to get into a wagon, but fell backward exclaiming, "My God, they will butcher me." Little Crow's son, a boy between fifteen and sixteen, ran up and shot him, and another Indian riding past jumped off his horse, sunk his tomahawk into his brain with a force that made him bound from the ground, leaped on his horse again, and joined in the pursuit. The wadding from the gun set Stone's clothes on fire, and one of the half-breeds endeavored to extinguish it by rubbing it with bunches of grass, which were afterward found near the body.

That night they encamped near Cedar Mills, and next morning advanced to Hutchinson, which they reached about ten o'clock. They burned a large portion of the town, and attacked Strout's company and others in the fort. Oma-ni-sa, a young Indian, called out in English to the garrison to come on the open field and fight like men. The whites came forth in squads and drove them back without the loss of any of their number. One of the Indians was severely wounded. He was carried as far as Lac qui Parle, where he died.

On the preceding day (the 3d), about two o'clock in the morning, the Indians, against whom Strout had been warned, numbering some fifty warriors, attacked Forest City, wounded two men, burned several buildings, and carried off a great deal of plunder.

The Hutchinson party, after skirmishing most of the day around that place, returned to their camping-place near Cedar Mills. They were joined during the night by the party who had attacked Forest City the preceding day. One of these, Kah-shak-a-wa-kan, brought Mrs. Adams as a prisoner. He had taken her child with her, but afterward murdered it in her presence.

Next morning the Indians again divided and returned home—Little Crow, with his party, by way of the Lower Agency, which he reached that night.

One of the scouts, while riding along, was startled by his horse jumping aside. He looked for the cause, and saw a white man lying in a pile of grass, which he had pulled up and heaped around him for concealment. Close to him were ears of green corn partially eaten. He was a young man; his hands were small; his hair was long and fair; but his garments were tattered and torn with long journeyings, and the face was haggard and pale. He was asleep, with his cheek resting on his hand; so soundly asleep, so intensely engaged, perhaps, in happy dreams—for thus, sometimes, does our nature compensate for the sufferings of our wakeful hours—that the trampling of the Indian's horse did not arouse him. "What do you here, my friend?" sounded in his ear in the loud voice of the savage. The sleeper raised his head and gazed with startled apprehension in the face of his threatening foe, whose presence he had shunned with bated breath for many a weary league; and before that expression had time even to change, the whirring axe dashed out the brains which gave it life. Then the murderer, dismounting, with his knife cut off the head; but even then that startled look did not change, for death had frozen it there, and nothing but corruption's effacing hand could sweep it away. The shuddering half-breeds who followed afterward passed by on the other side, and Crow said, "Poor fellow! his life ought to have been spared; he was too starved to have done us harm." But they left it there unburied, in its pool of blood, staring upward through the gathering darkness with its fixed, wild eyes, alone in the vast desolation, ringed by distant skies, there to remain until Nature, by storm and frost, should transform it to original clay, and by the blessed sunlight "reconcile it to herself again with the sweet oblivion of flowers."

Fort Abercrombie had been in a continued state of siege by the Sissetons since the 25th of August, and communication with it cut off, but the remainder of the country had been but little visited by the Indians since they left New Ulm on the 24th of August; and this fact, and the presence of the force on the frontier, had quieted the fears of the people, and induced many to return to their homes; but the attacks at Birch Coolie, Acton, Hutchinson, Forest City, and the massacre of citizens at Hilo, twenty miles above St. Peter's, and in the Butternut Valley, far within Sibley's lines, occurring on the 2d, 3d, and 4th of September, threw the whole country again into the most intense excitement. Portions even of Ramsey County was depopulated, and citizens on the outskirts of St. Paul moved into the interior of the city. General Sibley's family, living in Mendota, went one night to Fort Snelling for protection. Far and wide the wild news spread, like the wrath of fire racing on the wings of the wind.*

* On the 3d of September Fort Abercrombie was attacked in force by several hundred Sissetons and Yanktonais.

CHAPTER X.

THE CAPTIVES.

COLONEL SIBLEY was compelled to remain many days inactive at Fort Ridgely for want of ammunition and supplies; nor did the Indians commit any extensive outrages in the mean time, for the reason that a correspondence was being carried on for the delivery of the captives and a cessation of hostilities.

Little Crow, could he have followed his own inclinations, would have been willing, even at the commencement of the outbreak, to have made terms of peace. He did not join in the war as a matter of choice, but was forced into it by circumstances, as has already been shown. His reputation was that of a great liar, but he was not naturally a cruel-hearted man. It is said that many an Indian, who went by his door without sufficient covering, received from the chief a blanket, though he had to take it from his own back. He rejoiced, it is true, that the traders and employés of the government had been killed, because he considered that they had been the cause of all the troubles of his people, but it is not believed that he was guilty of the murder of any unarmed white person. He informed Chaska of the peril of his friend Spencer, and tried to save Myrick's life, and, at the risk of his own, assisted Charles Blair to escape. He openly opposed the slaughter of unarmed settlers and their families. At the agency the next day after the massacre commenced, assembling his warriors together in council, he addressed them as follows:

"Soldiers and young men, you ought not to kill women and children. Your consciences will reproach you for it hereafter, and make you weak in battle. You were too hasty in going into the country. You should have killed only those who have been robbing us so long. Hereafter make war after the manner of white men."

Desirous as he might have been for the cessation of a hopeless contest, he dared not broach the subject in the beginning to his braves. The plunder they had acquired, the numerous bloody deeds they had committed, and the belief of success infused them with fierce joy, and determined them upon a continuance of the war. After the defeat at Fort Ridgely and New Ulm, the chief was more thoroughly convinced than before of the certainty of defeat; and Joseph Campbell told the writer that at his (Crow's) dictation, on their way to the Big Woods, on the 1st of September, he wrote letters to Governor Ramsey and Colonel Sibley, requesting a cessation of hostilities and a treaty of settlement, and that these letters Crow exhibited to his braves, and that they would not allow them to be sent.

From the first there was trouble between the Upper and Lower Indians. Besides the feeling of semi-hostility which exists between separate communities, and especially among Indians, who are always quarreling with one another, the pride of the former was hurt by the failure of the others to counsel with them before commencing the war. There was another ground of complaint more serious than this. The latter had acquired a large amount of plunder before the Upper Indians came down, and their chiefs sent word if they would join in the war there should be an equal distribution of the spoils. This promise the braves of the Lower Indians refused to carry out, on the ground that it would be unfair to share with those who had done nothing that which they had periled their lives to obtain. They did not surrender for a long time even that which belonged to the half-breed relatives of the others, nor until a "Soldiers' Lodge" was formed, and demanded it in an interview which seriously threatened a bloody termination.

Prominent among the disaffected was Paul Ma-za-ku-ta-ma-ne, a civilized Indian, and head deacon of Mr. Riggs's church. Paul was a man of great oratorical powers and unflinching nerve. He was the chief speaker of the Sissetons. Like Crow, and other intelligent and aged men, he believed in the hopelessness of the contest; nor was he at all chary in so expressing himself, for he had the protection of his people, who had not been so deeply implicated in the troubles as the others. At a council at the Lower Agency, soon after the Yellow Medicine Indians came down, Paul made the following speech to the Lower Indians:

"Warriors and young men!—I am an Indian, and you are Indians, and there should be no secrets between us. Why, then, did you not tell us that you were going to kill the whites? All of us will have to suffer for what you have done. The preachers have told us that there is to be an end of the world. The end of the world is near at hand for the nation of the Dakotas. Every Indian knows that we can not live without the aid of the white man. Why, then, have you acted like children? You have spoken, too, with false tongues. Two days ago you sent a message by Sha-ko-pee, one of your chiefs, that you had laid aside for us half of your plunder. We have come to get it, and we see nothing. If you choose to act by yourselves in this way, every man must do the same, and henceforth I shall think and look out for myself."

Little Crow was statesman enough to know that a main lever to the procurement of peace was the prosecution of a formidable war; and he was Indian enough to desire, if peace was not obtained, to inflict as much injury as possible upon his opponents. Policy, therefore, required that the Upper Indians should be encouraged and conciliated, and their aid secured.

To enforce his ideas he had a tongue of most persuasive power. "I am an orator!" said Red Jacket, proudly; "I was born an orator!" Not less sensible of his gift was the Sioux chieftain. At the councils years before, when other Indians were endeavoring to make themselves understood, the knowledge of his own superior ability would manifest itself in his countenance, and the superbly contemptuous manner with which he would wrap his blanket around him and stride away was a subject of remark among the white lookers-on. The Rev. Dr. Williamson, the oldest living missionary among the Sioux, has stated that, though he knew Little Crow's complicity in the war, he would almost have been afraid to have met him, for fear he would have convinced him of his spotless innocence. Paul's speech produced some effect among his people, but it was done away with by Crow, who addressed them at length, telling them that they could easily conquer the whites; that there was plenty more plunder in the country; and that all they had to do was to persevere, and they could camp the next winter with their squaws in St. Paul. He then read to them a letter which Jo. Campbell, at his dictation, had written to the English at Pembina. The letter said:

"Our fathers have told us that when the English fought the Americans the Sioux helped them, and captured a cannon, which they gave to them, and which was called the 'Little Dakota.' Do you recollect this? We have helped you when you were in trouble. My own grandfather periled his life in your cause. Now we are in difficulty, and want that cannon and your assistance. We shall soon send men to council with you, and to bring the cannon; and we want you also to give us plenty of powder and lead. With these we can defeat the Americans."

Colonel Sibley, on leaving the battle-ground at Birch Coolie with a view of obtaining the release of the captives, had attached to a stake a communication in the following words:

"If Little Crow has any proposition to make, let him send a half-breed to me, and he shall be protected in and out of camp.

"H. H. Sibley, Col. Com'g Mil. Ex'n."

This was found and delivered to Crow on his return from Hutchinson, and he at once dispatched, with the consent of his braves, whom the Birch Coolie affair had disheartened, two mixed bloods under a flag of truce, with a letter, of which the following is substantially a copy:

"Yellow Medicine, September 7th, 1862.

"Dear Sir,—For what reason we have commenced this war I will tell you. It is on account of Major Galbraith. We made a treaty with the government, and beg for what we do get, and can't get that till our children are dying with hunger. It is the traders who commenced it. Mr. A. J. Myrick told the Indians that they would eat grass or dirt. Then Mr. Forbes told the Lower Sioux that they were not men. Then Roberts was working with his friends to defraud us out of our moneys. If the young braves have pushed the white men, I have done this myself. So I want you to let Governor Ramsey know this. I have a great many prisoners, women and children. It ain't all our fault. The Winnebagoes were in the engagement, and two of them were killed. I want you to give me an answer by the bearer. All at present.

"Yours truly, Friend Little his × mark Crow."

Addressed, "Gov. H. H. Sibley, Esq., Fort Ridgely."

By these messengers Colonel Sibley sent the following reply:

"LITTLE CROW,—You have murdered many of our people without any sufficient cause. Return me the prisoners under a flag of truce, and I will talk with you then like a man.

"H. H. SIBLEY, Col. com'g Mil. Exp'n."

On the 12th of September, the same messengers who had appeared on the previous occasion made a second entry into camp as bearers of dispatches from the same source as before. The following is a literal copy of the communication:

"Red Iron Village, or May awaken.

"To Hon H H Sibley

"we have in mawakanton band One Hundred and fifty five presoners—not includ the Sisiton & warpeton presoners, then we are waiting for the Sisiton what we are going to do whit the priseners they are coming doun. they are at Lake quiparle now. The words that il to the govrment il want to here from him also, and I want to know from you as a friend what way that il can make peace for my people —in regard to prisoners they fair with our chilldren or our self jist as well as us Your truly friend LITTLE CROW

"per A J Campbell"

To this communication Colonel Sibley penned the

following reply, and sent it forward by the messengers of Little Crow upon their return to the encampment of that chief:

"Head-quarters Military Expedition, September 12, 1862.

"To Little Crow, Sioux Chief:

"I have received your letter of to-day. You have not done as I wished in giving up to me the prisoners taken by your people. It would be better for you to do so. I told you I had sent your former letter to Governor Ramsey, but I have not yet had time to receive a reply. You have allowed your young men to commit nine murders since you wrote your first letter. That is not the way for you to make peace. H. H. Sibley, Col. com'g Mil. Exp'n."

At the same time that the last letter was received from Little Crow, Mr. Robertson, one of the messengers from that chief, brought privately and in a clandestine manner the following note from Wabashaw and Taopee, one of the Farmer Indians:

"Mayawakan, September 10th, 1862.

"Col. H. H. Sibley, Fort Ridgely:

"Dear Sir,—You know that Little Crow has been opposed to me in every thing that our people have had to do with the whites. He has been opposed to every thing in the form of civilization or Christianity. I have always been in favor of, and of late years have done every thing of the kind that has been offered to us by the government and other good white people—he has now got himself into trouble that we know he can never get himself out of, and he is trying to involve those few of us that are still the friend of the American in the murder of the poor whites that have been settled in the border, but I have been kept back by threats that I should be killed if I did any thing to help the whites; but if you will now appoint some place for me to meet you, myself and the few friends that I have will get all the prisoners that we can, and with our family go to whatever place you will appoint for us to meet. I would say further that the mouth of the Red-Wood, Candiohi, on the north side of the Minnesota, or the head of the Cotton-wood River—one of these places, I think, would be a good place to meet. Return the messenger as quick as possible. We have not much time to spare.

"Your true friends, Wabashaw,
Taopee."

To this letter Colonel Sibley returned by the same messenger the following answer:

"Head-quarters Military Indian Expedition, September 12th, 1862.

"To Wabashaw and Taopee:

"I have received your private message. I have come up here with a large force to punish the murderers of my people. It is not my purpose to injure any innocent person. If you and others who have not been concerned in the murders and expeditions will gather yourselves, with all the prisoners, on the prairie in full sight of my troops, and when a white flag is displayed by you a white flag will be hoisted in my camp, and then you can come forward and place yourself under my protection. My troops will be all mounted in two days' time, and in three days from this day I expect to march. There must be no attempt to approach my column or my camp except in open day, and with a flag of truce conspicuously displayed. I shall be glad to receive all true friends of the whites, with as many prisoners as they can bring, and I am powerful enough to crush all who attempt to oppose my march, and to punish those who have washed their hands in innocent blood. I sign myself the friend of all who were friends of your great American Father.

"H. H. Sibley, Colonel commanding Expedition."

Wabashaw and Taopee were Lower Indians, and dared not do any thing openly in favor of a delivery of the prisoners; but there began now a fierce controversy on the subject between a part of the Upper Indians, headed by Paul, and the others. The Lower Indians saw from Colonel Sibley's letters that he demanded an unconditional surrender of the captives, and that he would not make terms by which any of the guilty might escape, and, knowing that they were all deeply implicated, determined that the captives should share whatever fate they suffered. Paul thought, if the Upper Indians could get possession of the captives and deliver them to the whites, most of them would escape with impunity. He sought to detach them from the others, and make them a unit on this point, and, to accomplish it, cunningly fanned the elements of separation which already existed.

While the discussion proceeded, the Lower Indians, in order to counsel about the matter, made a feast, and invited the others to attend. Nearly all the Annuity Sioux were present. The following speeches were made. Mazza-wa-mnu-na, of Shakopee's band, a Lower Indian, made the first speech.

"You men who are in favor of leaving us and delivering up the captives, talk like children. You believe, if you do so, the whites will think you have acted as their friends, and will spare your lives. They will not, and you ought to know it. You say that the whites are too strong for us, and that we will all have to perish. Well, by sticking together and fighting the whites, we will live, at all events, for a few days, when, by the course you propose, we would die at once. Let us keep the prisoners with us, and let them share our fate. That is all the advice I have to give."

Rda-in-yan-ka, Wabashaw's son-in-law, and a soldier of Crow's band, spoke next as follows:

"I am for continuing the war, and am opposed to the delivery of the prisoners. I have no confidence that the whites will stand by any agreement they make if we give them up. Ever since we treated with them their agents and traders have robbed and cheated us. Some of our people have been shot, some hung; others placed upon floating ice and drowned; and many have been starved in their prisons. It was not the intention of the nation to kill any of the whites until after the four men returned from Acton and told what they had done. When they did this, all the young men became excited, and commenced the massacre. The older ones would have prevented it if they could, but since the treaties they have lost all their influence. We may regret what has happened, but the matter has gone too far to be remedied. We have got to die. Let us, then, kill as many of the whites as possible, and let the prisoners die with us."

Paul was the next speaker. A great many Indians were present; and as he was anxious that all should hear, he stood up on a barrel, and spoke in a loud voice as follows:

"I am going to tell you what I think, and what I am ready to do, now and hereafter. You, M'dewakanton and Wahpekuta Indians, have been with the white men a great deal longer than the Upper Indians, yet I, who am an Upper Indian, have put on white men's clothes, and consider myself now a white man. I was very much surprised to hear that you had been killing the settlers, for you have had the advice of the preachers for so many years. Why did you not tell us you were going to kill them? I ask you the question again, Why did you not tell us? You make no answer. The reason was, if you had done so, and we had counseled together, you would not have been able to have involved our young men with you. When we older men heard of it we were so surprised that we knew not what to do. By your involving our young men without consulting us you have done us a great injustice. I am now going to tell you something you don't like. You have gotten our people into this difficulty through your incitements to its rash young soldiers without a council being called and our consent obtained, and I shall use all the means I can to get them out of it without reference to you. I am opposed to their continuing this war, or of committing farther outrages, and I warn them not to do it. I have heard a great many of you say that you were brave men, and could whip the whites. This is a lie. Persons who will cut women and children's throats are squaws and cowards. You say the whites are not brave. You will see. They will not, it is true, kill women and children, as you have done, but they will fight you who have arms in your hands. I am ashamed of the way that you have acted toward the captives. Fight the whites if you desire to, but do it like brave men. Give me the captives, and I will carry them to Fort Ridgely. I hear one of you say that if I take them there the soldiers will shoot me. I will take the risk. I am not afraid of death, but I am opposed to the way you act toward the prisoners. If any of you have the feelings of men, you will give them up. You may look as fierce at me as you please, but I shall ask you once, twice, and ten times to deliver these women and children to their friends. That is all I have to say."

White Lodge's eldest son, one of those engaged in the Lake Shetek massacre, was the fourth speaker. He said:

"I am an Upper Indian, but I am opposed to what Paul advises. I hope our people will not agree with him. We must all die in battle, or perish with hunger, and let the captives suffer what we suffer."

This was all that was said in this council. Paul had no other speaker to assist him, and the Lower Indians would not consent that the captives should be delivered.

Paul went home and communicated the result to those who coincided with him, and by their advice he killed an ox and invited the Indians to another feast and council. They met, and a similar discussion took place, in which Paul, in addition to what he had formerly stated, said that the captives should not be taken into the battle, as some of them threatened; that if he had to die, as they said he must, he would die in endeavoring to deliver them; and that, as one third of the Upper Indians would stand by him in this, they had better deliver them, if they desired to prevent a quarrel among themselves.

The danger of collision was imminent. Had it occurred, the prisoners would all have been murdered. The Upper Indians, who were opposed to a junction with the Lower ones, formed a Soldiers' Lodge, and commanded them not to proceed any farther into their country; and at Red Iron's village, that chief, and a hundred and fifty Sissetons on horseback, formed a line in front of their column, and fired their guns off as a signal to halt. They were afraid that they were going through to Big Stone Lake, and leave them to stand the brunt of the rage of the whites; for they had said at first that they would make a stand at Yellow Medicine, and die there if necessary.

On being assured that they would not go as far as Lac qui Parle, and giving Red Iron's men some of their plunder, the chief allowed them to camp at a spot which he selected. The plunder was at first refused, and only a small portion turned over, and that under a threat from Red Iron and his men, that unless it was done, when Standing Buffalo, who was on his way, came down with the other Sissetons, they

RED IRON.

would join together and take the prisoners by force, and make peace with the whites, and leave the others to shift for themselves.

At this time the prisoners stood in great peril, because many of the Lower Indians were in favor of killing them to remove the inducement they offered to the others to separate and make peace. As an additional argument, they said that the whites had starved them before, and that there was no use to take the bread from their own mouths to feed so many captives.

When Standing Buffalo and his warriors arrived, another council was called. The Sissetons were ranged on one side, the Wahpetons on another, and the Lower Indians by themselves. Paul was the first speaker. He said:

"Soldiers and young men of the Sissetons!—I told the Lower Indians my mind before your arrival, and am now going to repeat what I have said in your hearing. First of all, they commenced war upon the whites without letting us know any thing about it. The Sissetons didn't hear of it until several days afterward. Why should we assist them? We are under no obligations to do so. I am part Sisseton and part Wahpeton, and I know that they have never interested themselves in our affairs. When we went to war against the Chippeways they never helped us.

"Lower Indians!—You are fools. We want nothing to do with you. We belong to the same nation, but you started the massacre without telling us about it, and have bribed our young men to kill the whites, and thought that by so doing you could involve us all in the same trouble. You are mistaken. You must give up the prisoners, or we will fight you. I and a hundred others have made up our minds to wait here for the soldiers."

Some of the younger Indians, who were fully armed, made so many angry demonstrations here that it was feared that the council would have a bloody termination; but they were persuaded to leave the grounds, and, after quiet was restored, Paul continued:

"I want to know from you Lower Indians whether you were asleep or crazy. In fighting the whites, you are fighting the thunder and lightning. You will all be killed off. You might as well try to bail out the waters of the Mississippi as to whip them. You say you can make a treaty with the British government. That is impossible. Have you not yet come to your senses? They are also white men, and neighbors and friends to the soldiers. They are ruled by a petticoat, and she has the tender heart of a squaw. What will she do for men who have committed the murders you have? Your young men have brought a great misfortune upon us. Let *them* go and fight the soldiers. But you, who want to live and not die, come with me. I am going to shake hands with the whites. I hear some of your young men talking very loud, and boasting that you have killed so many women and children. That's not brave; it is cowardly. Go and fight the soldiers. That's brave. You dare not. When you see their army coming on the plains, you will faint with fright. You will throw down your arms, and fly in one direction and your women in another, and this winter you will all starve. You will see that my words will come true. Go back from the lands of the Sissetons. They have not buffaloes enough for themselves, and can not feed you. Fight the whites on your reservation if you are not afraid of them. Make your boasts good, and stop your lies."

Here the excitement of the Lower Indians became so great that some of them cried out, "Kill him! kill him!" But Paul, unfaltering, continued in a loud voice:

"Some of you say you will kill me. Bluster away. I am not afraid. I am not a woman, and I shall not die alone. There are three hundred around me whom you will also have to kill before you have finished."

Wabashaw's son-in-law, Rda-in-yan-ka, made the next speech. He said:

"We all heard what Paul said the other day, and we have had several councils to decide what to do, but have arrived at no conclusion, and we desire a little longer time to think over it. Before the treaties the old men determined these questions, but now I have no influence, nor have the chiefs. The young soldiers must decide it."

Wakin-yan-to-ci-ye, of Crow's band, was the next speaker. He said:

"You have asked for the prisoners several times, and you must make up your minds not to ask any more. We are determined that the captives shall die with us."

Mah-pi-ya-na-xka-xka, a soldier of the Lac qui Parle band, made the next speech. He spoke as follows:

"I am an Upper Indian, and have heard what Paul has said, and do not agree with him. He is for giving up the captives and making peace. It can not be done. We have gone too far. Since the treaties, when did we do the least thing, either in stealing cattle or in harming a white man, that we did not get punished for? Now the Indians have been killing men, women, and children, how many God only knows, and if we give ourselves up we shall all be hung. I have heard that there were four stores full of goods for us here. I come and find nothing. How is this?"

Little Crow was the next speaker. He said:

"Paul wants to make peace. It is impossible to do so, if we desired. Did we ever do the most trifling thing, and the whites not hang us? Now we have been killing them by hundreds in Dakota, Minnesota, and Iowa, and I know that if they get us into their power they will hang every one of us. As for me, I will kill as many of them as I can, and fight them till I die. Do not think you will escape. There is not a band of Indians from the Red-Wood Agency to Big Stone Lake that has not had some of its members embroiled in the war. I tell you we must fight and perish together. A man is a fool and a coward who thinks otherwise, and who will desert his nation at such a time. Disgrace not yourselves by a surrender to those who will hang you up like dogs, but die, if die you must, with arms in your hands, like warriors and braves of the Dakota."

Standing Buffalo, hereditary chief of the Upper Sissetons, spoke next, as follows:

"I am a young man, but I have always felt friendly toward the whites because they were kind to my father. You have brought me into great danger without my knowing of it beforehand. By killing the whites, it is just as if you had waited for me in ambush and shot me down. You Lower Indians feel very bad because we have all got into trouble; but I feel worse, because I know that neither I nor my people have killed any of the whites, and that yet we have to suffer for the guilty. I was out buffalo-hunting when I heard of the outbreak, and I felt as if I was dead, and I feel so now. You all know that the Indians can not live without the aid of the white men, and therefore I have made up my mind that Paul is right, and my Indians will stand by him. We claim this reservation. What are you doing here? If you

STANDING BUFFALO.

want to fight the whites, go back and fight them. Leave me at my village at Big Stone Lake. You sent word to my young men to come down, and that you had plenty of oxen, and horses, and goods, and powder, and lead, and now we see nothing. We are going back to Big Stone Lake, and leave you to fight the whites. Those who make peace can say that Standing Buffalo and his people will give themselves up in the spring."

Wanata, the mixed Sisseton and Yanktonais chief, from the vicinity of Lac Traverse, was the next speaker. He said:

"You ask me to fight the whites. I want to ask you a question. You said you had plenty of powder and lead for us. Where is it? You make no answer. I will. You have it all. Go, then, you, and fight the whites with it. You are unreasonable to ask me to do so, for two reasons: first, I have no powder and lead; second, I can't live without the whites. You have cut my throat, and now you ask my assistance. You can't have it. I am going home. Above Lac qui Parle the country belongs to us. Stay on your own lands and don't come on ours. You can fight, and I will give myself up in the spring and shake hands with the whites. I have finished."

Wasou-washta and Wa-kein-to-wa, Spencer's friend, were the only ones, besides Paul, who spoke openly in favor of delivering the prisoners. After this council the Lower Indians held one by themselves, and sent four Indians to Paul to know if his party would join them in the war, and he gave them the same answer. Then they accused him and the others of cowardice, and the interview ended in a quarrel. Paul also told them that he had heard that Wabashaw and Taopee had written a letter to Colonel Sibley, but they said that it was not true; that they had heard the same thing, and had asked Wabashaw about it, but he denied it.

As time progressed the excitement increased, and the fate of the captives grew more hopeless. After Standing Buffalo arrived, a large number of Sissetons came in from Abercrombie. One of their squaws was loud in her incitements to battle. She had a white man's whiskers tied to a pole, which she had obtained at that fort, and flourished over her head while she sang a song to the purport that the whites had made the Indians mad, and that they would cut them into bits.

Little Crow did not cease to encourage his men, for he perceived that there was no other course left open but battle. He stated that there were from two to three thousand British soldiers at Lac Traverse, who would soon be down to assist them, and that he believed, from signs he had seen at the Big Woods, that the Chippeways were co-operating with them. He urged that the Winnebagoes would also rise and go down the west side of the Mississippi, while he would take care of the country on the east, and that the other Sioux would capture the forts on the Missouri.

There was a Yankton present who was a very fluent speaker. He addressed the Indians at great length in support of Crow's views. He traced on the ground a map of the country, showing the course of the Missouri, and the locality of the different forts. He also marked out the ocean, and stated that a great nation was coming across this to help them, and its people would bring them plenty of ammunition. Crow's brother ridiculed the courage of the whites, and narrated, with much glee, how he cut off the limbs of the men with one stroke of a cleaver, and that they made no resistance, but stared at him like poor dumb beasts. The young braves kept themselves in a high state of excitement by their war orgies. These they no longer conducted on foot, but upon the horses which they had stolen and trained to dance.

Other letters, indicating the condition of affairs in the camp, and the anxiety and peril of the captives, were received from the friendly Indians from time to time, of which the following are copies:

"Maya-wakan, September 14, 1862.

"DEAR SIR,—The first time that the young braves that brought the prisoners in camp I was opposed to it, but Crow opposed it and other things. I am afraid to come back on my reserve, but you will decide this for me. You told us that you wanted the priserners, so we quit fighting. Some of the prisoners have run away from our camp. There is three parties out, but when they come back we will quit the war for good. In regard to half-breeds, if you say that I should give them, I will do so. My friend, you know Wabashaw—that I am not a bad man. I am a kind-hearted man. I know myself that the poor women ain't the blamed for the fight. I am always in for good. If you want to make peace with the Friendly Indians, we want to hear from you in regard to it. I am trying to do what is right. I hope that you will do so, and deal honestly with us. I want you to write me a good letter.

"Yours truly, WABASHAW" his × mark.

"Red Iron's Village, September 15th, 1862.

"Ex. Governor Sibley:

"HON. SIR,—I have just seen your letter to Wabaxa and the other two chiefs. They intend to raise the white flag. It is our intention to join these bands; but if your troops do not reach here till the last of the week, it may be too late for our rescue. The Red Iron and the lower bands have held two councils already about killing off the captives, which includes the whites, half-breeds, and all those that have dressed like the whites. I have tried all that I could to get the captives free; have held two councils with the lower bands, but Little Crow won't give them up. Eight have come to me for protection till they can get better from their own people. I keep them in my family. I have tried to send a letter to you several times, but am watched very close. This letter, or rather a copy of it, was sent one day by a young man, but he could not get away from the other Indians in safety, so he returned. The half-breeds, and all the white captives, are in the greatest danger, for they declare they will put them to death as soon as your troops appear. We shall do as you requested as soon as practicable (that is, to raise the flag). Now, dear sir, please let me know what time we may expect you, for our lives are hazarded if we move before we can receive aid. I am glad you are powerful and strong, for, if God helps, you will conquer. As Christians, we are looking to him, and trust he will send you to free us. We have held meetings every Sabbath since the missionaries left. Oh! deliver us, if possible, from our savage foes, and we shall try to show you how much we honor our great American Father.

"Very respectfully, MA-ZA-KU-TA-MA-NE, or PAUL."

"September 18th.

"HON. SIR,—We think it just to witness our hands to the above, and also to state that this is the fourth letter we have written for him to send to you, but, as he said, he could not send it. Paul held a council with some of the lower chiefs, and talked very bravely to them. They wished to know if he was going to join the whites, telling him, at the same time, that chiefs had given themselves up and been killed (we didn't believe it). He told them plainly he should join them. They said he was no brave; says Paul, 'I am not brave to murder, and do such wicked acts as your people do, but you shall see I am brave to do right.' His life is in danger every moment from his speech. Paul requests us again to urge you to write immediately when he may expect you, so he can get his band ready, if possible, before the slaughter commences among the captives. We dare not give our names in full, but Rev. Mr. Riggs will know, for he married John and ——. M. A. BUTLER."

"September 18th.

"The Lower Friendly Indians to Hon. Governor Sibley:

"DEAR SIR,—We are in trouble about putting up the white flag. Some of the young men say they will go along with us, and, when near enough, will commence firing at your troops, so you see we are betrayed. Do let us know what we shall do; we are in jeopardy every moment. Great excitement last night about killing the captives, but nothing done. Please understand about the flag, and a part of the soldiers making you believe we are the enemies; so do write what we shall do. We hope you will hasten on, and spare the lives of the innocent." (*No signature.*)

"Red Iron's Village, September 19th, 1862.

"Colonel H. H. Sibley:

"I would like to see you in person this day, but I am in a hurry and can not come, so I send you a letter, which will answer the purpose. My brother, I talk to you on this paper to let you know that I have not forgotten that you are my friend. I still remember it was with the white man's provision that I have lived through the severe winter; for that reason, my friendship to you is unshaken. Although

I have known of one bad thing this day, it was none of my fault. I had nothing whatever to do with it. I came down here to this place to find out who disturbed the peace between us, and for what reason. I have now found out, and am in a hurry to return. The nation is about to sacrifice itself for the sake of a few foolish young men. As for me, my great Father wished me to live, therefore he gave me provisions and money; and now it seems as though they had suddenly taken it from me, and thrown it into the water. My heart is sad, not only because I have not seen my goods, but because this day I have seen the destitution of our half-breeds. They are our flesh and blood, and therefore we are anxious for their welfare. My heart is still made more sad at the sight of the many captives; but they are not my captives, and, were my band strong enough, they should be released. My brother, I want to say something which I hope you will regard. I heard of this trouble while I was away from home, but did not believe it, and so I came down to see for myself; and now that I have seen and heard, I am in a hurry to get back, and tell my relatives the straight of it. Although they have tried to shake our friendship, yet I am anxious to renew it, and let it be stronger than ever. You are anxious to punish the offenders; but I ask a favor—that is, to wait on me until I have gathered my people and relatives together, for they are many and scattered. I ask this favor because I am fearful lest your hurry should fail my intentions.

"TATANKA NAJIN (Standing Buffalo), Chief of the Sissetons."

"Red Iron's Village, September 24th.

"Ex. Gov. Sibley: Hon. Sir:

"I have written some three or four letters to you, but never could send them. From the first I was anxious to extend and renew our friendship, and that of all the whites, and also are my friends, the Lower chiefs, that wish for peace. I held two councils as soon as the enemies came to our peaceful republic, in order to get the captives free, willing to hazard my own life could I obtain the liberty of the poor captives. The enemy are holding a council this morning, and wanted us to join them. They are rebels. We prefer our own councils and writing our own letters. The captives have been coming to us for safety until we have the greatest number, and so we are in danger of a battle from them immediately. Now, dear sir, please come right away without delay, or we may all fall victims, for fight we must soon. The enemy are not large in numbers, but you well know they are cruel savages (and the women, in the writer's opinion, can fight as well as the men). All the Indians, with the exception of these, are friendly, and, were we prepared for defending ourselves, we should conquer; and if you don't hasten, our women and all the captives will suffer. Yours respectfully,

"MA-ZA-KU-TA-MA-NE,
"TAOPEE, and
"WAKE-WAN-WA.

"Hon. Ex. Gov. Sibley, Col. commanding.

"This letter is at the request of all our people. Maza-moni and Akipa are desirous of having their names put down with the Friendly Indians, feeling that they have had trouble enough, and are desirous of peace. All in great haste."

LITTLE PAUL.

CHAPTER XI.

UPWARD MARCH AND BATTLE OF WOOD LAKE.

On the afternoon of the 18th of September the camp at Fort Ridgely was broken up, and the expedition, disgusted with the long inactivity, joyfully started on its upward march after the foe. As crossing above might be attended with an ambuscade, a boat was constructed near the fort, and the expedition there ferried over. Just as the last of the train was leaving, a man was seen coming from the west. The scouts rode toward him to ascertain who he was. He proved to be a fugitive German almost starved. When they approached he supposed that they were Indians, and was hacking away at his throat with his knife to commit suicide, but the edge was too dull to effect his purpose.

The first camp was two miles above, and darkness came on before we were all across. Next morning we started with the dawn, and camped early in the afternoon a few miles below the agency. None of the enemy appeared during the day. Some of the men visited the houses of the "Farmer Indians," which were in the edge of the woods, and returned laden with buffalo robes and trinkets. A few miles above they found and buried the remains of Mr. Prescott, the government farmer. He had been concealed at the agency by his wife, a mixed blood, in an oven during the massacre, and then started for the fort.

The Indians met him. He pleaded long and earnestly for his life, but without avail. He was killed, and his head cut off and placed upon a pole, with the face toward St. Paul, "in order," as his murderers said, with grim facetiousness, "that he might watch for their money." He was an old man, and had lived many years among them. Soon after dark the presence of Indians was made manifest by their firing one of the buildings in the woods a mile from the camp. It was done to lure our men into an ambush, but it failed of success.

Early the next morning we proceeded on our way. On passing Prescott's grave we found several hundred little sticks thrust in the fresh dirt, indicating the number of Indians who had visited it.* All that day about a dozen of the enemy, well mounted, were seen two or three miles ahead. They were scouts from the camp above Yellow Medicine. Our route lay over a rolling prairie. Up every high hillock before us these scouts would gallop, watch our movements until we approached near, and then scud away. All objects on a prairie seem larger by reason of the absence of standards of comparison, and are more distinctly limned against the sky than elsewhere. The picturesque appearance of these horsemen—the knowledge that they were foes—the mystery associated with a different race, and the fact that they were probably possessed of secrets of movements of vital importance, invested them with strange and romantic interest. On a fence near the Red-Wood River they left a message of defiance, telling us to come on, and that the braves were ready for us at Yellow Medicine. They

* "These Indians were the ones alluded to in Wabashaw's letter.

also amused themselves with firing several bridges to impede our progress. These were smoking when we came up, but not materially injured.

The train stopped for dinner a mile and a half from the Red-Wood River, and young Myrick, one of the scouts (a cousin of the trader of that name, who was killed at the Lower Agency), in company with another person, galloped ahead to the brow of the bluff overhanging the Red-Wood River. Here there was a deep, spacious, valley-like gorge, a mile and a half across, caused by the meanderings of the stream. The bluffs were belted thickly with trees, and in the valley were large marshes of tall grass, and cornfields, and great patches of dense underbrush, with rocky acclivities rising above them. On a number of these were houses. The place was just the one for an Indian ambuscade. Where the horsemen stood there were fresh ears of green corn partially eaten, and sticks of kin-ne-kin-nic from which the Indians had recently whittled the bark.

As Myrick and his companion stood there, they saw Other Day on horseback visiting the different houses to their right, and they immediately observed to one another that he was committing a very hazardous and foolish act, for it would be so easy for the enemy to pick him off. Presently he rode to where they were standing, and they, forgetting their comments on his conduct, proposed to go farther up the valley to the house of John Moore. To this the Indian assented, and the three forded the Red-Wood, and rode to the foot of the rocks upon which the house was situated. Here Other Day fastened his horse to a plum-tree, threw himself upon the ground, and began eating the rich fruit which lay in great abundance below. The others followed his example. In a few moments he ran up the rocks to the house, leaving his horse fastened. Myrick's companion said it was dangerous to leave their horses there, as they had seen Indians all the morning ahead, and, close to where they now were, had observed a fresh moccasin track in the road, and plum-stones from which the fruit had just been eaten, and that it was best to have their horses with them.

So saying, he led his horse up to the house, and stood holding him at the door. Other Day was then up stairs. Myrick ran up presently. He said he had been debating whether to tie his horse or bring him along, and had finally concluded to leave him there without hitching. He then went up stairs and left the other at the door. The rough rocks were not inviting, nor were any of the surroundings. The windows were all smashed to pieces, and the floor littered with various articles. On the outside was the trunk belonging to Prescott, whom we had buried the evening before. It had been broken open and emptied, and scattered around were many letters bearing his superscription. These suggested his fate, and the presence of the warriors who had visited his grave, and the question of the possibility of escape if they saw them. To a mind rendered morbidly active by the horrors which had been enacted, the effect was somewhat exciting. The expedition was two miles away, and could not afford relief, and flight through the wild morass was almost an impossibility. After a long search in the garret, Other Day and Myrick passed down into the cellar; Myrick, as he did so, saying that it was a very foolish proceeding, but that it wouldn't do for white men to be beaten in temerity by an Indian.

They staid in the cellar some little time, when the silence was broken by the clattering of Myrick's horse up the rocks. The horses could not be seen from the house, nor therefore the cause of this proceeding perceived; but Myrick's companion immediately cried out, "Myrick, here comes your horse; there is something wrong." Both hurried from the cellar, and Other Day ran down the rocks, then hurried back, his face blazing with excitement, and crying, in startling tones, "Sioux! Sioux!" seized his gun, motioned the others back toward the house, as if they should there make a stand, and rushed down the rocks. Presently he was heard talking in a loud voice, and the others, no longer able to restrain their curiosity, ran to the edge of the eminence, holding their horses, and there, four hundred yards out in the marsh, were two Indians, mounted on Other Day's horse, which they had taken within fifty feet of the house. Other Day was trying to call them back, but they made off the faster, and then he discharged his rifle at them without effect. Its echoes rang through the valley, and were followed instantly by two discharges from Myrick (his companion had only a revolver). These were likewise without effect, and the Indians passed into the woods and made their escape. Hope of successful pursuit across the marsh there was not, and if there had been, an ignorance of the number of the foe would have rendered it too hazardous an undertaking to attempt. The horse was gayly decorated with a red head-dress, which its owner had found in one of the houses. It was a great prize to the captors, not merely for its value, but because it was taken from one whom they hated for joining the whites, and of whom they were all afraid. He was a desperate man in a quarrel; had killed several of the tribe years before, and went always armed, so as not to be caught unprepared. An Indian afterward stated that the captors were concealed in the grass while the three were eating plums, and that one of the two had his gun aimed at Myrick to shoot, but was made to desist by his companion, for fear one of them would be shot by Other Day, and also because the firing would call the attention of our troops.

Then the three made their way toward the camp, avoiding as far as possible the spots where a foe might be concealed. Fearing to cross at the ford, as Indians would naturally lie there in ambush, they endeavored ineffectually to cross the Red-Wood at other points. The opposite bank was too steep for the horses to clamber. Myrick's companion, when returning from the other shore, caught sight of some horsemen half a mile away, and pointed them out to Other Day. He jumped upon a little eminence, looked at them a moment, said they were white men, then crossed the river on a tree which had fallen across it, and took his way quickly toward the train. The horsemen disappeared from view almost immediately, and this led the two to doubt the correctness of Other Day's judgment. They thought that they must have heard the guns, and, if white men, would ride down to see what the trouble was. They debated for some time what to do, but finally rode over toward them through the tall corn, with their arms cocked and ready for use, and were delighted on finding them to be our advanced scouts. They had not heard the discharge of the guns. Poor Other Day was now under a temporary cloud, for Colonel Sibley laughed at his losing his horse, saying the enemy were too sharp for him, and compelled him to walk. He was much chagrined, as all the expedition knew him, and had noticed the gaudy head-dress of his horse; but he simply said that when they neared the enemy he would have two horses for one.

The next day we found George Gleason's body on the prairie, and buried it. He was wasted almost to a skeleton. Two heavy stones were imbedded in his skull. He was Mr. Galbraith's clerk at the Lower Agency, and well known throughout the state.

On the evening of the 22d we camped on the Lonetree Lake, two miles from Wood Lake, and two from the Yellow Medicine River. Next morning, between six and seven o'clock, as we were taking our breakfast, several foraging teams, with their guards, when about half a mile from camp, were fired upon by Indians, who lay concealed in the grass. The guards returned the fire, while the teams were urged to their utmost speed. The 3d regiment, under Major Welch, which had joined us at the fort, hurried out, without orders from the commander of the expedition, crossed a ravine, and was soon engaged with the foe. The general impression at first was that the attack was by a small number of the enemy, and that the soldiers were wasting their ammunition, for the firing soon became rapid. The 3d were ordered back into camp; and just then the enemy appeared in great numbers on all sides, and were gathering in the ravine between the regiment and the camp. The battle, which was known as that of Wood Lake, had now fairly begun. The balls flew thick and fast, some of them penetrating the tents.

Captain Hendricks's cannon now opened fire, as did the howitzer, under the direct supervision of Colonel Sibley. Then Hendricks boldly advanced his gun to the head of the ravine, and the brave Lieutenant Colonel Marshall, with three companies of the 7th, and

LIEUTENANT COLONEL W. R. MARSHALL.

Captain Grant, of the 6th, charged amid a shower of balls, on the double-quick, through the ravine, and put the foe to rout. The contest lasted for an hour and a half. The number actually engaged on each side was about eight hundred, many of our men being held in camp in reserve. Our loss was four killed and between forty and fifty wounded. Among the wounded was Major Welch, who was shot in the leg early in the fight while bravely leading his men forward. The command then devolved upon Lieutenant Olin, who distinguished himself by his gallant conduct.

The 3d regiment had acted in a very boisterous manner ever since it joined us, paying little regard to orders. This was owing to the fact that they felt reckless from their unjustifiable surrender at Murfreesborough, and because they were without officers, Lieutenant Olin being the only one present belonging to the regiment (Welch had been recently assigned to the command). In this fight they nobly did their whole duty. They and the Renville Rangers, under Captain James Gorman, bore the brunt of the fray, and sustained most of the losses. A small body of the enemy threatened another portion of the camp, but were successfully repelled by Major M'Laren and Captain Harvey B. Wilson. Colonel Sibley's staff were active in carrying his orders, and were specially commended in his dispatches.

Other Day nobly redeemed the pledge he had made two days before. He took with his own hand two horses from the enemy, and slew their riders. He was often in their midst, and so far in advance of our men that they fired many shots at him, in the belief that he was one of the foe. No person on the field compared with him in the exhibition of reckless bravery. He was a warrior worthy to have crossed cimeters with Saladin, or dashed with Arabia's mad prophet through the shock of Eastern war. He seemed to be instinct with the spirit of the fierce, resistless steed, "who saith among the trumpets 'ha! ha!' and smelleth the battle from afar off, the thunder of the captains and the shouting." He was clothed entirely in white; a belt around his waist, in which was placed his knife; a handkerchief was knotted about his head, and in his hand he lightly grasped his rifle. His teeth glistened like finest ivory through the slightly-parted lips; his eye was ablaze with fire; his face of bronze radiant with the joy of battle; his exulting utterances came thick and fast, in a sort of purr, pitched upon a high key, and soft as the dulcet tones of an Italian woman. As he bounded along with the graceful spring of a tiger-cat, there came to mind Djalma, the Prince of Java, when, in the theatre at Paris, at the time of the escape of the panther Le Mort, he leaped upon the stage with the returning ardor of his native jungles, and struck his dagger to the heart. With the exuberant, riotous health of Bulwer's Margrave, and the airy wildness of the Faun, he looked the perfection of all the creatures of the woods and fields, and the incarnation of the ideal of the Indian God of War.

It was the taunts of the Friendly Indians who forced on the fight while we were in camp. Little Crow's plan was to ambuscade us while passing through the deep gorge of the Yellow Medicine. Had this advice been followed many of our number would have been slain. They insisted that if the Lower Indians were really brave they ought to attack us on the open plain. Just before the battle their medicine-man went through certain incantations and predicted success. In one of the wagons the Sioux carried a British flag. Had they been a unit in their feelings the battle would have continued much longer; but the Upper Indians, as soon as they found the day was going against them, abandoned the field, and were followed by the others.

Simon, a Sioux who had joined us at Fort Ridgely, went from Colonel Sibley's forces during the progress of the fight to ascertain what the friendly-disposed Indians were going to do. It will be recollected that they had sent word that they would display a white flag and leave the others. He distinctly stated that it would be better for them to abandon the others, and that the innocent ones would not be punished. The young braves evinced great hostility, and threatened to kill him; but he said that they might do so; that he was an old man, but would do his duty whatever might happen. His conduct is represented to have been cool and daring in the extreme. At the conclusion of the contest they requested leave to carry away their dead, but were refused. Fifteen Indians were found upon the battle-field, and a wounded one brought in as a prisoner. The dead ones were gathered together and buried. They were all scalped. One person, in his eagerness, tore off the entire skin from the face with the scalp, and carried it to his tent under his vest. It seemed a hard thing to exult over the dead, but the soldiers could not help feeling satisfaction that the hunt after the miscreants who had committed so many murders with impunity was having a practical result. The sensation experienced was very much like that felt by the hunter when he proves that he has succeeded in killing some wily animal by an exhibition of the animal itself, or by the fisherman, who produces the fish to listeners who would otherwise be dubious as to the reception of bites. So many large stories about the killing of Indians had been told, without any person having actually seen their natural confirmation — the bodies — that the people were getting very incredulous on the point. The mutilation of the dead enemy was discountenanced by the officers. It was done in the excitement of the moment, and after seeing the horrible manner in which the foe had carved up the soldiers which they killed.

The wounded Indian lived several days. He was shot through the lungs, and the breath and the bubbling blood could be heard issuing from the wound. He was lying in a tent, guarded, shivering with cold, and almost perishing for water. James Gorman, of the Renville Rangers, and another person, gave him some water, and threw an overcoat over him. A grateful look came into his dying eyes. He had not expected this. The soldiers on the outside thought this act of charity an outrageously culpable thing. How precious a cup of cold water may sometimes be, and what contumely attend its bestowal! Among the fatally wounded of the Indians who were carried away was one of the "Farmers," who had been a devoted friend of the captives. He was not engaged himself, but took a club and drove some of the cowardly Lower Indians into the midst of danger, saying, "You said we were not brave, and now I will show you where to go." Red Iron, who had also been our friend, was with him.

After burying our dead and remaining one day at Wood Lake, we marched to the Indian camp near Lac qui Parle, which, by the route we had taken, was about two hundred and twenty-five miles from St. Paul.

INDIAN CAMP TAKEN BY COLONEL SIBLEY.

CHAPTER XII.

CAMP RELEASE.

On the 26th of September we reached the Indian camp. It was located nearly opposite the mouth of the Chippeway River, and numbered about one hundred tepees. Just before we arrived, a war party, composed of a portion of those who had placed the sticks on Prescott's grave, had passed by, leaving a prisoner with the inmates.* Little Crow and some two hundred men and their families hurriedly fled the day after the battle. Some of the fugitives were still in sight when we came up. A few hundred cavalry could easily have captured these, and put an immediate end to the war.

Colonel Sibley frequently urged the necessity of a mounted force, and Governor Ramsey was energetic in his endeavors to comply with his demand. The failure to do so resulted from the preoccupation of the federal government in a more important war. General Pope, who was placed in command of the department some time afterward, dispatched several hundred cavalry to Colonel Sibley, but the season was too far advanced to follow Crow. It was unfortunate that the energetic and influential ex-Senator Rice had not been placed early in charge of the

* This party had murdered several persons in the neighborhood of Hutchinson on the day of the battle of Wood Lake. The others committed depredations at Medalia.

department, as was suggested. He was fully alive to the necessity of such a force, and would have taken care that Colonel Sibley should have had the requisite number in time.

Our own camp, which was called "Camp Release," was pitched about a quarter of a mile from that of the Indians, which our cannon commanded. Their camp was filled with wagons and cattle which they had stolen. The tents were well supplied with carpets, and different kinds of goods and household utensils. Soon after our arrival, the commander, with his staff and body-guard, rode over and took formal possession.

OLD BETZ.

CAMP RELEASE.

INDIAN BOY.

Wondering squaws and children stared at the newcomers, and tall, gayly-painted braves were profuse in their declarations of friendship. "Old Betz," a very aged squaw, since dead, who was well known throughout the state, and who, it was said, had been kind to the captives, was among the former. A formal demand which was made for the captives was instantly complied with. They were nearly two hundred and fifty in number. They had been compelled to wear the Indian dress during their captivity, but had now been permitted to resume their former habiliments.

The poor creatures wept for joy at their escape. They had watched for our coming for many a weary day, with constant apprehensions of death at the hands of their savage captors, and had almost despaired of seeing us. The woe written in the faces of the half starved and nearly naked women and children would have melted the hardest heart. They were taken to our camp, where they remained until sent below a few days subsequently. The sleepless nights which the commander passed in scheming for their deliverance, and the steadfastness with which he resisted all counsels for a sudden attack, which would have compromised their safety, received in their deliverance a rich reward.

George Spencer, who was saved by his Indian friend at Red-Wood (the only white man among the captives), said, if we had marched to the camp immediately after the battle, most of the prisoners would have been killed. It will be recollected that many of them were in the Lower Indians' exclusive possession, and that they had resolved that they should die with them.

The apprehensions of the captives after the first rage of their captors was over were greater than their actual sufferings. They fared as well as the Indians in the main. Only one person was killed—a little boy whom a warrior had adopted. The Indian was in the habit of painting his face, and one morning the little fellow cried because it was not done, and, enraged, the savage shot him. He was only wounded, and the Indian boys beat him to death with clubs and pitched him over the bluff. The grosser outrages were mostly committed by the younger portion of the tribe.

Indians are not all lost to humanity. Simon, Lorenzo Lawrence, Robert Hopkins, Paul, Spencer's comrade, Chaska, and the noble Other Day, risked their lives in behalf of their white friends. History is full of such instances. The heroic Pocahontas interposed her own person between the axe of the executioner and the imperiled Smith. The great Virginia massacre of 1662 was limited in its extent by an Indian revealing the plot to a friend whom he wished to save, and Philip of Pokanoket wept with sorrow when he heard of the death of the first Englishman who was killed. These acts and numberless others will suffer no diminution of effect by comparison with any sacrifices that whites have made for Indians.

Many of our men insisted that Colonel Sibley would be justifiable in making any treaty he could to obtain the captives, and when that was done, kill all the Indians, men, women, and children; one of them quoting a saying, which he attributed to the great Indian-fighter Harney, that "nits make lice." Our people, luckily, are disciplined; and the broad, sober sense of the leaders, which reaches beyond the present hour, generally restrains acts of atrocity.

Indians pay little regard to the chiefs and older men. Prominent intellects they have, but no commanders—no men with power to enforce their views. Passion, unrestrained by judgment, therefore rules. In vain Tecumseh sought, with more effort than the white man Proctor, to stay the massacre on the River Raisin; and Crow's exhortations to spare women and children fell unheeded on the ears of the braves. The murder of white soldiers who have surrendered in good faith is due to the inability of the chiefs to enforce obedience to their orders.

A military commission of inquiry was at once appointed to ascertain the guilty parties, and testimony against about a dozen obtained. A commission for the trial of these and of any others who might be accused was then organized, and some thirty or forty immediately arrested. The remainder in camp were sent down to the Yellow Medicine Agency under charge of Agent Galbraith, as the stock of provisions was fast becoming exhausted.

Many other Indians came in voluntarily with their squaws from time to time, and gave themselves up; and others were surprised in the night by our expeditions, and placed with the others in a second camp near our own.

The evidence before the commission indicating that the whole nation was involved in the war, Colonel Crooks, by order of the commander, silently surrounded the second camp in the night, disarmed the men, and placed them in a log jail which had previously been erected in the midst of our camp. The guns taken from them were nearly all loaded with ball, and the shot-pouches also filled with them. Among the guns were some of the rifles which had been taken from Marsh and Strout. A similar proceeding was ordered at Yellow Medicine, and safely accomplished by assembling all the braves within the walls of the agency buildings, under pretense of holding a council. Rattling Moccasin, taking alarm, had decamped from there a few days before with a portion of his band.

The prisoners were linked together in pairs by chains forged to their ankles. As the proud but now crestfallen braves hobbled along, the soldiers would derisively salute them with "*Left!*" "*Left!*" They were designated, whenever spoken of, as "*Los*," from "Lo! the poor Indian, whose untutored mind," etc.

A number of half-breeds were among the accused, and these were looked upon with more hatred than the Indians, because related to the whites. The object of most bitter malediction was the negro, or, rather, mulatto Godfrey or Gussá, who was also a prisoner and chained to an Indian. He had been foremost among the attacking party at New Ulm, and Indians said he was braver than any of them. He had boasted that he had killed nine adults and a number of children, but of the latter he said he kept no account, because he thought they did not amount to any thing. The Indians had given him the name of Otakle, *i. e.*, "he who kills many." He admitted being in the battles, but denied that he had killed any one. Where persons are murdered in a house, the Indians give the credit of the affair to the man who first enters, on account of the superior daring thereby indicated, just as, for the same reason, they say a brave who first touches the body of the slain *kills* the person, although the deed may have been committed by another. The man attacked may be only feigning death. Indians often do so. Godfrey said he acquired his name by entering first into a house near New Ulm by direction of the Indians, where a number were killed by them. I have but little doubt that he entered into the massacres with as much zest as the Indians themselves after he once commenced. He was brought up among them, could speak their language, and was married to a squaw. Two very intelligent girls, who were captured by a party of Indians on the first day of the massacre, between Reynolds's place on the Red-Wood and New Ulm, said that Godfrey, who was with the Indians, driving the team in which they were placed, was painted for war, and wore a breech-clout; and that he chuckled over their captivity, and seemed to enter fully into the spirit of their captors. He was leaning composedly against a wagon-box when we entered the Indian camp. He was about the medium height, stoutly built; had very dark complexion, curly hair, lips of medium thickness, eyes slightly crossed, but not enough to disfigure, and a voice of most marvelous sweetness. He wore moccasins, but otherwise had resumed the dress of the whites. An old plush cap, with large ear-flaps, was placed on one side of his head. This is the story which Godfrey told:

CHAPTER XIII.

GODFREY'S STORY.

"I AM twenty-seven years old. I was born at Mendota. My father was a Canadian Frenchman, and my mother a colored woman, who hired in the family of the late Alex. Bailley. I was raised in Mr. Bailley's family. My father is, I think, living in Wisconsin; his name is Joe Godfrey. My mother is also living at Prairie du Chien. I last saw my father and mother at Prairie du Chien seven years ago. I lived with Mr. Bailley at Wabashaw, and also at Hastings and Faribault. I had lived at the Lower Agency five years. I was married, four years ago, to a woman of Wabashaw's band—daughter of Wa-kpa-doo-ta.* At the time of the outbreak I lived on the Reservation on the south side of the Minnesota River, between the Lower Agency and New Ulm, about twenty miles below the agency and eight above New Ulm.

"The first time I heard of the trouble I was mowing hay. About noon an Indian was making hay near me. I went to help him, to change work; he was to lend me his oxen. I helped him load some hay, and as we took it to his place we heard hallooing, and saw a man on horseback, with a gun across his legs before him. When he saw me he drew his gun up and cocked it. The Indian with me asked him 'What's the matter?' He looked strange. He wore

* Afterward executed.

a new hat—a soft gray hat—and had a new white leather ox or mule whip. He said all the white people had been killed at the agency. The Indian with me asked who did it, and he replied the Indians, and that they would soon be down that way to kill the settlers toward New Ulm. He asked me which side I would take. He said I would have to go home and take off my clothes, and put on a breech-clout. I was afraid, because he held his gun as if he would kill me. I went to my house and told my wife to get ready, and we would try to get away. I told my wife about what the Indian told me. I told her we would try to get down the river. She said we would be killed with the white people. We got something ready to take with us to eat, and started—we got about two hundred yards into the woods. (The old man, my wife's father, said he would fasten the house and follow after.) We heard some one halloo. It was the old man. He called to us to come back. I told my wife to go on, but her mother told her to stop. I told them to go ahead; but the old man called so much that they stopped and turned back. I followed them.

"I found my squaw's uncle at the house. He scolded my wife and her mother for trying to get away; he said all the Indians had gone to the agency, and that they must go there. He said we would be killed if we went toward the white folks; that we would only be safe to go and join the Indians. I still had my pants on. I was afraid; and they told me I must take my pants off and put on the breech-clout. I did so. The uncle said we must take a rope and catch a horse.

"I started with him toward New Ulm, and we met

a lot of Indians at the creek, about a mile from my house. They were all painted, and said I must be painted. They then painted me. I was afraid to refuse.

"They asked me why I didn't have a gun, or knife, or some weapon. I told them I had no gun—the old man had taken it away. One Indian had a spear, a gun, and a little hatchet. He told me to take the hatchet, and that I must fight with the Indians, and do the same they did, or I would be killed. We started down the road. We saw two wagons with people in them coming toward us. The Indians consulted what to do, and decided for half of them to go up to a house off the road, on the right-hand side. They started, but I stopped, and they called me and told me I must come on. There was an old man, a boy, and two young women at the house—Dutch people. The family's name was something like 'Masseybush.' The boy and two girls stood outside, near the kitchen door. Half of the Indians went to the house, half remained in the road. The Indians told me to tell the whites that there were Chippeways about, and that they (the Indians) were after them. I did not say any thing. The Indians asked for some water. The girls went into the house, and the Indians followed and talked in Sioux. One said to me, 'Here is a gun for you.' Dinner was on the table, and the Indians said, 'After we kill, then we will have dinner.' They told me to watch the road, and when the teams came up to tell them. I turned to look, and just then I heard the Indians shoot; I looked, and two girls fell just outside the door. I did not go in the house; I started to go round the house. We were on the back side of it, when I heard the Indians on the road hallooing and shouting. They called me, and I went to the road and saw them killing white men. My brother-in-law told me I must take care of a team that he was holding; that it was his. I saw two men killed that were with this wagon. I did not see who were killed in the other wagon. I saw one Indian stick his knife in the side of a man that was not yet dead; he cut his side open, and then cut him all to pieces.* His name was Wakantonka (great spirit). Two of the Indians that killed the people at the house have been convicted. Their names are Waki-ya-ni and Mah-hwa. There were about ten Indians at the house, and about the same number in the road. I got into the wagon, and the Indians all got in. We turned and went toward New Ulm. When we got near to a house the Indians all got out and ran ahead of the wagons, and two or three went to each house, and in that way they killed all the people along the road. I staid in the wagon, and did not see the people killed. They killed the people of six or eight houses—all until we got to the 'Travelers' Home.' There were other Indians killing people all through the settlement. We could see them and hear them all around. I was standing in the wagon, and could see three, or four, or five Indians at every house.

"When we got near the 'Travelers' Home' they told me to stop. I saw an old woman with two children—one in each hand—run away across the yard. One Indian, Maza-bom-doo, who was convicted, shot the old woman, and jumped over and kicked the children down with his feet. The old woman fell down

* Afterward executed.

as if dead. I turned away my head, and did not see whether the children were killed. After that I heard a shot behind the barn, but did not see who was shot. I supposed some one was killed. After that the Indians got in the wagon, and told me to start down the road. We started on, and got to a house where a man lived named Schling—a German—an old man. The Indians found a jug in the wagon, and were now almost drunk. They told me to jump out. I jumped out and started ahead, and the Indians called me to come back. They threw out a hatchet, and said I must go to the house and kill the people. Maza-bom-doo was ahead. He told me there were three guns there that he had left for some flour, and we must get them. I was afraid.

"I went into the house. There was the old man, his wife and son, and a boy and another man. They were at dinner. The door stood open, and the Indians were right behind me, and pushed me in. I struck the old man on the shoulder with the flat of the hatchet, and then the Indians rushed in and commenced to shoot them. The old man, woman, and boy ran into the kitchen. The other man ran out some way, I did not see how; but when we went back to the road, about twenty steps, I saw him in the road dead. He was the man I struck in the house. I heard the Indians shoot back of the house, but did not see what at. After we started to go to Red-Wood, one little Indian, who had pox-marks on his face, and who was killed at Wood Lake, said he struck the boy with a knife, but didn't say if he killed him. He told this to the other Indians.

"We saw coming up the road two wagons, one with

a flag in it. The Indians were afraid, and we started back, and went past the 'Travelers' Home.' We got to a bridge, and the Indians got out and laid down in the grass about the bridge. I went on up the road. The wagons, with white men, came on up and stopped in the road, where there was a dead man, I think; then they sounded the bugle and started to cross the bridge, running their horses. The foremost wagon had one horse, of a gray color; three men were in it, and had the flag. Just as they came across the bridge, the Indians raised up and shot. The three men fell out, and the team went on. The Indians ran and caught it. The other wagon had not got across the bridge. I heard them shoot at the men in it, but I did not see them. After the Indians brought the second wagon arcoss the bridge, three Indians got in the wagon. After that all of them talked together, and said that it was late (the sun was nearly down), and that they must look after their wives and children that had started to go to Red-Wood. Many of these Indians lived on the lower end of the reservation. The two-horse team that they had just taken was very much frightened, and they could not hold them. They told me I must take and hold them, and drive them. I took the team, and then they all got in. We then had four teams. We started from there, and went on up. When we got to where the first people were killed, the Indians told me to drive up to the house. The two girls were lying dead. I saw one girl with her head cut off; the head was gone. One Indian, an old man, asked who cut the head off; he said it was too bad. The other Indians said they did not know. The girls' clothes were turned up. The old man put them down. He is now in prison; his name is Wazakoota; he is a good old man. While we stood there one wagon went to another house, and I heard a gun go off.

"We started up the road, and stopped at a creek about a mile farther on. We waited for some of the Indians that were behind. While we were there we saw a house on fire. When the Indians came up they said that Wak-pa-doo-ta, my father-in-law, shot a woman, who was on a bed sick, through the window; and that an old man ran up stairs, and the Indians were afraid to go in the house; they thought he had a gun, and they set fire to the house and left it. We then started on from that creek, and went about seven miles to near a little lake (about a hundred yards from the road). We saw, far away, a wagon coming toward us. When it was only two miles from us we saw it was a two-horse wagon, but the Indians didn't know if it was white people. When it came nearer they told me to go fast. The Indians whipped the horses and hurried them on. Two Indians were ahead of us on horseback. Pretty soon we came near, and the team that was coming toward us stopped and turned round, and the Indians said it was white men, and they were trying to run away. The two on horseback then shot, and I saw a white man—Patville—fall back over his seat; and after that I saw three women and one man jump out of the wagon and run. Then those in the wagon with me jumped out and ran after the women. We got up to the wagon. Patville was not dead. The Indians threw him out, and a young Indian, sentenced to be hung, stuck a knife between his ribs, under the arm, and another one, who is with Little Crow, took his gun and beat his head all to pieces. The other Indians killed the other white man near the little lake, and brought back the three women—Mattie Williams, Mary Anderson, and Mary Swan.

"Patville's wagon was full of trunks. The Indians broke them open and took the things out; there were some goods in them (Patville was a sort of trader on the reservation). They put one woman in the wagon. I drove. The other two were put separately in the other wagons. The one in my wagon (Mary Swan) was caught by Maza-bom-doo. Ta-zoo had Mattie Williams. We then went on, and stopped at a creek about a mile ahead to water the horses. Then they called me to ask the woman that was wounded if she was badly hurt. She said 'Yes.' They told me to ask her to show the wound, and that they would do something for it. She showed the wound. It was in the back. The ball did not come out. She asked where we were going. I said I didn't know, but supposed to Red-Wood. I asked what had been done at the agency. She said they didn't know; that they came around on the prairie past Red-Wood. I told her I heard that all the whites at the agency were killed and the stores robbed. She said she wished they would drive fast, so she could have a doctor do something for her wound; she was afraid she would die. I said I was a prisoner too. She asked what would be done with them. I said I didn't know; perhaps we would all be killed. I said maybe the doctor was killed, if all the white people were. After that we started on, and got to the Red-Wood Agency about nine o'clock. It was dark. Then the Indians looked round, and did not see any people. We went on to Wacouta's house. He came out, and told me to tell the girl in my wagon to go into his house—that the other two girls were in his house. I told the girl; but she was afraid, and said she thought the other women were somewhere else. I told her that Wacouta said they were in his house, and she had better go. Wacouta told her to go with him, and she got out and went with him. I then went on to Little Crow's village, where most all of the Indians had gone. I found my wife there. We staid some time there, and then started for the fort. They asked me to go to drive a team. After we got there they commenced to fight. They broke in the stable, and told me to go and take all the horses I could. I got a black mare, but an Indian took it away from me. They fought all day, and slept at night in the old stable under the hill. The next morning they fought only a little; it was raining. We then went back to Red-Wood. In about six days after all the Indians started, and said they would go to Mankato. They came down toward the fort on that side of the river, and crossed near the 'Travelers' Home.' When they got opposite the fort they stopped, and talked of trying to get in again, but did not. About noon they went on to New Ulm. I saw no white people on the road. I got to New Ulm about two hours after noon. They burned houses, and shot, and fought. They slept at New Ulm that night, and the next day went back to Little Crow's village. (This was the last fight at New Ulm; Godfrey says he was not there at the first fight. He was then at Little Crow's village.) After a few days we went to Rice Creek; staid there a few days, and started again to come to Mankato. After crossing the

Red-Wood we went up the hill, and saw wagons on the prairie on the other side of the river. After the Indians had all crossed the Red-Wood, half staid there all night, and half went over the Minnesota to where they saw the wagons. Those that staid back went over early the next morning. I went with them. We got there at sunrise. We heard shooting just before we got there. They were shooting all day. They killed all the horses. (This was the battle of Birch Coolie.) At night the Indians killed some cattle, and cooked and ate some meat. Some talked of trying to get into the camp, and some tried it all night. Others talked of watching till they should drive them out for want of water. Three Indians were killed that day—so the Indians said. I saw some wounded—I should think five. In the morning some more talk was had about trying to get in. In the mean time we saw soldiers coming up, and half of the Indians started to try and stop them, and the other half staid to watch the camp at Birch Coolie. They went down to try and stop the soldiers, and afterward came back and said 'twas no use—that they couldn't stop them. Some wanted to try and get the whites into Birch Coolie, but others thought they had better go back. They fired some shots, and then started back. The Sissetons got to us while we were there the second day, about two or three hours before the Indians all left. The Indians left a little before sundown. They crossed the river at the old crossing, and went up to the site of Reynolds's house, the other side of the Red-Wood, and camped. They started about midnight to go to Rice Creek. Got there about sunrise. Staid there several days.

"While we were at Birch Coolie Little Crow was at the Big Woods. He got back to Rice Creek two days after we did. We went from Rice Creek to Yellow Medicine; staid there about two weeks. While there ten or twenty started every day to see if soldiers were coming. When they reported that soldiers were on the way, we moved our camp to where Mr. Riggs lived; then up to Red Iron's village; then to a little way from where the *friendly* camp was. After the scouts reported that soldiers had crossed the Red-Wood, Little Crow made a speech, and said that all must fight; that it would be the last fight, and they all must do the best they could. Scouts reported about midnight that soldiers were camped at Rice Creek. In the morning we all started down to Yellow Medicine; got there a little before sundown. Some were there earlier. We staid at Yellow Medicine all night. Some wanted to begin the attack in the night, but others thought 'twas best to wait till morning. In the morning the fight began. After the fight, went back to the old camp at Camp Release. Little Crow tried to get all to go with him, but they would not. Little Crow started away in the night. I didn't see him go. I never was out at any of the war parties except once at New Ulm (the last fight), once at the fort, at Birch Coolie, and Wood Lake. They thought that the Winnebagoes would commence at Mankato and attack the lower settlements."

CHAPTER XIV.

CAPTIVITY OF THE FAMILY OF JOSEPH R. BROWN.

MAJOR JOSEPH R. BROWN'S wife and children were among the captives at Camp Release. They suffered very little ill treatment, for the reason that they were related to the Sissetons, and had powerful friends among them. They lived in a very fine stone house, elegantly furnished, a few miles below the Yellow Medicine Agency, on the opposite side of the river, which was afterward destroyed by the savages. Samuel Brown, one of the sons, a remarkably intelligent boy of about fifteen years of age, narrated to the writer the following particulars connected with the affair:

"On Monday, the 18th day of August, I went to Yellow Medicine with my sister Ellen upon an errand. We met on the way an Indian named Little Dog, who told us that the Indians had killed a family at Beaver Creek, and were going to kill the whites as far as St. Paul, and that we must not tell any one about it, or they would kill us. He said he warned us at the risk of his own life. This was about noon. Soon after our arrival at Yellow Medicine, an old squaw told us that we had better be getting away, as there would soon be trouble. We asked many of the other Indians about it, but they said they had heard of nothing of the kind. Another squaw afterward told us that she thought it must be the Yanktonais who were coming down to take the agency. We left there about half past three o'clock. George Gleason had just left with Mrs. Wakefield and her children for below. When we reached home we told mother what we had heard. She was very much scared, and didn't sleep any that night. About four o'clock next morning I heard some one outside calling in a loud voice a number of times for my mother, and then I heard Charles Blair, my brother-in-law (a white man), ask what was the matter, and the man, who was a half-breed named Royer, said that four hundred Yanktonais had arrived at the Upper Agency, and were killing every body. We then became very much alarmed, and had our oxen yoked at once to the wagon, put every thing in it we could, and started for Fort Ridgely. We had all the neighbors warned, and they went with us. They had three wagons with ox-teams. Four or five white men overtook us on the way, among them Garvie's cook. (Garvie was the trader wounded at the agency, who died at Hutchinson.)

"When we had gone about five miles we saw some men two miles ahead, near the bank of the river, but supposed they were farmers. The Yanktonais, whom we were afraid of, lived above us. We thought nothing more about the men until we saw an Indian on a hill ahead of us. He beckoned to others, and before we knew it we were surrounded. De-wa-nea, of Crow's band, and Cut-nose, and Shakopee, three of the worst among the Lower Indians, came to us first. We were in the head wagon. Mother told them who we were, and they said we must follow them, and that we were all as good as dead. De-wa-nea said that the whites had taken him prisoner a good many times,

CUT-NOSE.

and that it was now his turn. He wanted the rest of the Indians to kill us all.

"There was an Indian in the party, John Moore's brother-in-law, who took our part, and he and his friends saved us from the others. This Indian had once come to our house when he was freezing, and my mother took him in and warmed him. He told the other Indians that he remembered this, and that we should live. They insisted that my brother Angus should shoot one of the white men, but he refused to do so. Each of the Indians had one of the white men picked out to shoot as they came up. My mother said they were poor men, and it would do no good to kill them. John Moore's brother-in-law said they should live if she wanted them to. The Indians made a great fuss about it, and said she ought to be satisfied with what she had got, but afterward consented, and told the men to start off. The women staid with us. After the men had got off a little, Leopold Wohler, who had a lime-kiln at the agency, came back to the wagon after his boots, and an Indian told him if he didn't go away he would kill him. He started off with one boot, and came back again after the other, and the Indian drove him away again with the same threat. He went a short distance, and returned a third time to kiss his wife. The Indians then became very much enraged, and acted so fiercely that he was glad to escape without farther difficulty.

"There were ten Indians close to us, and twenty-five or thirty near, running into the houses. They made Angus and Charles Blair, who were riding horses, dismount and give them up. De-wa-nea put on my sister's bonnet, and began singing a war song. He was very merry. He said the Indians were now going to have a good time, and if they got killed it was all right; that the whites wanted to kill them off, and were delaying the payment in order to do it by starvation, and that he preferred to be shot. We saw three men and a woman on the road terribly hacked up. This party had committed the murders. The men had been mowing together; their scythes and pitchforks lay near. Cut-nose showed us his thumb, from which a piece had been bitten near the nail, and he said it was done by one of these men while he was working the knife around in his breast; that he was very hard to kill, and he thought he would never die.

"Cut-nose afterward went to a wagon, and told a Scotch girl who was in it that he wanted her for his wife, and to get out and follow him. She refused, and then he drew his knife and flourished it over her, and she got out and went away with him. That was the last I saw of him until we got to camp. He was called Cut-nose because one of his nostrils had been bitten out. This was done by Other Day in a quarrel.

"When we got to the camp of the Rice-Creek Indians, four miles above the Red-Wood River, they told us that the Agency Indians had sent word for all to come down there, and that those who did not come would be taken care of by the 'Soldiers' Lodge.' They were then about starting, and an Indian made Angus and myself hitch up a mule-team which he said he had taken from Marsh's men the day before. He said they had just heard a cannon at the fort, and they wanted to go down and whip the whites there. This was about noon. We then went down to John Moore's house (this was where Other Day's horse was stolen), and they put us up stairs, where they had two or three women, captives. We were there about an hour, when three Indians told us to come up to their camp on the hill, where we were to stop with John Moore's mother or grandmother. We followed them, and when we got half way up suddenly missed them. We supposed they hid from us, and we wandered on. We met a German woman who had seven or eight children with her, all under eight years of age—two on her back, one under each arm, and two following behind. They came along with us. We went to

Moore's relative, but she said she knew nothing about us, and couldn't take us, and that we had better go down to Crow's village. We started, not knowing where to go, when a squaw, who was crying about the troubles, met us, and took us home with her. The Indians sent our team back to the camp. They gave Angus and I blankets and moccasins, and we put them on and went down to see Little Crow. He told us to bring our folks down there, and no one should hurt us. This was Tuesday evening about seven o'clock. He was in his own house, and the camp was pitched around it. We went back and brought our folks down. Crow put us up in the top room of the house, and gave us buffalo robes and every thing to make us comfortable. He brought us a candle as soon as it was dark; he was very kind to us; he said he would take as good care of us as he could, but that he didn't believe he could keep Charley Blair alive until morning. He gave him a breech-clout and leggins, which he put on.

"During the night an Indian or a half-breed came in the room down stairs where Crow was, and told him that we ought to be killed. We overheard what they said. The man was very ugly, and said no prisoners ought to be taken, and that we were related to the Sissetons, and had no claim on the Lower Indians, and there was no reason why we should be spared. He said he wanted Crow to call a council about it immediately. Crow told him that he saved us because we were his friends, and that he would protect us; that it was too late to hold a council that night, and he compelled him to leave.

"He gave us plenty to eat, and came up several

times during the night to see how we were getting along. We begged him to let Charley Blair go. He said he couldn't; that the Indians knew he was there, and would kill him (Crow) if he allowed it. We coaxed him for a couple of hours, when he consented, and brought an Indian who took Charley down to the river and left him in the brush. He made his escape from there to the fort. Crow told us not to say any thing about it, for the Indians would kill him, and that he did it because he had known our folks and Charley so long. He said the young men started the massacre, and he couldn't stop them. A week after that, Akipa, an Upper Indian, came down from the Yellow-Medicine Agency and took us up with him. From that time until our deliverance we remained with our relatives, and were well treated by them."

CHAPTER XV.

MRS. HUGGINS'S STORY.

AMONG the captives who were brought in several days after our arrival at Camp Release was Mrs. Sophia Josephine Huggins, the wife of the estimable missionary who was killed at Lac qui Parle. She has published the following narrative of her adventures. It is interesting for the minuteness of the details of her captivity:

"The 19th day of August, 1862, dawned on me full of hope and happiness. It was the twenty-fourth anniversary of my birth. But before its close it proved to be the saddest day of my life. News of the war which broke out at the Lower Agency on the 18th did not reach Lac qui Parle until the next day. Then it came with fearful suddenness and fearful reality.

"On the afternoon of that day three men from Red Iron's village came in, each carrying a gun. They were quite friendly and talkative, seeming very much interested in the sewing-machine Julia was using, and asked a great many questions about it. About four o'clock Amos came home from the field. Then the men went out; and soon after we heard the report of two guns. The Indians rushed in, looking so wild and frightened that my first thought was that the Chippeways were upon them. They said to us, 'Go out, go out; you shall live — but go out. Take nothing with you.' When I went out, the oxen my husband had been driving were standing at the side of the house, and near them was Julia on her knees, bending over the motionless body. She looked up and said, 'Oh Josephine, Josephine!' What an ocean of grief rolled over me.

* * * * *

"We were driven away, Julia and I. We ran over to De Cota's. Julia went first, carrying Letta. I staid behind until I saw they were really going to shoot me. Then, after hastily spreading a lounge cover that I had been sewing on, and had carried out with me, over the lifeless form of my dear one, I fled with Charlie in my arms. When I reached De Cota's, he and his wife were starting back with Julia. I wanted to go with them, but they thought it would not be safe. I knew Julia would see that every thing which it was possible to do should be done, so I yielded to their judgment.

"Mr. De Cota came home shortly. I asked him if he could not take us to the Yellow Medicine. He said that we would be killed on the road. I then suggested that he should take us across the river, and go across the country to the white settlements. He answered that perhaps he would start to the Red River the next day.

"When Julia returned, she told me that Walking Spirit and others had buried Amos. The old chief was full of sorrow, and said that if he had been there they should have killed him before they could have killed Mr. Huggins.

"Our house was full of plunderers. Indians from the Lac qui Parle villages were there as well as the murderers. Julia went in, and was able to get a few things, which afterward proved valuable to me.

"It was thought we would be safer at Walking Spirit's than at De Cota's, so we went over in the evening. Mrs. De Cota intended to go with us, but her husband prevented it, probably thinking he would not be safe if she left him. She sent her brother, Blue Lightning, with us. He did not offer to carry either of the children.

"We had not gone far before Ke-yoo-kan-pe came up to us, and, taking Charlie out of my arms, carried him until we reached the village. As we passed through it, a great many women came out to shake hands with me. Some of them laid their hands on their mouths and groaned. The men paid no attention to me. When we reached the chief's house he received us kindly, shaking hands with me and with the children. His wife hurried to spread a buffalo robe at the farther end of the room for us to sit on. All the time that I was with Walking Spirit my seat was, whether in a tent or in a house, at the end farthest from the door—the most honorable place. We slept on the robe, but were furnished with pillows by the chief's wife, one of which I recognized as having been mine. She gave me several other articles which had been mine.

"There was a great deal of noise in the village during the night—loud talking, singing, and yelling; but the children slept soundly, not realizing what had befallen them, nor the dangers before them. Men went and came through the whole night long to talk to the chief.

"The next morning we had beef for breakfast

which had been killed at our house the evening before. They gavē me, as they always did, bountifully of the best they had.

"In the afternoon Mr. John Longee invited us over to his house across the river, thinking we would be safer there than in the Indian village. Walking Spirit told us to do as we thought best, and we finally concluded to go. One woman packed Letta all the way; another packed Charlie as far as Lame Bear's village. As we passed through it I saw a great deal of fresh beef hanging up to dry. My husband's writing desk was there; also many of our chairs. I saw Indian children dressed in my children's clothes. I could hardly bear these reminders of the home which had been so cruelly torn from me. I did not, however, see any Indians that I knew except 'Old Fuss.' He shook hands with me, and made a speech, of which I understood nothing but Amos's name.

"We staid at Longee's until Friday, and had a quiet, lonely time. We saw no Indians while there except the woman who packed Letta over. She staid with us all the time. Julia and I were in constant alarm. Longee and a Frenchman always slept with their guns beside them, in readiness for use, or staid outside watching. Thursday, Mr. Longee went over to the village, and brought back dreadful accounts of the war below. It was reported that the missionaries and the whites at both agencies were killed. Oh what a day that was — full of grief, anxiety, and surprise. Julia had saved two pocket Bibles from the hands of the plunderers. One of them was my husband's. How precious it was to me! Precious for the sake of him who had once pondered its sacred pages, as well as for the blessed teachings and glorious promises it contained.

"In the evening Julia's brother came up from below, dressed like an Indian. He said that he had come for her, and that if she put on the Indian dress, and staid with him, she would be safe, but that it would not be prudent for me to accompany them. Mr. De Cota was there, and invited me to live in his family. It was decided that I should do so.

"A white man, who had escaped from Big Stone Lake, came in that night. Mr. Longee gave him a pair of moccasins and some food. Every one advised the Frenchman to go with him, but he refused to do so. After a few weeks he went with Mr. Longee to Red River.

"Friday morning Julia left me. She had been my comforter, my adviser, my help in all my troubles. Now I was left alone. I realized more than ever my need of strength and fortitude, and prayed that I might be prepared for whatever I might be called to pass through.

"After Julia had gone, Mr. Longee and I started to Walking Spirit's village. We went on horseback, carrying the children. How I suffered with fear as we trotted along through the woods. It seemed as if every tree hid some skulking foe, ready to spring out and murder us. When we reached Lame Bear's village, Longee thought it best not to go any farther, as there were a good many men about, and we should be noticed on horseback. After finding an Indian woman to go with me and pack Letta, he bade me good-by. I carried Charlie in my arms, and as I had eaten nothing that day, I felt faint and sick. As we were passing through the village a woman called after me. I looked around, and then went on. She ran after me, and finally made me understand that she wished me to go to her house and eat. I told her as well as I could that I was going to Walking Spirit's, and would eat there. She seemed satisfied and went back. Presently another woman hailed me. When she came up she took Charlie and put him on her back, motioning me to follow, which I did as well as I could. When we came to the strip of woods that lies between the two villages, the women were afraid of something, I don't know what. They told me to go before; so I led the way, trembling with fear. When I reached De Cota's, Mrs. De Cota, who was standing outside of the tent, motioned me to go to the chief's house. What did it mean? Did they not invite me there? Mr. De Cota was sitting near by, but as he did not look at me, I passed on without speaking. I felt so hurt—so much disappointed! What should I do if I received as cold a reception at Walking Spirit's? How thankful I was when I went in and met a kind welcome from the chief's wife. Here I found food and water for myself and children. I was so tired, so sad, that I did not try to speak or ask for any thing; but she seemed to understand how I felt, and kindly, even tenderly supplied my wants.

"Walking Spirit was not at home, and did not come home until several days afterward. When he came and saw me, his cheery 'Ho-ho-ho,' as he held out his hand to me, sounded very pleasantly. Then he talked to me very kindly, I know, though I could not understand much of what he said. I understood that he told me to stay there in his house, and that when he could he would take me to my friends below. My poor, weary, anxious heart felt comforted. This old man was my friend and protector. I could here find something like rest and security.

"For the next six weeks I found a home in Walking Spirit's family. True, I was a captive in an enemy's country, longing for deliverance — subject to many inconveniences, many hardships; but the chief and his wife were kind to me, and made my life as light as possible. Here my husband's Bible was my constant companion.

"Walking Spirit's family consisted of himself and wife, and his wife's mother, and one son, Na-ho-ton-ma-ne, a boy fourteen or fifteen years old. These, with myself and children, made a family of seven. Besides, the chief had children and grandchildren in the village, who were in to see us so often as to form a part of the same family. We had also many other visitors. If they spoke to me at all, it was with kindness and respect. They frequently said, 'The white woman feels sad; I want to shake hands with her.'

"I soon learned to adopt myself to the life and circumstances about me, and make one in the society in which I lived. I always tried to be cheerful and pleasant to others, and in so doing found enjoyment and even happiness myself. I assisted the chief's wife in sewing, cooking, and bringing water from the brook. I was seldom asked to do any thing, but did what I chose to do.

"The chief and his wife never seemed displeased with me but once. Then I had gone over to Sacred Nest's, and had staid nearly all day. When I went back the chief said that I did not do right to go away and stay so long—that it was good for me to stay in his house. His wife remarked that the Sissetonwans would come down, and they might kill me if I did not stay there. After that I did not go to the neighbors' tepees unless I was sent for to eat, and then I did not stay long.

"The children, who were not afraid of any one, were petted and caressed. Letta was taught to call the chief grandfather, and his wife grandmother. The chief's son she called uncle.

"One day, a few weeks after I went there, the chief's wife's brothers came in, bringing a Frenchman, who spoke some English, for interpreter, and asked me if I would not give him one of my children. He said he lived up north; that he had no children; and if I would give him one of mine, he would keep it as his own child. I saw that the man was really in earnest, and I answered very decidedly, 'No; I can not give either of them to any one.' After waiting a few minutes, I said, 'What is he going to do about it—what does he say?' The Frenchman replied, 'He will not take them if you do not give them to him.' The chief was in, and I thought perhaps this was his answer instead of the other man's.

"They talked some time with the chief, but did not say any thing more to me. Afterward the old woman seemed displeased about it. She said, 'I thought you would have given Letta to him, but you did not.' She had often before asked me something about Letta which I did not understand. I now know that she had wanted me to give her to her son. She never forgave this offense, but often reminded me of it. She had loved both the children very much before this, but now she treated them with great indifference, and sometimes was quite cross to them. I did not pay any attention to this, and so we had no quarrels. But I was very much afraid my children would be stolen. I was afraid to leave them with the old woman when I went for water, as I had often done before. I was afraid to see them packed around by the Indian women, as they often were; and at night, I was afraid they would be taken from me while I slept.

"Indian living did not agree with Charlie. It was not long before he became quite unwell, and he did not regain his health during our stay with the Indians. For many days together we had no bread. We lived mostly on corn and potatoes, of which we had plenty. Sometimes we had beef and sometimes dog meat. Once in a while we had coffee and sugar. When our neighbors had something better than we had, they often sent some to me, or, more frequently, sent me to go and eat with them.

"One night, at bedtime, some one came for me to go out and eat. I was not hungry, but never refused to go when sent for. Walking Spirit was invited, and went also. We had a good supper. There was a piece of nice carpet spread for me to sit on, and a white towel to put my plate on. I had one of my plates that I used to have to eat on, and one of my sauce-plates to drink out of. We had potatoes, rice, dried apples, and cold water for supper. The chief carried home the remains of his supper to his wife, but I always left what I and my children could not eat.

"Sometimes, when I thought of the dirty dishes my food was on, the dirty kettles it was cooked in, and the dirty hands that prepared it, my stomach rebelled. But I tried to keep away such troublesome thoughts, and make the best of what I had.

"When I first went to Walking Spirit's, I was perplexed to know what to wash in. They had neither wash-basin nor tub. Seeing my difficulty, the chief's wife went to one of the neighbors and brought home the half of a powder-keg, which she gave me. This I found a great convenience as long as I staid there. When I wanted to wash my children's clothes, I cleaned out and used an old iron heater that was used as a dog's dish. Sometimes I had soap and sometimes I had none. Once or twice the chief's wife borrowed a tub and washboard for me from the Frenchman's wife that lived in the village. The washboard was one that had been mine. I was thankful to get clean clothes for myself and children, though they were unironed.

"The Indian dress that De Cota had promised me I never got. I wore my own clothes all the time. There were a good many articles of clothing given to me while I was in the village, most of those things that had been plundered from our house. I never asked for any thing, though I frequently saw some of my things that I and my children really needed worn by the Indian women and their children. Sometimes I saw Indian men wearing articles of clothing that had belonged to Mr. Huggins.

"Sacred Nest and wife were out on a buffalo hunt when I went to the village, and did not come home for a week or two afterward. When they came to see me I felt that I had met with loving, sympathizing friends. They sat down and wept with me. Letta was overjoyed at seeing again her *Indian mother*, as she called Sacred Nest's wife. She took her in her arms and stroked her, and said, 'Poor thing—poor thing!' Sacred Nest said to me, 'It is hard, very hard!' And then he said, 'God is good, though all men are bad. With Him it is light, though all was dark here.' The same day they sent for us to eat with them. When we came away they gave Letta as much buffalo meat as she could carry home.

"Sabbath days in our village were very much like other days. I tried to keep the time and remember the Sabbath, but I found afterward that I had got one day behind the time. I do not know how many Mondays I kept for Sunday.

"One day the chief's wife called me out to see something. On the road, coming down from the north, was a great company of Indians. The women of the village gathered around me, and told me I must stay in the house very closely while they were going past—that I must not let them see me. I went into the house, but presently the chief's wife came and hurried me into the tent that stood by, and told me to be very quiet—that I must not let the children cry or even talk loud. The Northerners were coming right to the village. I could see a great many warriors on horseback, a great many carts, and a great many people on foot. It looked to me like a very great multitude. I almost smothered the children trying to keep them quiet, for they would talk and cry to go out. At last I frightened them into something like quietude by telling them that there were wicked men out there who would hurt them.

"On, on came the host, right past where we were, and then stopped a little distance off. The children were frightened into silence by the noise they made. I could look out of a hole in the tent and see almost as well as if I had been on the outside. There were very few women among them—I think not more than one woman to six men. There was great excitement in the village; men, women, and children were running about as if they did not know what to do. Many of them were preparing and carrying food to our formidable visitors. I think the Indians were frightened as well as myself. The warriors galloped about as if to show themselves, frequently firing off guns. Then I heard one chief's voice sounding loud above all others. I could see him. He was holding his head high, walking slowly back and forth, making a speech. I wondered what he was talking about, but I understood nothing. Before noon they were gone, and our village was again quiet.

"A day or two after the Northerners had gone down, all the men in the village went away—Walking Spirit on his old horse, Na-ho-ton-ma-ne on his colt, and Mrs. Walking Spirit on foot, packing food, followed the rest. For three days and two nights the old woman and I were left alone. This was before I had offended her, and she was very kind to me and my children. I suffered terribly from fear—from morning till night and from night till morning I was afraid—but nothing came to disturb us.

"Between one and two weeks after the Northerners went down, some of these passed up north, and stopped at our village. I was not taken to the tent this time. Walking Spirit told me they were coming to his house to eat after a while, but that I need not be afraid; he would not let any one hurt me. An hour or two afterward he came in and said, 'They are coming now; they will sit here, and here, and here; they will fill up the house; you must come and sit here behind me.' His place was near the door, on the right-hand side. He kept two guns by him, and told me several times that I need not be afraid; if any one tried to harm me, he would shoot him.

"So the children and I got in behind him, and awaited the coming of the guests. It was as the chief said it would be; the men filled the house; some of them were Walking Spirit's soldiers; the rest were Northerners. The women carried food to the door, but did not come in. The dinner consisted of fried bread and coffee. Walking Spirit, and several others that sat near, gave the children bread, and let them drink out of their cups of coffee. There were several speeches made, but I did not understand what they talked about. The Northerners went away first. After they were gone, the chief turned to me and said, 'These are all my soldiers.' Perhaps he intended to let me know that the danger was past. After talking a little while the men all left, and things went on as usual.

"One day, when we were all out braiding corn, some one brought a letter to the chief. As he could not read it himself, he handed it to me to look at. It was a nice-looking letter, written in Dakota, directed to Walking Spirit. When I told him I could not read it, he said he would take it to Sacred Nest; he would read it to him. I waited anxiously to hear the news from this letter, hoping that it might bring some word to me from friends below.

"When the chief came back, he said that Good

Day, a man who lived at the Yellow Medicine, had written the letter. Then he said to me, 'That letter made me very angry. He wants you to go and live with him.' Presently he said, 'Do you want to go?' I said I did not know, and asked him if Good Day was a good man. He said, 'No, he is a bad man.' Seeing that I still thought about it, and did not understand all he said, he went and brought the Frenchman to tell me in English. He said, 'Good Day wanted to buy me for a wife; that he already had a wife; and the chief was very angry at Good Day because he had thought of such a thing.' Then the old chief showed me how he had thrown the letter in the fire, because he was so very angry.

"One day, when the old woman and I were alone in the house, she started out, saying that she would soon be back; that I must stay in the house, for there was a bad man in the village who would kill me. This is what I understood her to say, but I did not understand her fully. Very soon afterward the blanket door of the house was thrown up, and there came in a young man with a drawn sword in his hand. He looked very fierce, and his face was painted most frightfully. One of the neighbor's children followed him in, and looked at him and then at me with a look of terror; then he ran out.

"Walking Spirit was in another part of the village, and the little boy ran as fast as he could, and told him that there was an angry man in his house going to kill the white woman. I supposed this to be the man the old woman had told me of, and that he had come on purpose to kill me. I wonder now at the presence of mind I felt then. I made a great effort to show no fear, no surprise. I looked up at him once, and then bent my face again over my sewing, though I trembled so violently that it was with difficulty I held my needle.

"After looking at me a moment without speaking, he went away. I drew a long breath then, and thought, 'He is gone, and I and my children are saved alive.' A moment after and the chief came running. He sprang in at the door, puffing and panting, with his hair all blown over his face. I looked up and smiled, saying, 'You frighten me, coming up in such a hurry.' '*You frighten me*,' he replied, as he sat down to rest; 'I was afraid you would be killed before I got here.'

"The women came in presently and told us all about the angry man. He did not want to kill *me*, but *his wife*, who had run away from him. He had come into the chief's house in search of her. He found her soon afterward, but did not kill her; he only cut up her pack with his sword.

"I met with several such frights as this, but always passed through unharmed. When there were strangers about I was frequently hid in the tent that stood by the house. I never tried to hide unless I was told to do so, and then I remained in my hiding-place until they told me the danger was past.

"Several days before we started north they told me that the Indians were all going north—that Julia, and her brothers, and the white prisoners below were all going. They told me of a great many white soldiers that were down below somewhere. They said that Mr. Riggs and Dr. Williamson were among them. I did not understand the half of what they told me.

I could only conjecture, and wish, and wonder. Walking Spirit told me several times that if Mr. Riggs and Dr. Williamson sent for him, he would take me and the children in a wagon and go. I thought I could not do better than to wait patiently until the time of my deliverance came.

"The whole village was now preparing for their journey, gathering and burying corn and potatoes, pounding corn off the cob to take with them, and bundling up their goods. Some kept their wagons partly loaded all the time. Every one was in a hurry, and I helped all I could. The chief's wife and I, with some assistance from her mother and the chief himself, pounded corn until we had filled five sacks, for our provisions by the way. We had as many sacks of potatoes, but no meat or flour.

"The women seemed to regret very much leaving home, and said they were going to a bad country, where they would have no wood, and very little to eat. At last word came that the white prisoners were all killed, and that the Indians who did not flee north would be killed in consequence. A great many Indians were on the road that day, and most of our village went. The chief was almost the last to go.

* * * * * *

"At night we camped in a valley, pitched our tent, staked out the animals, and ate a supper of skunk and potatoes. Oh how lonely and quiet it was that night. I enjoyed the solitude, and peaceful trust filled my heart. I loved to think of God's beautiful works all around and above us, and of his protecting, loving care guarding and guiding us.

"Early the next morning a man rode up to the tent

and called out something that made the family all start to their feet. They pulled down the tent, hurried things into the wagon, and started as quickly as possible. We soon joined a company of Indians, and traveled until afternoon without stopping. I had a little parched corn for the children, but they, as well as myself, were tired and hungry. Charlie was sick and fretful.

"We traveled on for four days, over beautiful prairies, and in sight of beautiful lakes. Sometimes I felt cheerful, and sometimes very sad and desponding. Charlie was growing weaker every day. I feared he could not endure Indian life much longer, and I saw no prospect of rescue. How hard it was to think that my darling might die. Then, too, came the fear that we might all starve during the coming winter. Another fear was that Little Crow's people, or some of the Northerners, would overpower Walking Spirit, and take me. How I suffered when I thought of these things. But, generally, I felt hopeful that some way would be provided, and we be rescued to our friends, who, I knew, were earnestly praying for our release.

"Sometimes, as we were traveling, my Indian friends would see what they supposed might be enemies, and they would bid me lie down and cover up. I always hid when they told me to, without waiting to see what or where the danger was.

"One day our company had stopped for dinner, and some other Indians came into camp. Among them were Sacred Nest and his wife. Letta ran to meet them, reaching out her arms, and screaming, 'My Indian mother, my Indian mother.' Mrs. Sacred Nest took her up, and kissed her most affectionately, and gave her a piece of bread wrapped in white cotton. She had brought it from home on purpose for Letta.

"The last night before we started back we camped in company with a great number of Indians. They had a great many wagons, horses, and cattle. I counted about eighty yoke of oxen. Mrs. Walking Spirit said there were a great many bad Indians there. In the morning, a man brought some news which I did not understand; and when the chief's wife told me something about it, and asked if I was glad, and wanted to go, I said, 'I don't know.' When we started that morning, we left the rest of the company and turned back. I did not know what it meant, and was afraid to hope. Still I did hope, and was in a feverish state of anxiety and surprise. At noon we camped, and the family bustled about preparing for visitors. We seated ourselves in the tent. Oh, how my heart burned with surprise and delight when Enos Good Hail, Lazarus Rusty, and, in a moment, Robert Hopkins and David Renville, entered. They looked so pleased and happy that I knew they had good news. When they were seated, Enos drew two letters from his pocket; one for Walking Spirit, from Colonel Sibley, written in English, and translated by Mr. Riggs. Walking Spirit sent for Sacred Nest to come and read his letter to him. While it was being read twice — once by Sacred Nest and once by Enos, the pipe was passed around the circle, each smoking in his turn. The chief handed it to me, saying that he was sent for, and was going, and then inquired who had written my letter, and what it contained.

"Colonel Sibley was then camped with his soldiers near Lac qui Parle, and had sent for me by these

Friendly Indians. Here, then, was deliverance. I could not sleep that night, my thoughts were so busy. Next morning, while the chief's wife prepared breakfast, I mended the chief's clothes, so that he might appear as respectably as possible. I finished, and gave her the thread and scissors. She handed the scissors back, telling me to keep them. They shall always be a remembrance of her.

"Then I bade my friends good-by, and went with the men who had been sent for me. Sacred Nest generously gave his wagon for our use. Enos Good Hail brought two German girls and a half-breed boy to go with us. He cried as if his heart would break to leave the woman who had taken care of him. In a short time I succeeded in comforting him. The girls talked in German almost continually.

"The first night we camped near where the old trading posts at Big Stone Lake had been. Lame Bear and some of his people were camped there. We were very hospitably entertained by them. Some one lent us a tent. Enos Good Hail made a bed for me and my children, and assisted us in every way possible. I was very tired and almost sick.

"The day before we reached Camp Release we passed twelve men seated on the ground smoking. They were fine-looking fellows, painted most savagely. They looked like warriors and murderers. I was sure Good Hail was afraid of them, though he stopped to talk and smoke with them. When he went on he drove very fast, frequently looking back, as if he feared pursuit. That night we camped in sight of Lac qui Parle. We left the wagon, and camped some distance from the road, at the foot of a hill. (This was

Dakota precaution against enemies.) The children and I had all the bedding there was; but the night was cold, and we had no tent, so that we suffered somewhat. I lay awake nearly all night, in great fear of the men we saw the day before.

"When we passed the place the next day which I once called home, Enos and Walking Spirit went with me to the grave of my husband. We drove in stakes to protect it as well as we could. Then I walked around the desolated place where our houses had been —went to the stream where Amos used to catch fish, and to every familiar spot. Much was unchanged, and yet how much was changed—how much was gone!

"An hour's ride brought us to Camp Release. I was worn down, faint, and sick, for the fatigue and excitement of the last three days had quite prostrated me. During the two weeks which we spent in the camp, Charlie and I gained in health and strength. Then we proceeded on our way to join our friends below."

In addition to the above facts, showing the kind treatment which Mrs. Huggins received during her captivity, she tells us how delicately her need of a shawl was supplied by an Indian woman, who came up behind her, and placed one on her shoulders. Another Dakota woman, Amanda, often sent milk to Letta and Charlie. She also went down to the Yellow Medicine to get flour for the white woman who had sought their protection.

"We have a white woman with us," she said, "and we keep her very carefully; we don't allow a young man to speak to her."

WILD-GOOSE-NEST LAKE.

CHAPTER XVI.

HOMEWARD BOUND.

ON the 21st of October a perfect hurricane swept over our camp. The air was dark with cinders and smoke from the burning prairies. Trees were torn up by the roots, and the tents blown down over our heads. Through this storm Lieutenant Colonel Marshall and two hundred men, who had been on an expedition into Dakota Territory, arrived with a crowd of prisoners, whom he had captured upon Wild-Goose-Nest Lake. We were only waiting his arrival to break up our camp,* and on the 23d the tents were struck, and, with the Indian prisoners in wagons, we commenced our homeward march. At Yellow Medicine we took in the other prisoners. The march this day was terrible, and rapidly extracted the joke of soldier life. Old Æolus seemed to be re-enacting the same lively little operation which Virgil describes him doing at the instigation of the cruel Juno, except that he now mingled the land instead of the sea with the sky. The dust drove in darkening clouds across the prairie, filling the eyes, ears, noses, and faces of our poor soldiers, and giving them the appearance of having been suddenly resurrected from dirty graves; and the cold was so intense that they shivered as if in fear that Death was hurrying fast behind, to re-consign

* Before we left, Colonel Sibley received news of his appointment to the position of brigadier general.

them to the abodes which they had prematurely left. Horses would turn from the road, back up against the wind, and neither whip nor spur could urge them forward; and so we left them, soon to fall upon the prairies, and remain melancholy memorials of our army's returning march. But the next day the sun shone brightly; the clear autumn air was calmly at rest; and great flocks of geese, and brant, and vari-colored ducks, and cranes, with their clattering cry, wheeled over our heads and drew the soldiers' fire. That night we pitched our tents in the valley of the Red-Wood.

The Indian camp, consisting principally of women and children, had been previously removed to this place from Yellow Medicine. When the squaws caught sight of our train, and saw their fathers, and uncles, and brothers chained in the wagons, they began to weep, and set up a dismal wail. "See our poor friends," they said; "they are prisoners, and hungry and cold." Antoine Frenier, the interpreter, told them that there were forty-five white men, women, and children lying unburied on the other side of the Minnesota, who had been cruelly murdered by these same men, and that they then shed no tears, and that they had better recollect this and remain quiet. This effected a quietus.

Two or three days before our arrival, a woman was found, with her two little daughters, on the opposite side of the river. They had been in the woods over nine weeks, and knew nothing of what had transpired. When discovered, they were in a house which they had entered to die. The whites they supposed to be Indians when they first entered, and they covered up

INDIAN CAMP AT RED WOOD.

their heads to receive the fatal blow. The poor creatures were starved to mere skeletons, and it seemed as if the convulsions of joy which they experienced at their rescue would break their hearts. Strong-minded men, as they gazed at their emaciated, sorrow-stricken faces, bowed their heads and shed tears like girls. When the mother fled from the massacre she had another child, an infant, which she carried in her arms. The other children "walked and ran painfully along by her side through the tangled brush and brier vines. They lived on wild plums and berries, and when those were gone by the frost, on grape tendrils and roots. At night they cowered like a brood of partridges, trembling, starving, nearly dead. The infant was taken home to heaven. The mother laid its body under a plum-tree, scraped together a heap of dried leaves and covered it, placed a few sticks over them to prevent the rude winds from blowing them away, then, looking hastily around, again fled with the survivors."

Several weeks were spent at the Lower Agency, the trials still progressing. Here was the most comfortable camping-ground that had fallen to our lot during the campaign. We were located on a high plain, and wood and water were within easy access. The ferry was put in running order, and thereby was furnished an easy transit for foraging parties and those desirous of going to Fort Ridgely. The buildings left by the savages were occupied for hospital and other purposes. Stoves in abundance were obtained, and protruded their blackened pipes from the tent-tops. For those who desired fireplaces, convenient bricks were at hand for their construction. Colonel Crooks had one of these in his tent, and the blazing brands reminded one of home, and suggested gay, hilarious times. Men will make themselves comfortable in camp. If logs are not to be found, they will build houses from sods and dig holes in the ground, as some of our men did at Camp Release. We still continued to find victims of the massacre. On the 29th a foraging party crossed the river, and eleven miles above discovered the remains of twelve persons. In one house a skull lay upon the bed, and in the same room lay a dead hog, who had probably been feeding on the dead. Close to the house the party were saluted by two howling, half-starved dogs. The next day they went out again, and, a short distance above the same place, found the bones of thirteen more bodies. One skeleton was evidently that of a strong, powerful man; the skull was fractured into bits. Cattle were running around almost as wild as buffaloes. An ox was writhing on the ground in agony, and frothing at the mouth, apparently with hydrophobia. Many of the dogs there are said to have gone mad. Desolation reigned supreme. A flag of truce would not have saved the murderers had they made their appearance on that scene of inhuman butchery. Many other bones were found in that neighborhood, and among them those of the persons which Antoine Frenier saw on his way to Yellow Medicine. The house where the little children were had been burned, and the charred remains were in the ruins. Henceforth, for many a year on our borders, Indian hunters will be found who will emulate those of whom the early history of our country tells, bent on war to the death with the savage foe. Men

THE COURT-HOUSE OF THE MILITARY COMMISSION.

whose wives and children have been brutally murdered, and hearthstones blasted forever, will never rest till blood has answered for blood. God's fierce avengers in the future! success to their unerring rifles.

Soon after our arrival the Indians were brought down from the Red-Wood River, and their camp placed near ours, around the walls of the church which charitable and pious hands had reared for their benefit. The male prisoners were confined in the jail which had recently been constructed, and the trials were conducted in a log building heretofore occupied by the murdered mixed-blood, La Batte, for unromantic kitchen purposes, but now destined to pass into history and be immortalized. The avenging Nemesis had brought the guilty to an appropriate spot, and that on eagle wings, for here it was that the mad saturnalia first began. The fire had scarcely died out in the ruins of the goodly buildings which they destroyed, or the blood of their murdered, mangled victims sunk in the ground. A few hours after our arrival the charred bones of a victim were taken from the ruins of one of the houses, and the unburied remains of one of Marsh's men found near the ferry. Almost within stone's throw was the battle-ground of Birch Coolie. The dirt on the graves of the slain was yet fresh. You could see, as if it was done but yesterday, behind every little bush and hillock the marks where the savages had lain when they fired upon the camp, and the trails which they made over the grass in crawling toward it. The splinters made by the bullets were still hanging upon the trees, and the dead horses massed around and through the intrenchments, though much wasted, were easily distinguishable from one another. All that was needed to complete the deep tragedy of the spot was the erection of a mighty gallows—one partaking of the gigantesque—and the culprits launched together from it into eternity, there to hang until the elements should scatter their dust to the winds.

The only enemy that threatened us here was the prairie fire. Lighting up the heavens with lurid flames, roaring through the tall, dry grass, it came down upon us like "an army with banners" with the rush of the storm. The whole force turned out to "fight fire with fire," but a lucky wind changed it to another direction.

On the 7th of November, Colonel Marshall, with the inmates of the Indian camp, about 1500 in all, consisting of women and children, and a few innocent males, started for Fort Snelling. When the outrage broke out the Indians said that they would winter their squaws near St. Paul. The prediction was to be accomplished, but the fact was not to be as agreeable as supposed.

At six o'clock our drums were beating for forward march. The general was one of the earliest of risers. He had all the camp aroused and at breakfast before four. It was a disagreeable morning; "the owl through all his feathers was a-cold," and so were bold "sojer" boys. We soon cantered away, and left the aforesaid quondam kitchen, but henceforth immortalized court-house, in which three of us had slumbered cozily for many a pleasant night (and which the general therefore playfully characterized as a "den"), probably forever. When the command passed New Ulm the inhabitants were engaged in disinterring the

PRAIRIE ON FIRE.

dead from the street for more appropriate burial. Hearing that we were passing by, they all rushed forth, men, women, and children, armed with clubs, pitchforks, hoes, brickbats, knives, and guns, and attacked the prisoners. The women were perfectly furious; they danced around with their aprons full of stones, and cried for an opportunity to get at the prisoners, upon whom they poured the most violent abuse. Many rushed forward and discharged a shower of stones. One woman, who had a long knife in her hand, was especially violent in her demonstrations, and another pounded an Indian in the face till she broke his jaw, and he fell backward out of the wagon. They were the brutal murderers of their friends. The prisoners cowered low, and the negro Godfrey, who lived in the neighborhood of this theatre of his exploits, and was well known in New Ulm, took good care to cover his head with his blanket, and crouch close down in his wagon. The expedition soon reached Mankato, near which a permanent camp for the winter was established, called "Camp Lincoln." Here the trial of a number of the Winnebagoes was held.

As no other murders were committed until the following spring, this is an appropriate place to state the estimated losses in 1862.

I take Mr. Galbraith's figures.

Citizens massacred: In Renville County, including Reservations, 221; in Dakota Territory, including Big Stone Lake, 32; in Brown County, including Lake Shetek, 204; in the other frontier counties, 187—644. *Soldiers killed in battle:* Lower Sioux Agency, Captain Marsh's command, 24; Fort Ridgely and New Ulm, 29; Birch Coolie, 23; Fort Abercrombie, Acton, Forest City, Hutchinson, and other places, including Wood Lake, 17—93. Total, 737.

Mr. Galbraith says, "Here, then, we have seven

hundred and thirty-seven persons whom I am certainly convinced have been killed by the Indians. More there may be, and I think there are, yet I confine myself to the facts I have. Are they not enough? Many of this number were full-grown men, and boys over twelve years of age; the rest women and children—the mother, the maiden, the little boy or girl, and the innocent infant. Are they not enough?"

During the winter of 1862 and '63 Congress made an appropriation, though greatly insufficient in amount, for the indemnification of the losses incurred by the settlers, and appointed three commissioners to audit the claims, who commenced their sessions in the state early in the season.

Justice demands complete reparation. The federal government, through the maladministration of the Indian Department, is largely responsible for the excitement of the Indians against the whites. Besides, it exercises exclusive jurisdiction over them, and is responsible for their good conduct. Alas! what human power can compensate for the precious lives extinguished, for the desolated homes, for the blasted virtue, for all the anguish, and sorrow, and heart-desolation entailed. In the month of September alone, 8231 persons, who had been living in comparative affluence, were dependent on the support which the state furnished. Many charitable donations were received from abroad. Among the good men who contributed to the support of the sufferers was Mr. Minturn, of New York City. The names of the donors will live in the memory of a grateful people.

On the Reservation the property destroyed has been estimated by the agent at over one million of dollars.

THE ATTACK AT NEW ULM.

The direct and indirect loss to the remainder of the state can hardly be estimated. Millions will not cover it.

If the stories told by the whites of the number of Indians killed in different encounters during the season were correct, their loss would be several hundred. But the number was grossly exaggerated. An Indian with his head bound with grass, and hugging the prairie, and availing himself, with practiced eye, of every inequality in its surface for protection, and shifting his position every time he discharges his gun, is a very difficult mark for an experienced shot, let alone for those who were not accustomed to the use of arms.

In order to get, if possible, other information upon the subject, at Fort Snelling I gathered the Indians of different bands together, and asked them to enumerate their losses. They did so willingly, and the manner in which they did it convinced me of their sincerity. They went over the bands one by one, and gave the names of the slain, each refreshing the recollections of the others. An Indian ascertains and remembers such things much better than a white man, because there are comparatively few things to occupy his mind, and prominent among these is what pertains to battles. They do not confine themselves to one place, but are continually wandering around and associating with one another, and can tell the locality of every band. Their knowledge of distances, and of what Indians went upon different war paths, and their numbers, and what they did, I found to be astonishingly correct.

The conversation and details of the affair at Acton was narrated to me by an Indian, who told me he had heard it many times. It was from one of them, too, that I obtained the speeches which were made.

Their estimate of the killed upon the field corresponded with the number found by us at the different places of contest. I have heard some say that there were more found at New Ulm, Ridgely, and Abercrombie, but I looked in vain for a man who could tell me he had seen them. I was at Ridgely myself shortly after the battles, and was told that more than here stated had been discovered, but I could not find them after a diligent search.

Here are the figures as given by the Indians. They include those who were carried away wounded from the battle-field, and afterward died.

Admitted loss of the enemy in 1862: At the battle of Red-Wood Ferry, 1; at New Ulm (including half-breeds), 5; at Fort Ridgely, 2; at Birch Coolie, 2; Big Woods, at or near Forest City, 1; at battle of Acton with Strout, 1; at Hutchinson, 1; at Spirit Lake, 1; at Lake Shetek, by Duly, 1; near Omahaw, where several went to steal horses, not knowing of the outbreak, 1; at Abercrombie, 4; between Fort Ridgely and New Ulm, half-breed, 1; at Wood Lake, 22. Total, 42.

CAMP LINCOLN.

CHAPTER XVII.

TRIALS OF THE PRISONERS.

THE Military Commission, which organized, as stated in the order creating it, "to try *summarily* the mulatto, mixed bloods, and Indians engaged in the Sioux raids and massacres," consisted at first of Colonel Crooks, Lieutenant Colonel Marshall, Captains Grant and Bailey, and Lieutenant Olin. The writer acted as recorder.

After twenty-nine cases were disposed of, Major Bradley was substituted for Lieutenant Colonel Marshall, who was absent on other duty.

The prisoners were arraigned upon written charges specifying the criminating acts. These charges were signed by Colonel Sibley or his adjutant general, and were, with but few exceptions, based upon information furnished by the Rev. S. R. Riggs. He obtained it by assembling the half-breeds, and others possessed of means of knowledge, in a tent, and interrogating them concerning suspected parties. The names of the witnesses were appended to the charge. He was, in effect, the Grand Jury of the court. His long residence in the country, and extensive acquaintance with the Indians, his knowledge of the character and habits of most of them, enabling him to tell almost with certainty what Indians would be implicated and what ones not, either from their disposition or their relatives being engaged, and his familiarity with their language, eminently qualified him for the position.

Major Forbes, of General Sibley's staff, a trader of long standing among the Indians, acted as provost marshal, and Antoine Frenier as interpreter. The charges were first read to the accused, and, unless he admitted them, evidence on oath introduced.

Godfrey was the first person tried. The following was the charge and specifications, which will serve as a sample of the others:

"*Charge and Specifications against O-ta-kle, or Godfrey, a colored man connected with the Sioux tribe of Indians.*

"*Charge.* MURDER.

"*Specification 1st.* In this, that the said O-ta-kle, or Godfrey, a colored man, did, at or near New Ulm, Minnesota, on or about the 19th day of August, 1862, join in a war party of the Sioux tribe of Indians against the citizens of the United States, and did with his own hand murder seven white men, women, and children (more or less), peaceable citizens of the United States.

"*Specification 2d.* In this, that the said O-ta-kle, or Godfrey, a colored man, did, at various times and places between the 19th of August, 1862, and the 28th day of September, 1862, join and participate in the murders and massacre committed by the Sioux Indians on the Minnesota frontier. By order of

"COL. H. H. SIBLEY, Com. Mil. Expedition.

"S. H. FOWLER,* Lt. Col. State Militia, A. A. A. G.

"*Witnesses:* Mary Woodbury, David Faribault, Sen., Mary Swan, Bernard la Batte."

* Colonel Fowler was formerly in the regular army, and rendered General Sibley efficient aid in the organization of the expedition.

On being asked whether he was guilty or not guilty, he made a statement similar to the one heretofore detailed.

Mary Woodbury testified that she saw him two or three days after the outbreak at Little Crow's village with a breech-clout on, and his legs and face painted for a war party, and that he started with one for New Ulm; that he appeared very happy and contented with the Indians; was whooping around and yelling, and apparently as fierce as any of them. When they came back there was a Wahpeton, named Hunka, who told witness that the negro was the bravest of all; that he led them into a house and *clubbed* the inmates with a hatchet; and that she was standing in the prisoner's tent door, and heard the Indians ask him how many he had killed, and he said only seven; and that she saw him, once when he started off, have a gun, a knife, and a hatchet.

Mary Swan and Mattie Williams testified that when the war party took them captive, though the prisoner was not armed, he appeared to be as much in favor of the outrages as any of the Indians, and made no intimation to the contrary in a conversation the witnesses had with him.

La Batte knew nothing about him.

David Faribault, Sen., a half-breed, testified as to his boasting of killing seven with a tomahawk, and some more—*children;* but these, he said, didn't amount to any thing, and he wouldn't count them. Witness saw him at the fort and at New Ulm, fighting and acting like the Indians; and he never told him (Faribault) that he was forced into the outbreak.

Godfrey, it will be recollected, stated, before witnesses were called, that he was at the fort, New Ulm, Birch Coolie, and Wood Lake, but was compelled to go; and that he had struck a man with the back of a hatchet in a house where a number were killed, and that he spoke of killing in the Indian acceptation of the term, as before explained, and boasted of the act in order to keep the good will of the Indians.

He had such an honest look, and spoke with such a truthful tone, that the court, though prejudiced against him in the beginning, were now unanimously inclined to believe that there were possibilities as to his sincerity. His language was broken, and he communicated his ideas with some little difficulty. This was an advantage in his favor, for it interested the sympathetic attention of the listener, and it was a pleasure to listen to his hesitating speech. His voice was one of the softest that I ever listened to.

The court held his case open for a long time, and, while the other trials were progressing, asked every person who was brought in about him, but could find no person who *saw* him kill any one, although the Indians were indignant at him for having disclosed evidence against a number of them, and would be desirous of finding such testimony.

Finally, the court found him not guilty of the first specification, but guilty of the charge and the second specification, and sentenced him to be hung, accompanying the sentence, however, by a recommendation of a commutation of punishment to imprisonment for ten years. It was afterward granted by the President.

The trials were elaborately conducted until the commission became acquainted with the details of the different outrages and battles, and then, the only point being the connection of the prisoner with them, five minutes would dispose of a case.

If witnesses testified, or the prisoner admitted, that he was a participant, sufficient was established. As many as forty were sometimes tried in a day. Those convicted of plundering were condemned to imprisonment; those engaged in individual massacres and in battles, to death.

If you think that participation in battles did not justify such a sentence, please to reflect that any judicial tribunal in the state would have been compelled to pass it, and that the retaliatory laws of war, as recognized by all civilized nations, and also the code of the Indian, which takes life for life, justified it. The battles were not ordinary battles.. The attacks upon New Ulm were directed against a village filled with frightened fugitives from the surrounding neighborhood, and the place was defended by *civilians*, hastily and indifferently armed, and were accompanied by the wanton burning of a large portion of the town, and by the slaughter of horses and cattle, and the destruction of all property which came within the power of the enemy. A number of persons from the country, who endeavored, while the attack was progressing, to make their way into the town, where alone was possible safety, were shot down and horribly mutilated. The attacks upon the forts were also accompanied by similar acts.

The battle of Birch Coolie commenced with an attack, just before daylight, upon a small party of soldiers and civilians who had been engaged in the burial of the dead at the Red-Wood Agency, by over three hundred Indians, who started for the purpose of burning the towns of New Ulm, Mankato, and St. Peter, and butchering the inhabitants. The war party to the Big Woods marched a distance of eighty miles on a general raid through the settlements. They murdered and mutilated a number of unarmed fugitives, burned many houses, stole a large quantity of horses and cattle, killed a portion of Captain Strout's company at Acton, and partially destroyed the town of Hutchinson. On all these occasions, as they were attacked by largely superior numbers, the whites would have surrendered could "quarter" have been expected. It was with the utmost resistance of despair that the defense of Fort Rigdely and New Ulm was sustained after the burning of all the outbuildings, and an attempt to set fire to the fort itself. The timely arrival of re-enforcements alone saved the party at Birch Coolie from total massacre. One hundred and four bullet-holes through a single tent, the slaughter of over ninety horses, and the loss of half the party in killed and wounded, indicate the peril of their situation. The purpose of these Indians, as frequently stated, was to sweep the country as far as St. Paul with the tomahawk and with fire, giving the men "no quarter;" and these battles were but a part of the general design, and rendered the acts of one the acts of all. The fact that those engaged in such a mode of warfare acted together in organized bands, and directed their attempts against a large number of whites, was *not* a matter of mitigation, but of *aggravation*, arising from increased ability and opportunity to accomplish their purpose.

Besides, most of these Indians must also have been engaged in individual massacres and outrages. Those who attacked New Ulm on the second day after the outbreak, and Fort Ridgely on the third day, were undoubtedly parties who had scattered through the neighborhood in small marauding bands the day before. The extent of the outrages, occurring almost simultaneously over a frontier of two hundred miles in length and reaching far into the interior, and whereby nearly one thousand people perished, can not be accounted for without their participation. The fact that they were *Indians*, intensely hating the whites, and possessed of the inclinations and revengeful impulses of *Indians*, and educated to the propriety of the indiscriminate butchery of their opponents, would raise the moral certainty that, as soon as the first murders were committed, all the young men were impelled by the sight of blood and plunder—by the contagion of example, and the hopes entertained of success—to become participants in the same class of acts.

In at least two thirds of the cases the prisoners admitted that they fired, but in most instances insisted that it was only two or three shots, and that no one was killed; about as valid an excuse as one of them offered who was possessed of an irresistible impulse to accumulate property, that a horse which he took was only a very little one, and that a pair of oxen which he captured was for his wife, who wanted a pair. In regard to the third who did not admit that they fired, their reasons for *not* doing so were remarkable, and assumed a different shape every day. One day all the elderly men, who were in the vigor of manly strength, said their hair was too gray to go into battle; and the young men, aged from eighteen to twenty-five, insisted that they were too young, and their hearts too weak to face fire. The next day would develop the fact that great was the number and terrible the condition of those who were writhing in agony with the bellyache on the top of a big hill. A small army avowed that they had crept under a wonderfully capacious stone (which nobody but themselves ever saw) at the battles of the fort, and did not emerge therefrom during the fights; and a sufficiency for two small armies stoutly called on the Great Spirit (Wakan-tonka), and the heavens and the earth (patting the latter emphatically with the hand), to witness that they were of a temper so phlegmatic, a disposition so unsocial, and an appetite so voracious and greedy, that, during the roar of each of the battles at the fort, New Ulm, Birch Coolie, and Wood Lake, they were alone, within bullet-shot, roasting and eating corn and beef all day! A fiery-looking warrior wished the commission to believe that he felt so bad at the fort to see the Indians fire on the whites, that he immediately laid down there and went to sleep, and did not awake until the battle was over! Several of the worst characters, who had been in all the battles, after they had confessed the whole thing, wound up by saying that they were members of the Church!

One young chap, aged about nineteen, said that he used always to attend divine worship at Little Crow's village, below St. Paul, and that he never did any thing bad in his life except to run after a chicken at Mendota a long time ago, and that he didn't catch it. The evidence disclosed the fact that this pious youth had been an active participant in some of the worst massacres on Beaver Creek.

All ages were represented, from boyish fifteen up

to old men scarcely able to walk or speak, who were "fifty years old," to use the expression of one, "a long time ago, and then they stopped counting." Two of these old gentlemen were once brought in together, who were direct opposites in physiognomy—the face of one running all to nose, which terminated sharply, giving him the pointed expression, while that of the other was perfectly flat, and about two feet broad, and fully illustrated (what I always considered a fable) the fact of persons being in existence who couldn't open or shut their eyes and mouths at the same moment. This specimen was apparently asleep the whole time, with his lower jaw down; and closed eyes being his normal condition, he had to be punched up every two minutes, when the president of the commission was interrogating him, as he wished to look in his eyes to judge if he was telling the truth.

"*Wake him up! stir him up!*" was the continual injunction to the interpreter. This lively little proceeding kept the old gentleman's face in continued action, eyes and mouth alternately opening and shutting with a jerk. If he was simply *told* to open his eyes, the operation was slow. The lids peeled up like those of some stupid noxious bird gorged with carrion, and would shut again before they were fairly open, the mouth following suit *pari passu.* Nothing was proved against him, and the president said, in a loud voice, "Lead him out." The startled tones awakened him, but the eyes shut again, and they led him away wrapped in profound slumber.

Another equally antiquated specimen, but by no means terrific in appearance, and not of the smallest account to himself or any body else—sore-eyed, and of lymphatic temperament—astonished the court by stating that he was the sole cause of the Sioux difficulty; that he was living near New Ulm upon the charity of the whites; that the whites were, in fact, lavishingly kind to him, and to such an extent that the other Indians were jealous of him, and became so excited thereby that they brought on the war.

Two semi-idiots were tried. Nothing was elicited concerning one of them except that he was called "white man," and was picked up when an infant alone on the prairies. He claimed to be a white, but looked like a "Red, and a very cross-eyed, ugly-phized "Red" at that. The other had wit enough to kill a white child, and, unfortunately for him, the plea of idiocy was not recognized by the commission.

An innocent-looking youth was tried on a charge of robbery. The following examination took place:

Ques. "What goods, if any, did you take from Forbes's store?"

Ans. "Some blankets."

Q. "Any thing else?"

A. "Yes; some calico and cloth."

Q. "Any thing else?"

A. "Yes; some powder, and some lead, and some paint, and some beads."

Q. "Any thing else?"

A. "Yes; some flour, and some pork, and some coffee, and some rice, and some sugar, and some beans, and some tin cups, and some raisins, and some twine, and some fish-hooks, and some needles, and some thread."

Q. "Was you going to set up a grocery store on your own account?"

A. A stupid and inquiring look from the Indian, but no words.

Ten years in prison was given him to meditate on his reply.

Let it not be supposed, because facetiæ were sometimes indulged in, that the proceedings were lightly conducted. The trial of several hundred persons for nearly the same class of acts became very monotonous. The gravest judge, unless entirely destitute of the juices of humor, sometimes a while

> "Unbends his rugged front,
> And deigns a transient smile."

Many cases there were where there was occasion enough for display of solemn sorrow.

The most repulsive-looking prisoner was Cut-nose, some of whose acts have been detailed by Samuel Brown. He was the foremost man in many of the massacres. The first and second days of the outbreak he devoted his attention particularly to the Beaver Creek settlement, and to the fugitives on that side of the river. I will give a single additional instance of the atrocity of this wretch and his companions. A party of settlers were gathered together for flight when the savages approached; the defenseless, helpless women and children, huddled together in the wagons, bending down their heads, and drawing over them still closer their shawls. Cut-nose, while two others held the horses, leaped into a wagon that contained eleven, mostly children, and deliberately, in cold blood, tomahawked them all—cleft open the head of each, while the others, stupefied with horror, powerless with fright, as they heard the heavy, dull blows crash and tear through flesh and bones, awaited their turn. Taking an infant from its mother's arms, before her eyes, with a bolt from one of the wagons they riveted it through its body to the fence, and left it there to die, writhing in agony. After holding for a while the mother before this agonizing spectacle, they chopped off her arms and legs, and left her to bleed to death. Thus they butchered twenty-five within a quarter of an acre. Kicking the bodies out of the wagons, they filled them with plunder from the burning houses, and, sending them back, pushed on for other adventures.*

Many of those engaged in the Patville murder were tried. Patville started from Jo. Reynolds's place, just above Red-Wood, for New Ulm, on the morning of the outbreak, with three young ladies and two other men, and on the way they were attacked by the Indians, as detailed by Godfrey. Patville was killed near the wagon, and the other men at the edge of the woods, while trying to escape. One of the girls was wounded, and all three taken prisoners and brought to Red-Wood. Here the three were abused by the Indians; one, a girl of fourteen, by seventeen of the wretches, and the wounded young lady to such an extent that she died that night. Jo. Campbell ventured to place her in a grave, but was told that if he did so, or for any of the other bodies which were lying exposed, his life should pay the forfeit. The two other young ladies were reclaimed at Camp Release, and sent to their friends, after suffering indignities worse than death, and which humanity shudders to name.

Others were tried who belonged to a band of eight that separated themselves from the main body which attacked the fort in the second battle, and went to-

* Harper's Magazine.

ward St. Peter's, burning the church, the Swan Lake House, and other buildings, and murdering and plundering. They attacked one party, and killed all the men, and then one of them caught hold of a young girl to take her as his property, when the mother resisted and endeavored to pull her away. The Indians then shot the mother dead, and wounded the girl, who fell upon the ground apparently lifeless. An Indian said she was not dead, and told her first captor to raise her clothes, which he attempted to do. Modesty, strong in death, revived the girl, and she attempted to prevent it, but as she did so the other raised his tomahawk and dashed out her brains—a blessed fate in comparison with that which was otherwise designed.

An old man, shriveled to a mummy, one of the criers of the Indian camp, was also tried, and two little boys testified against him.

One of them, a German, and remarkably intelligent for his years, picked him out from many others at Camp Release, and had him arrested, and dogged him till he was placed in jail, and when he was led forth to be tried, with the eye and fierceness of a hawk, and as if he feared every instant that he would escape justice.

These boys belonged to a large party, who came from above Beaver Creek to within a few miles of the fort, where the Indians met them, and said if they would go back with them to where they came from, and give up their teams, they should not be harmed. When they were some distance from the fort, they fired into the party, and killed one man and a number of women, and took the remainder prisoners. The old wretch was made to stand up, looking cold and impassable, and as stolid as a stone, and the boys, likewise standing, placed opposite. They stood gazing at each other for a moment, when one of the boys said, "I saw that Indian shoot a man while he was on his knees at prayer;" and the other boy said, "I saw him shoot my mother."

Another was recognized by Mrs. Hunter as the Indian who had shot her husband, and then took out his knife and offered to cut his throat in her presence, but finally desisted, and carried her away into captivity.

A party of five was also tried, who all fired and killed a white man across the river. The party consisted of three half-breeds, Henry Milard, Baptiste Campbell, and Hippolyte Auge, and two Indians.

One of the Indians was first examined, and, as he was going out of the door, said hastily that there was a white man with him, and gave the name of Milard. He was at once arrested, and brought before the court the next day, and the Indian called as a witness. On being interrogated as to whether he knew the prisoner, he turned around, and, after leisurely scanning him from head to foot, said he never saw him before. Milard had previously made some rather damaging admissions, and being asked whether he desired any witnesses, mentioned the name of Campbell, who being brought in, stolidly told the whole thing, saying that they were sent over the river by Little Crow after cattle, and saw the white man, and all fired at the same time, and the man fell, and that he was sure the Indian shot him, as he had gotten where he could get a better shot. He said, with the utmost *sang froid*, that he aimed to hit, but unfortunately failed. Auge had gone to St. Peter's, but was arrested and convicted.

Several of the Renville Rangers were also arraigned, who deserted from the fort, and were in all the battles. One of these, about eighteen, built like a young Hercules, stated that he went from the fort to cut kin-ne-kin-nic, and the Indians, surrounding the fort while he was out, prevented his getting in, and that his presence in the battles was compulsory, and stoutly denied having been guilty of any wrong act. The evidence showed that he was of a decidedly belligerent character, having been engaged in war parties against the Chippeways, and that at Wood Lake he had scalped the first man killed, one of the Renville Rangers, an old gray-headed German (and very likely was the one who had cut his head and hands off), and had received therefor one of two belts of wampum which Little Crow had promised to those who should kill the first two white men. He called his Indian uncle in his defense, but he, much to his disgust, admitted that he had received the wampum.

The female sex was represented in the person of one squaw, who, it was charged, had killed two children. The only evidence to be obtained against her was camp rumor to that effect among the Indians, so she was discharged. Her arrest had one good effect, as she admitted she had taken some silver spoons across the river, and ninety dollars in gold, which she had turned over to an Indian, who, being questioned concerning it, admitted the fact, and delivered the money over to the general.

But the greatest institution of the commission, and

the observed of all observers, was the negro Godfrey. He was the means of bringing to justice a large number of the savages, in every instance but two his testimony being substantiated by the subsequent admission of the Indians themselves. His observation and memory were remarkable. Not the least thing had escaped his eye or ear. Such an Indian had a double-barreled gun, another a single-barreled, another a long one, another a short one, another a lance, and another one nothing at all. One denied that he was at the fort. Godfrey saw him there preparing his sons for battle, and recollected that he painted the face of one red, and drew a streak of green over his eyes. Another denied that he had made a certain statement to Godfrey which he testified to. "What!" said Godfrey, "don't you recollect you said it when you had your hand upon my wagon and your foot resting on the wheel." To a boy whom he charged with admitting that he had killed a child by striking it with his war spear over the head, and who denied it, he said, "Don't you remember showing me the spear was broken, and saying that you had broken it in striking the child?" To another, who said he had a lame arm at New Ulm, and couldn't fire a gun, and had such a bad gun that he could not have fired if he desired, he replied, "You say you could not fire, and had a bad gun. Why don't you tell the court the truth? I saw you go and take the gun of an Indian who was killed, and fire two shots; and then you borrowed mine, and shot with it; and then you made me reload it, and then you fired again."

I might enumerate numberless instances of this kind, in which his assumed recollection would cause his truthfulness to be doubted, if he had not been fully substantiated. It was a study to watch him, as he sat in court, scanning the face of every culprit who came in with the eye of a cat about to spring. His sense of the ridiculous, and evident appreciation of the gravity which should accompany the statement of an important truth, was strongly demonstrated. When a prisoner would state, in answer to the question of "Guilty or not guilty," that he was innocent, and Godfrey knew that he was guilty, he would drop his head upon his breast, and convulse with a fit of musical laughter; and when the court said, "Godfrey, talk to him," he would straighten up, his countenance become calm, and, in a deliberate tone, would soon force the Indian, by a series of questions in his own language, into an admission of the truth. He seemed a "providence" specially designed as an instrument of justice.

The number of prisoners tried was over four hundred. Of these, three hundred and three were sentenced to death, eighteen to imprisonment. Most of those acquitted were Upper Indians. There was testimony that all these left their homes and went upon war parties, but the particular acts could not be shown, and they were therefore not convicted. Some people have thought that the haste with which the accused were tried must have prevented any accuracy as to the ascertainment of their complicity. I have already shown that the point to be investigated being a very simple one, viz., presence and participation in battles and massacres which had before been proven, and many of the prisoners confessing the fact, each case need only occupy a few moments. It was completed when you asked him if he was in the battles of New Ulm and the fort, or either, and fired at the whites, and he said "yes." The officers composing the court were well known to the community as respectable and humane gentlemen. They resided a long distance from the scene of the massacres, and had no property destroyed or relatives slain. They were all men of more than average intelligence, and one of them (Major Bradley) was not only a gallant soldier, but had long been rated among the first lawyers of the state. Before entering upon the trials they were solemnly sworn to a fair and impartial discharge of their duties. It would scarcely be supposed that such men as these, after such an oath, would take away human life without the accused were guilty.

The fact that in many instances the punishment of imprisonment was graduated from one to ten years, and that in nearly one quarter of the cases the accused were acquitted, argues any thing but inattention to testimony and blind condemnation.

Mr. Riggs, their missionary, who furnished the grounds for the charges, had free intercourse with them, and as he was well known to all of them personally or by reputation for his friendship and sympathy, those who were innocent would be likely, of their own accord, to tell him of the fact, and those who were members of his church, or those whose characters were good, specially interrogated by him as to their guilt; and a gentleman of such kind impulses, and who took such a deep interest in their welfare, would not have hesitated to have had the defensive or excusatory fact brought to the attention of the court, and he did not. One instance was that of Robert Hopkins, a civilized Indian, and a member of the Church. He helped to save the life of Dr. Williamson and party, and when he was tried Mr. Riggs had this adduced in his favor.

Where so many were engaged in the raids, the fact of any one staying at home would be a circumstance much more marked than that of going — a circumstance quickly noticed, and calculated to impress the memory, and therefore easily proven.

It is the height of improbability to believe that any Indian would be accused, especially by Mr. Riggs, and the subject of his guilt or innocence canvassed among the half-breed witnesses who had been present through the whole affair, and be conducted by Provost Marshal Forbes, who understood the Indian language, and was well acquainted with them, a distance of a quarter of a mile from the prison to the court, without the fact of innocence, if it existed, being noticed and called to the attention of the court, and in no instance was there suggestion made of any defensive testimony but what the court had it produced, and gave to it due weight and consideration.

No one was sentenced to death for the mere robbery of goods, and not to exceed half a dozen for mere presence in a battle, although the prisoner had gone many miles to it, or on a general raid against the settlements. It was required that it should be proven by the testimony of witnesses, unless the prisoner admitted the fact, that he had fired in the battles, or brought ammunition, or acted as commissary in supplying provisions to the combatants, or committed some separate murder.

Where defensive testimony was offered, the defendant's case generally appeared worse against him. The reader will recollect the instances where the half-breed Milard sent for Baptiste Campbell, and the deserter from the Renville Rangers for his Indian uncles. Robert Hopkins's case, too, was unfortunate. He had helped Dr. Williamson to escape, but he fired in battles; and David Faribault swore that while he was between New Ulm and Red-Wood he heard a gun fired near a house a short distance off, and shortly afterward Hopkins and another Indian approached, and one of them (I think Hopkins) said that he (Hopkins) had first shot a white man at that house, and that there was another white man ran up stairs, and that Hopkins wanted the other Indian to follow, but he dared not; that Hopkins then proposed that they should set fire to the house, but the Indian refused to do so, as he said the white man might have a gun, and shoot one of them from the window.

Some have criticised the action of the court because of the great number of the condemned. Great also was the number of crimes of which they were accused.

Many of the presses in the East condemned the demands of the people of Minnesota for their execution as barbarous in the extreme. For their benefit let me cite a few instances from the history of their own ancestors under similar circumstances. See how the investigation and trial above detailed, and the refraining of the people to visit death summarily upon the criminals, or upon any one of them, compares with their conduct, and then judge.

In 1675 the New England army broke into King Philip's camp in the southern part of Rhode Island,

and fired five hundred wigwams; and hundreds of the women and children, the aged, the wounded, and the infirm, perished in the conflagration.

On the 5th of June, 1637, the soldiers of Connecticut forced their way into the Pequod fort, in the eastern part of the state, and commenced the work of destruction. The Indians fought bravely, but bows and arrows availed little against weapons of steel. "We must burn them," shouted Mason, their leader; and, applying a firebrand, the frail Indian cabins were soon enveloped in the flames.

The whites hastily withdrew and surrounded the place, while the savages, driven from the inclosure, became, by the light of the burning fire, a sure prey for the musket, or were cut down by the broadsword. As the sun shone upon the scene of slaughter it showed that the victory was complete.

About 600 Indians, men, women, and children, had perished, most of them in the hideous conflagration. Of the whole number within the fort, only seven escaped, and seven were made prisoners. *Two* of the whites were killed and twenty wounded. The remainder of the Pequods scattered in every direction; straggling parties were hunted and shot down like deer in the woods; their territory was laid waste, their settlements burned, and about 200 survivors, the sole remnant of the great nation, surrendering in despair, were enslaved by the whites, or forced to live with their allies.

CHAPTER XVIII.

EXECUTION.

THE records of the testimony and sentences of the Indians was sent to the President at an early day, but no action was taken for several weeks. Finally, thirty-eight were ordered to be executed at Mankato on the 26th day of February, 1863. On Monday, the 22d, the condemned were separated from the other prisoners to another prison. On the afternoon of the same day, Colonel Miller, the officer in command at Mankato, visited them, and announced the decision of the President.

Addressing the interpreter, the Rev. Mr. Riggs, he said:

"Tell these condemned men that the commanding officer of this place has called to speak to them upon a very serious subject this afternoon.

"Their Great Father at Washington, after carefully reading what the witnesses testified to in their several trials, has come to the conclusion that they have each been guilty of wantonly and wickedly murdering his white children. And for this reason he has directed that they each be hanged by the neck until they are dead, on next Friday; and that order will be carried into effect on that day, at ten o'clock in the forenoon;

"That good ministers are here—both *Catholic* and *Protestant*—from among whom each one can select a spiritual adviser, who will be permitted to commune

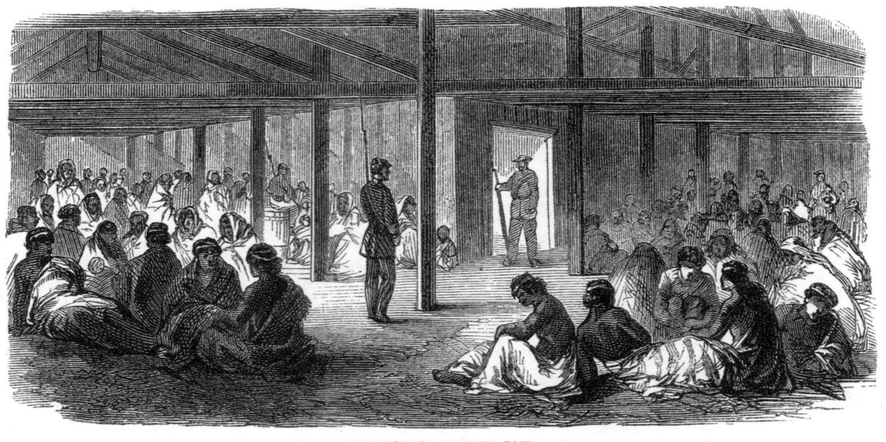

INTERIOR OF INDIAN JAIL.

with them constantly during the four days that they are yet to live;

"That I will now cause to be read the letter of their Great Father at Washington, first in English, and then in their own language. (The President's order was here read.)

"Say to them now that they have so sinned against their fellow-men that there is no hope for clemency except in the mercy of God, through the merits of the blessed Redeemer; and that I earnestly exhort them to apply to that, as their only remaining source of comfort and consolation."

The St. Paul Press, to which I am indebted for the details of the execution, says:

"Very naturally it would be expected that this scene would be peculiarly solemn and distressing to the doomed savages. To all appearances, however, it was not so. The prisoners received their sentence very coolly. At the close of the first paragraph they gave the usual grunt of approval; but as the second was being interpreted to them, they evidently discovered the drift of the matter, and their approval was less general, and with but little unction.

"Several Indians smoked their pipes composedly during the reading, and we observed one in particular who, when the time of execution was designated, quietly knocked the ashes from his pipe and filled it afresh with his favorite kin-ne-kin-nick; while another was slowly rubbing a pipeful of the same article in his hand, preparatory to a good smoke.

"The Indians were evidently prepared for the visit and the announcement of their sentence, one or two having overheard soldiers talking about it when they were removed to a separate apartment.

"At the conclusion of the ceremony, Colonel Miller instructed Major Brown to tell the Indians that each should be privileged to designate the minister of his choice; that a record of the same would be made, and the minister so selected would have free intercourse with him.

"The colonel and spectators then withdrew, leaving the ministers in consultation with the prisoners."

The following order was issued as per date:

"**Head-quarters Indian Post Mankato, December 22, 1862.**

"*General Order No.* 17.

"Colonel Benjamin F. Smith, of Mankato, Major W. H. Dike, of Faribault, Hon. Henry A. Swift and Henry W. Lamberton, Esq., of St. Peter's, Edwin Bradley and Major E. W. Dike, of Mankato, and Reuben Butters, of Kasota, together with such other good citizens as they may select, are hereby requested to act at this place on Friday, the 26th inst., as mounted citizen marshals, Colonel Benjamin F. Smith as chief, and the others as assistants.

"The colonel commanding respectfully recommends that they assemble at Mankato on the previous evening, and adopt such wholesome measures as may contribute to the preservation of good order and strict propriety during the said 26th instant.

"By order of the colonel commanding.

"J. K. ARNOLD, Post Adjutant."

On Monday a general order was promulgated by the commander of the post, forbidding all persons in Mankato, and in the adjoining district, extending a distance of ten miles, from selling intoxicating liquors.

Martial law was declared by the promulgation of the following order:

"Head-quarters of Indian Post Mankato, December 24, 1862.

"*General Order No.* 21.

"The colonel commanding publishes the following rules to govern all who may be concerned; and for the preservation of the public peace, declares martial law over all the territory within a circle of ten miles from these head-quarters.

"1. It is apprehended by both the civil and military authorities, as well as by many of the prominent business men, that the use of intoxicating liquors, about the time of the approaching Indian execution, may result in a serious riot or breach of the peace; and the unrestrained distribution of such beverages to enlisted men is always subversive of good order and military discipline.

"2. The good of the service, the honor of the state, and the protection of all concerned, imperatively require that, for a specified period, the sale, gift, or use of all intoxicating drinks, including wines, beer, and malt liquors, be entirely suspended.

"3. From this necessity, and for the said purposes, martial law is hereby declared in and about all territory, buildings, tents, booths, camps, quarters, and other places within the aforesaid limits, to take effect at three o'clock on Thursday morning, the 25th inst.

"4. Accordingly, the sale, tender, gift, or use of all intoxicating liquors as above named, by soldiers, sojourners, or citizens, is entirely prohibited until the evening of the 27th instant, at eleven o'clock.

"5. The said prohibition to continue as to the sale

or gift of all intoxicating liquors as before described to enlisted men in the service of the United States, except upon special written orders or permission from these head-quarters, until officially revoked by the commandant of this post.

"6. For the purpose of giving full scope and effect to this order, a special patrol will visit all suspected camps, tents, booths, rooms, wagons, and other places, and seize and destroy all liquors so tendered, given, sold, or used, and break the vessels containing the same, and report the circumstances, with the name of the offender, to these head-quarters.

"7. This order will be read at the head of every company of the United States' forces serving or coming within said limits.

"[Official.] STEPHEN MILLER,
"Col. 7th Regt. Min. Vol., Comd'g Post.
"J. K. ARNOLD, Adj't 7th Regt. Min. Vols., Post Adj."

All the prisoners, shortly before their execution, made statements to the Rev. Mr. Riggs as to their participation in the massacre. In the first eleven cases on his list I retained copies of the records of the trial, and in these I will give the statements made to Mr. Riggs, and what appeared against them before the commission.

1. Te-he-hdo-ne-cha (one who forbids his house) confessed, on trial, to having gone east of Beaver River with a party who committed murders, and that he took a woman prisoner, with whom he slept; and that he was in five battles, but denied firing a gun or killing any one. A woman swore he ravished her against her will, and was delighted with the acts of

the war party. (*Statement made to Mr. Riggs.*) He said he was asleep when the outbreak took place at the Lower Agency. He was not present at the breaking open of the stores, but afterward went over the Minnesota River and took some women captives. The men who were killed there were killed by other Indians.

2. Ta-zoo, alias Ptan-doo-tah (Red Otter). Prisoner was professional juggler and medicine-man, and was convicted of rape upon the testimony of the violated woman herself, and of participation in the murder of Patville. He tied her hands. The lady testified that he acted as if delighted with the acts of the others of the war party, and helped to plunder. Her testimony was fully corroborated by others, and her own reputation was stainless. Godfrey refers to this Indian in his account of the Patville murder. (*Statement.*) Prisoner said he had very sore eyes at the commencement of the outbreak, and was at that time down opposite Fort Ridgely. He was with the party that killed Patville and others. Maza-bom-doo killed Patville. He himself took Miss Williams captive. Said he would have violated the women, but they resisted. He thought he did a good deed in saving the women alive.

3. Wy-a-tah-ta-wa (his people) confessed to having participated in the murder of Patville, and to have been in three battles. (*Statement.*) He said he was at the attack on Captain Marsh's company, and also at New Ulm. He and another Indian shot a man at the same time. He does not know whether he or the other Indian killed the white man. He was wounded in following up another white man. He was at the

battle of Birch Coolie, where he fired his gun four times. He fired twice at Wood Lake.

4. Hin-han-shoon-ko-yag-ma-ne (one who walks clothed in an owl's tail). Convicted on the testimony of an eye-witness, Mrs. Alexander Hunter, of the murder of her husband, and with taking herself prisoner. Her testimony was corroborated. (*Statement.*) He said he was charged with killing white people, and so condemned. He did not know certainly that he killed any one. He was in all the battles.

5. Ma-za-bom-doo (iron-blower). Convicted of the murder of an old woman and two children at the Travelers' Home, near New Ulm, on the testimony of Godfrey. At the time he was with the party who killed Patville. (*Statement.*) He stated he was down on the Big Cottonwood when the outbreak took place; that he came to New Ulm and purchased various articles, and then started home. He met the Indians coming down. Saw some men in wagons shot, but did not know who killed them. He was present at the killing of Patville and others, but denied having done it himself. He thought he did well by Mattie Williams and Mary Swan in keeping them from being killed. They lived and he had to die, which he thought not quite fair.

6. Wah-pa-doo-ta (Red Leaf). This was Godfrey's father-in-law. Confessed that he was engaged in the massacres, and that he shot a white man. (*Statement.*) He said he was an old man. He was moving when he heard of the outbreak. He saw some men after they were killed about the agency, but did not kill any one there. He started down to the fort, and went on to the New Ulm settlement. There he shot at a

man through the window, but does not think he killed him. He was himself wounded at New Ulm.

7. Wa-he-hna (meaning not known). Prisoner confessed that he had been in three battles and fired at white people, "but never took good aim;" that he belonged to the Soldier's Lodge. David Faribault testified that he heard him say that he had shot a messenger (Richardson) going to the fort. (*Statement.*) He said that he did not *kill* any one. If he had believed he had killed a white man he would have fled with Little Crow. The witnesses lied on him.

8. Sna-ma-ne (Tinkling Walker). Convicted of the murder of two persons on the testimony of a boy, an eye-witness. (*Statement.*) He said he was condemned on the testimony of two German boys. They say he killed two persons. The boys told lies; he was not at the place at all.

9. Rda-in-yan-ka (Rattling Runner). David Faribault swore that prisoner was very active among those who shot at Marsh's men, and that he saw him firing in the battles of the fort, New Ulm, and Wood Lake; that he took a prominent part; was the exhorter, and did all he could to push the others ahead; that, before going to Wood Lake, he ran through the camp, urging the Indians to kill every body and take their goods; and that he made a speech, in which he offered two bunches of wampum, which he displayed, for the first scalp, and two bunches of crow's feathers (very precious) for the scalp of Sibley or of Forbes. Paul and Lorenzo testified that he opposed giving up the white captives. (He was a son-in-law of Wabashaw.) (*Statement.*) He said he did not know of the uprising on Monday, the 18th of August, until

they had killed a number of men. He then went out and met Little Crow, and tried to stop the murders, but could not. The next day his son was brought home wounded from Fort Ridgely. He forbade the delivery up of the white captives to Paul when he demanded them, and he supposed that he was to be hung for that.

10. Do-wan-sa (the Singer) confessed to having been in the battles of New Ulm, the fort, Birch Coolie, and Wood Lake, and on the war party of eight that went to the Swan Lake House, in Nicollet, and committed murders on the road. This was the party which committed one of the outrages detailed in the chapter upon the trials. Godfrey, who first stated the facts which led to the arrest, testified that prisoner told him that there were three women and two men in a wagon, and these were all killed; that he (prisoner) wanted to take one good-looking young woman home, and her mother interfered, and he told the others to shoot the mother, which they did, and, in doing so, wounded the daughter, who fell as if dead. That he went away, and one of the Indians said she wasn't dead; and on his running to her and pulling up her clothes, she jumped up, and another Indian split her head open with his tomahawk. The prisoner confessed that what Godfrey stated was true, only he didn't kill any body. (*Statement.*) He said he was one of six who were down in the Swan Lake neighborhood. He knew that they killed two men and two women, but this was done by the rest of the party, and not by himself.

11. Hapan (second child if a son). He confessed he was with the war party that killed Patville, and

that he took hold of one of the women by the arm "*to save her life.*" (*Statement.*) He said he was not in the massacre of New Ulm nor the agency. He was with the company who killed Patville and his companions. He took one of the women. O-ya-tay-ta-wa killed Patville.

Among the others were White Dog, who was said to have given the order to fire on Marsh's men at the Red-Wood ferry (he insisted on his innocence to the last), Cut-nose, Chaska, one of the two who shot George Gleason, and the half-breeds Baptiste Campbell, Henry Milard, and Hippolyte Auge, who was engaged in the murder of the white man opposite Crow's village, and Na-pe-shue, convicted of participating in the massacres, and who boasted of having killed nineteen persons. Those who were simply engaged in battles, with the exception of White Dog, were not included in the order. Mr. Riggs, in closing up his written account of their statements, says: "And now, guilty or not guilty, may God have mercy upon these poor human creatures, and, if it be possible, *save* them in the other world through Jesus Christ his Son. Amen.

"In making these statements, confessions, and denials, they were generally calm; but a few individuals were quite excited. They were immediately checked by others, and told they were all dead men, and there was no reason why they should not tell the truth. Many of them have indited letters to their friends in which they say that they are very dear to them, but will see them no more. They exhort them not to cry or change their dress for them. Some of them say they expect to go and dwell with the Good Spirit, and express the hope that their friends will all join them.

"On Tuesday evening they extemporized a dance with a wild Indian song. It was feared that this was only a cover for something else which might be attempted, and their chains were thereafter fastened to the floor. It seems, however, rather probable that they were only singing their death-song. Their friends from the other prison have been in to bid them farewell, and they are now ready to die."

Before the execution, Wabashaw's son-in-law (No. 9) dictated the following letter to that chief:

"WABASHAW,—You have deceived me. You told me that if we followed the advice of General Sibley, and gave ourselves up to the whites, all would be well; no innocent man would be injured. I have not killed, wounded, or injured a white man, or any white persons. I have not participated in the plunder of their property; and yet to-day I am set apart for execution, and must die in a few days, while men who are guilty will remain in prison. My wife is your daughter, my children are your grandchildren. I leave them all in your care and under your protection. Do not let them suffer; and when my children are grown up, let them know that their father died because he followed the advice of his chief, and without having the blood of a white man to answer for to the Great Spirit.

"My wife and children are dear to me. Let them not grieve for me. Let them remember that the brave should be prepared to meet death; and I will do as becomes a Dakota.

"Your son-in-law, RDA-IN-YAN-KA."

"On Wednesday, each Indian set apart for execution was permitted to send for two or three of his relatives or friends confined in the same prison for the purpose of bidding them a final adieu, and to carry such messages to absent relatives as each person might be disposed to send. Major Brown was present during the interviews, and describes them as very sad and affecting. Each Indian had some word to send to his parents or family. When speaking of their wives and children almost every one was affected to tears.

"Good counsel was sent to the children. They were in many cases exhorted to an adoption of Christianity and the life of good feeling toward the whites. Most of them spoke confidently of their hopes of salvation. They had been constantly attended by Rev. Dr. Williamson, Rev. Van Ravoux, and Rev. S. R. Riggs, whose efforts in bringing these poor criminals to a knowledge of the merits of the blessed Redeemer had been eminently successful. These gentlemen were all conversant with the Dakota language, and could converse and plead with the Indians in their own tongue.

"There is a ruling passion with many Indians, and Tazoo could not refrain from its enjoyment even in this sad hour. Ta-ti-mi-ma was sending word to his relatives not to mourn for his loss. He said he was old, and could not hope to live long under any circumstances, and his execution would not shorten his days a great deal, and dying as he did, innocent of any white man's blood, he hoped would give him a better chance to be saved; therefore he hoped his friends would consider his death but as a removal from this to a better world. 'I have every hope,' said he, 'of going direct to the abode of the Great Spirit, where I shall always be happy.' This last remark reached the ears of Tazoo, who was also speaking to his friends, and he elaborated upon it in this wise: 'Yes, tell our friends that we are being removed from this world over the same path they must shortly travel. We go first, but many of our friends may follow us in a very short time. I expect to go direct to the abode of the Great Spirit, and to be happy when I get there;. but we are told that the road is long and the distance great; therefore, as I am slow in all my movements, it will probably take me a long time to reach the end of the journey, and I should not be surprised if some of the young, active men we will leave behind us will pass me on the road before I reach the place of my destination.'

"In shaking hands with Red Iron and Akipa, Tazoo said: 'Friends, last summer you were opposed to us. You were living in continual apprehension of an attack from those who were determined to exterminate the whites. Yourselves and families were subjected to many taunts, insults, and threats. Still you stood firm in our friendship for the whites, and continually counseled the Indians to abandon their raid against the whites. Your course was condemned at the time, but now you see your wisdom. You were right when you said the whites could not be exterminated, and the attempt indicated folly; you and your families were prisoners, and the lives of all in danger. To-day you are here at liberty, assisting in feeding and guarding us, and thirty-nine men will die in two days because they did not follow your example and advice.'

"Several of the prisoners were completely overcome during the leave-taking, and were compelled to abandon conversation. Others again (and Tazoo was one) affected to disregard the dangers of their position, and laughed and joked apparently as unconcerned as if they were sitting around a camp-fire in perfect freedom.

"On Thursday, the women who were employed as cooks for the prisoners, all of whom had relations among the condemned, were admitted to the prison. This interview was less sad, but still interesting. Locks of hair, blankets, coats, and almost every other article in possession of the prisoners, were given in trust for some relative or friend who had been forgotten or overlooked during the interview of the previous day. The idea of allowing women to witness their weakness is repugnant to an Indian, and will account for this. The messages were principally advice to their friends to bear themselves with fortitude and refrain from great mourning. The confidence of many in their salvation was again reiterated.

"Late on Thursday night, in company with Lieutenant Colonel Marshall, the reporter visited the building occupied by the doomed Indians. They were quartered on the ground floor of the three-story stone building erected by the late General Leech.

"They were all fastened to the floor by chains, two by two. Some were sitting up, smoking and conversing, while others were reclining, covered with blankets and apparently asleep. The three half-breeds and one or two others, only, were dressed in citizens' clothes. The rest all wore the breech-clout, leggins, and blankets, and not a few were adorned with paint. The majority of them were young men, though several were quite old and gray-headed, ranging perhaps toward seventy. One was quite a youth, not over sixteen. They all appeared cheerful and contented, and scarcely to reflect on the certain doom which awaited them. To the gazers, the recollection of how short a time since they had been engaged in the diabolical work of murdering indiscriminately both old and young, sparing neither sex nor condition, sent a thrill of horror through the veins. Now they were perfectly harmless, and looked as innocent as children. They smiled at your entrance, and held out their hands to be shaken, which yet appeared to be gory with the blood of babes. Oh treachery, thy name is Dakota.

"Father Ravoux spent the whole night among the doomed ones, talking with them concerning their fate, and endeavoring to impress upon them a serious view of the subject. He met with some success, and during the night several were baptized, and received the communion of the Church.

"At daylight the reporter was there again. That good man, Father Ravoux, was still with them; also Rev. Dr. Williamson; and whenever either of these worthy men addressed them, they were listened to with marked attention. The doomed ones wished it to be known among their friends, and particularly their wives and children, how cheerful and happy they all had died, exhibiting no fear of this dread event. To the skeptical it appeared not as an evidence of Christian faith, but a steadfast adherence to their heathen superstitions.

"They shook hands with the officers who came in among them, bidding them good-by as if they were going on a long and pleasant journey. They had added some fresh streaks of vermilion and ultramarine to their countenances, as their fancy suggested, evidently intending to fix themselves off as gay as possible for the coming exhibition. They commenced singing their death-song, Tazoo leading, and nearly all joining. It was wonderfully exciting.

"At half past seven all persons were excluded from the room except those necessary to help prepare the prisoners for their doom. Under the superintendence of Major Brown and Captain Redfield, their irons were knocked off, and one by one were tied by cords, their elbows being pinioned behind and the wrists in front, but about six inches apart. This operation occupied till about nine o'clock. In the mean time the scene was much enlivened by their songs and conversation, keeping up the most cheerful appearance. As they were being pinioned, they went round the room shaking hands with the soldiers and reporters, bidding them 'good-by,' etc. White Dog requested not to be tied, and said that he could keep his hands down; but of course his request could not be complied with. He said that Little Crow, Young Six, and Big Eagle's brother got them into this war, and now he and others are to die for it. After all were properly fastened, they stood up in a row around the room, and another exciting death-song was sung. They then sat down very quietly, and commenced smoking again. Father Ravoux came in, and after addressing them a few moments, knelt in prayer, reading from a Prayer-book in the Dakota language, which a portion of the condemned repeated after him. During this ceremony nearly all paid the most strict attention, and several were affected even to tears. He then addressed them again, first in Dakota, then in French, which was interpreted by Baptiste Campbell, one of the condemned half-breeds. The caps were then put on their heads. These were made of white muslin taken from the Indians when their camps were captured, and which had formed part of the spoils they had taken from the murdered traders. They were made long, and looked like a meal-sack, but, being rolled up, only came down to the forehead, and allowed their painted faces yet to be seen.

"They received these evidences of their near approach to death with evident dislike. When it had been adjusted on one or two, they looked around on the others who had not yet received it with an appearance of shame. Chains and cords had not moved them—their wear was not considered dishonorable—but this covering of the head with a white cap was humiliating. There was no more singing, and but little conversation and smoking now. All sat around the room, most of them in a crouched position, awaiting their doom in silence, or listening to the remarks of Father Ravoux, who still addressed them. Once in a while they brought their small looking-glasses before their faces to see that their countenances yet preserved the proper modicum of paint. The three half-breeds were the most of all affected, and their dejection of countenance was truly pitiful to behold.

"At precisely ten o'clock the condemned were marshaled in a procession, and, headed by Captain Redfield, marched out into the street, and directly across through files of soldiers to the scaffold, which had been erected in front, and were delivered to the officer of the day, Captain Burt. They went eagerly and cheerfully, even crowding and jostling each other to be ahead, just like a lot of hungry boarders rushing to dinner in a hotel. The soldiers who were on guard in their quarters stacked arms and followed them, and they, in turn, were followed by the clergy, reporters, etc.

"As they commenced the ascent of the scaffold the death-song was again started, and when they had all got up, the noise they made was truly hideous. It seemed as if Pandemonium had broken loose. It had a wonderful effect in keeping up their courage. One young fellow, who had been given a cigar by one of the reporters just before marching from their quarters, was smoking it on the stand, puffing away very coolly during the intervals of the hideous 'Hi-yi-yi,' 'Hi-yi-yi,' and even after the cap was drawn over his face he managed to get it up over his mouth and smoke. Another was smoking his pipe. The noose having been promptly adjusted over the necks of each by Captain Libby, all was ready for the fatal signal.

"The solemnity of the scene was here disturbed by an incident which, if it were not intensely disgusting, might be cited as a remarkable evidence of the contempt of death which is the traditional characteristic of the Indian. One of the Indians, in the rhapsody of his death-song, conceived an insult to the spectators which it required an Indian to conceive, and a dirty dog of an Indian to execute.

"The refrain of his song was to the effect that if a body was found near New Ulm with his head cut off, and placed in a certain indelicate part of the body, he did it. 'It is I,' he sung, 'it is I;' and suited the action to the word by an indecent exposure of his person, in hideous mockery of the triumph of that justice whose sword was already falling on his head.

"The scene at this juncture was one of awful interest. A painful and breathless suspense held the vast crowd, which had assembled from all quarters to witness the execution.

"Three slow, measured, and distinct beats on the drum by Major Brown, who had been announced as signal officer, and the rope was cut by Mr. Duly (the same who killed Lean Bear, and whose family were attacked)—the scaffold fell, and thirty-seven lifeless bodies were left dangling between heaven and earth. One of the ropes was broken, and the body of Rattling Runner fell to the ground. The neck had probably been broken, as but little signs of life were observed; but he was immediately hung up again.

ONE OF THE EXECUTED INDIANS.

While the signal-beat was being given, numbers were seen to clasp the hands of their neighbors, which in several instances continued to be clasped till the bodies were cut down.

"As the platform fell, there was one, not loud, but prolonged cheer from the soldiery and citizens who were spectators, and then all were quiet and earnest witnesses of the scene. For so many, there was but little suffering; the necks of all, or nearly all, were evidently dislocated by the fall, and the after struggling was slight. The scaffold fell at a quarter past ten o'clock, and in twenty minutes the bodies had all been examined by Surgeons Le Boutillier, Sheardown, Finch, Clark, and others, and life pronounced extinct.

"The bodies were then cut down, placed in four army wagons, and, attended by Company K as a burial-party, and under the command of Lieutenant Colonel Marshall, were taken to the grave prepared for them among the willows on the sand-bar nearly in front of the town. They were all deposited in one grave, thirty feet in length by twelve in width, and four feet deep, being laid on the bottom in two rows, with their feet together, and their heads to the outside. They were simply covered with their blankets, and the earth thrown over them. The other condemned Indians were kept close in their quarters, where they were chained, and not permitted to witness the executions.

"The forces of the militia were disposed during the time of the execution as follows: Colonel Wilkin, in command of the 9th and several companies of the 6th, present at half past eight, took position in line of battle in front of the scaffold, and also occupied the river front. Colonel Baker, in command of the 10th regiment, took up a position on the north side. Lieutenant Colonel Marshall, in command of four companies of the 7th regiment, took position on the south side. Lieutenant Colonel Jennison, in command of one company of the 7th and one of the 10th, took position in the yard of the prison, and, after the platform fell, was relieved by Major Bradley, in command of two companies of the 10th. Major Buell, in command of three companies of the Mounted Rangers, disposed of his forces around the forces of infantry. Captain White's mounted company of the 10th regiment acted as patrol guards. The whole force formed a large square, with the scaffold in the centre, from which all persons who had no business within the lines were excluded. The number present is estimated as follows: 6th regiment, under command of Lieutenant Colonel Averill, 200; 7th regiment, Colonel Miller, 425; 9th regiment, Colonel Wilkin, 161; 10th regiment, Colonel Baker, 425; Captain White's mounted men, 35; Mounted Rangers, Major Buell, 273; in all, about 1419 men.

"The arrangement for the execution of so many persons at the same instant were most perfect, and great credit is due Colonel Miller for devising, and carrying out so successfully, his well-digested plan. Neither can too much credit be given to Captain Burt, the officer of the day, Lieutenant Colonel Marshall, Major Brown, and Captain Redfield, the provost marshal.

"All day and night on Thursday, and on the morning of Friday up to the time of the execution, people were continually arriving to witness the hanging. Troops were constantly coming in from all points, and the streets were densely crowded. The roofs and windows of all buildings in the vicinity, and all other eligible places, were early occupied by anxious spectators, including the sand-bar in the river and the opposite bank. All was quiet and orderly. Owing to the strict enforcement of martial law, not a single case of drunkenness or disorderly conduct occurred, and after the bodies had been cut down they began to return from the scene, many leaving town immediately. All expressed themselves as satisfied that the execution was being carried out, and there were no threats or apparent wishes to execute summary vengeance on the others."

In the spring the other condemned were taken down the Mississippi to Davenport, and are now closely confined. The people desired their execution as an example to other neighboring tribes, and to prevent their again perpetrating other outrages. Perhaps the effect of the first has been obtained by the executions already had; and if the confinement of the others remains secure, they have no complaint to make, although they think a much easier solution of the question, and one consonant with justice, would have been to carry out the sentence of the commission. Soon after, the inmates of the camp at Fort Snelling were removed high up the Missouri, as were also the Winnebagoes, where they were placed upon adjoining reservations. It is a horrible region, filled with the petrified remains of the huge lizards and creeping things of the first days of time. The soil is miserable; rain rarely ever visits it. The game is scarce, and the alkaline waters of the streams and springs are almost certain death.

CHAPTER XIX.

DEATH OF LITTLE CROW.

In the territory of Dakota, nearly five hundred miles northwest of St. Paul, is the celebrated Mini-wakan, or Devil's Lake. It is full sixty-five miles in length, and its waters are salt as those of the ocean. The immediate shores are equally divided between prairie and timber; but a mile beyond, the country is one vast rolling plain, destitute of trees, and dotted over with little lakes of salt water. This inland sea is filled with fish; and gulls, and ocean birds, and flocks of great white swan are continually skimming over its waves. The beach is covered with the petrified remains of wood, and of the bones of fish and animals.*

To this neighborhood Little Crow and his followers, after the defeat at Wood Lake, made their way and encamped, where they were joined by nearly all the Minnesota Sioux who had not surrendered or been captured, numbering some four thousand souls, and by the Yanktonais. During the winter the chief sent presents to many of the Western tribes, and endeavored to enlist them in a general war; and about the first of June went in person to St. Joseph and Fort Garry, in the British possessions, and requested ammunition. It was refused him.

When at St. Joseph, Little Crow had on a black

* Pioneer and Democrat.

DEVIL'S LAKE.

coat, with velvet collar; a breech-clout of broadcloth; a fine ladies' shawl was wrapped around his head, and another knotted around his waist. He had discarded the rifle, and carried in his hand a "seven-shooter," one of the trophies of the last summer's raid. He was aware of the deportation of his friends to the Missouri, of which the white residents there had not yet received the news. A swift-footed "good Indian" had outstripped the mails. Little Crow and sixty of his braves accompanied him to Fort Garry, where they had a "war-dance," after which the chief made a speech, saying "that he considered himself as good as dead, but that he had plenty of warriors yet to rely on, and would not be caught during the summer." He had before been refused a tract of land in the British dominions to settle on, and now the only request he said he had to make was a little ammunition "to kill Americans" with. With the chief were three white captives—young boys—who were liberated by the noble charity of "Father Germaine," a Catholic missionary at St. Joseph. A horse was given as ransom for the two younger, and a horse and two blankets for the eldest. The good priest allowed himself no rest for several days and nights in order to accomplish his charitable object. He gave his all, and ran in debt to obtain the means of their liberation. The following is a letter which he wrote upon the subject to Mr. Joseph le May, the collector of the port at Pembina:

"St. Joseph, D. T., June 3, 1863.

"MR. LE MAY,—DEAR SIR,—I would be most happy to give you many details of my present position, but my occupations do not permit me. I am here continually on the "look-out." I examine the different rumors; I lend a very attentive ear to the Indian meetings, etc. The very murmur of the waters, the rustling of the leaves—in fact, the least noise, rouses my fears.

"You are aware that '*Petit Corbeau*,' with his bloodthirsty reputation, came to pay a visit to our mountain. Still, his attitude is not indeed very sinister. Far from attempting to trouble the peace of the half-breeds, he, on the contrary, seems very anxious to gain their sympathy. I profited by his peaceful disposition to put into execution a design that I had formed some time since. Having heard that those barbarians had torn away from parental affection that which is most dear, I knew that those Sioux had children of civilization under their fierce and tyrannical power. Consequently, in order to rescue those poor children from such slavery, I gave all the money I possessed for their ransom. I dressed them with my own clothing, keeping for myself but what is strictly necessary.

"I have my cross and my breviary; thus I feel happy and content. My privations are amply recompensed. My efforts have been crowned with success."

A network of fortifications now existed along the whole frontier, garrisoned by two thousand soldiers, and early in June General Sibley, with a force of between two and three thousand men, started for Devil's Lake, by way of the Minnesota River and Fort Abercrombie. About the same time, General Sully, with a large body of cavalry, passed up the Missouri to cooperate with Sibley, and cut off the retreat of the savages.

Early in the spring small squads of Indians made their way back to the state, and, penetrating far into the interior through our defensive lines, renewed the massacres of the previous years. They continued their depredations throughout most of the season, killing some thirty whites, with a loss of about a dozen of their own number. So bold did they become, that they lighted their camp-fires within twelve miles of St. Paul.

The horrible details of the attack upon the Dustin

ST. JOSEPH, FROM PEMBINA.

family, in M'Leod County, show that the outrages were accompanied by all the barbarities of the previous season. The family were traveling in an open lumber box-wagon, and were attacked on Monday, the 29th of June. It was not until the Wednesday following that they were found, and the sight of their decomposed and mangled bodies were truly awful.

Amos Dustin, the father, was sitting in the front part of the wagon, dead, with an arrow sticking in his body, and a deep wound in his breast, probably made by a tomahawk or war-club. His left hand had been cut off, and carried away by the Indians.

Beneath his seat crouched a little child of six years, who had concealed herself there when the attack was made. The life-blood of her father had streamed down, covering her face and clothes, and her shoes were literally filled with the blood that had trickled from the mangled body. She says that the Indians saw her, and looked quite sharply at her, but did not offer violence. It is probable that she is mistaken about this, as she is the only member of the family uninjured, and from the displays we have had of savage ferocity, we should not infer that they would knowingly spare a victim in their power.

In another part of the wagon lay the corpse of Mrs. Dustin, the grandmother of the children. An arrow was in her body also, and her head was hanging over the side of the wagon, her long hair disheveled and streaming in the air, filled with the clotted blood that had flowed from her wounds.

The mother, and a child twelve years of age, were in the wagon, still alive, but so badly wounded that no hopes are entertained of their recovery. For two days they had lain and suffered beside the dead bodies of their friends, unable to procure sustenance or assistance.*

Captain Cody, of the 8th regiment, was shot dead while gallantly leading a small squad of his men to rout a party of the marauders from some bushes where they lay concealed.

It was in view of such facts that Adjutant General Malmros offered a reward for every Indian killed, and, with characteristic energy and zeal, organized a band of state scouts for service on the frontier. Commenting on his order for this corps, one of the editors of the St. Paul Press wrote as follows:

"While General Sibley's army is moving on, with solemn steps and slow, like a terrific Brobdignag, to crush the Sioux Lilliput under the ponderous heel of strategy, and at the dignified leisure of commissary trains, his nimble adversary is crawling through his legs and running all around him, and with a total disregard of military science, Hardee's tactics, lines of defense, and all that, are burrowing the country behind him with deadly ambuscades, and reviving all the terrors of Indian warfare along our whole frontier.

"A score or two of these copper-faced assassins, multiplying themselves by the swiftness and secrecy of their movements, are apparently more than a match for our whole northwestern army; and a single Indian, lurking in the grass, safely and contemptuously defies our whole system of garrisons and outposts to stop him in his career of murder and mischief; and the humiliating fact stares us in the face, that after all our vast and elaborate preparations to rid the state of

* St. Paul Press.

FORT GARRY.

these infernal red devils, our frontier settlements, except some few fortified villages, are almost as defenseless against the peculiar modes of Indian warfare as if we hadn't a single military guard in the state.

"The state authorities have at last come to the conclusion that there is no sort of use in trying to catch this sort of vermin with horse-rakes, and that henceforth we must try the virtue of fine-tooth combs. The general order of the adjutant general for a corps of scouts is intended to supply the inherent defects of the regular military organizations, and to follow and hunt Indians wherever they can find them, without regard to bases of supplies or the necessities of a regular service."

Little Crow's manner at St. Joseph's on the 1st of June, in speaking of his foe, was haughty and defiant, and he said, if General Sibley desired to know his whereabouts, he would find him soon at Yellow Medicine.

On Friday evening, July 3d, as Mr. Lampson and his son Chauncey were traveling along the road, six miles north of Hutchinson, they discovered two Indians.

The ground where the Indians were discovered is a little prairie opening in the woods, interspersed with clumps of bushes and vines, and a few scattering poplars. The Indians were picking berries, and did not discover the Messrs. L. Concealing themselves immediately, Mr. L., after reflecting a moment on the best course to be pursued, taking advantage of the cover offered by a poplar surrounded with bushes and vines, crept quietly forward until he reached the tree. Steadying his gun against the tree, and taking deliberate aim, he fired. The Indian instantly threw back his hands with a yell, and fell backward to the ground, severely wounded. Not knowing how many Indians there might be, Mr. L. thought best to retreat a little, to obtain the shelter of some bushes. In doing this, he had to pass over a little knoll.

The wounded Indian crept after to obtain a shot at Mr. L., who was still partially shielded by the poplar-tree and vines. In crossing the little knoll just referred to, Mr. L. was obliged to expose himself, and both Indians and Chauncey L. fired simultaneously. Chauncey's ball instantly killed the wounded Indian; the Indian's ball whistled close by Chauncey's cheek, while a buckshot from the other Indian's gun struck Mr. L. on the left shoulder-blade, making a flesh-wound perhaps two inches and a half in length. The other Indian then mounted his horse and rode rapidly away. Mr. L. dropped when the shot struck him, and Chauncey, thinking his father was killed, and not knowing how many Indians there might be around them, and having no more ammunition, his father, who was at some distance from him, having the ammunition, now thought it best to retreat and give the alarm.

He reached Hutchinson about ten o'clock at night with the exciting news, and in a short time a squad of Company E, accompanied by a number of the citizens, were marching rapidly toward the scene of the recent conflict, while others of the troops and citizens started immediately to warn the citizens of Cedar Settlement to be on their guard, and others went to Lake Preston for a squad of cavalry.

But we must now return to Mr. L., whom we left

wounded on the field. Mr. L., after being wounded, crawled into the bushes, and, secreting himself, reloaded his gun, drew his revolver, and waited for the Indian to come on. Thus he waited for some time. After remaining in his concealment until he could profit by the cover of coming night, he laid aside his gun, threw off his white shirt, lest it might lead to his discovery by prowling Indians, and, after a circuitous and toilsome march, reached home at two o'clock on Saturday morning.*

The detachment of cavalry immediately visited the spot, and found the dead body, and tore off the scalp. The Indian was above the medium height, and between fifty and sixty years of age. His hair was sprinkled with gray; his front teeth were double, like the back ones, and both arms were deformed; the bones of the right arm had been broken and never set, which precluded the use of the hand, and the other arm was withered.

The body was carried to Hutchinson, and formed the centre of attraction for several hours. It was then carried a little distance below the village, and thrown into a pit used as a receptacle for the bones and offal of slaughtered cattle. About a week afterward the head was pushed off with a stick, and left lying on the prairie for several days, the brains oozing out in the broiling sun. It was afterward picked up and deposited in a kettle of lime preparatory to a process to render it suitable for a place in the rooms of the Historical Society, and the body was thrown into the river, to remain until the flesh sloughed off, and the bones were in a condition for preservation.

* Correspondence of the St. Paul Press.

The remains thus unceremoniously treated were those of the foremost hunter and orator among the Sioux. He was one who had been forced into the war by circumstances against his own better judgment and desires, yet who did not slink from responsibility by a cowardly denial of the part he had taken, but boldly classed himself among the worst, and justified their acts even when fortune pressed him sorest, saying in his letter to Sibley, "If the young braves have pushed the whites, I have done it myself." The remains were those of Tah-o-ah-ta-doo-ta (his scarlet people), or Little Crow,* who had made his promise to return to the settlements good, and died in the land of his fathers before the extermination of his race, following up his foe like a warrior and brave of the Dakota.

The Indian who escaped was his son Wa-wi-nap-a (one who appeareth). He was picked up by a party of soldiers nearly a month after, in a half starved condition, near Devil's Lake. This is the statement which Wa-wi-nap-a made in reference to his father, and the manner of his death, and his own flight:

"I am the son of Little Crow; my name is Wa-wi-nap-a; I am sixteen years old; my father had two wives before he took my mother; the first one had one son, the second a son and daughter; the third wife was my mother. After taking my mother he put away the first two; he had seven children by my

* Little Crow was a nickname bestowed upon the chief's grandfather by the Chippeways from wearing a crow's skin upon his breast, and the name descended to his grandson. Little Crow formerly lived at Kaposia, four miles below St. Paul, and his band was called the Lightfoot Band.

mother; six are dead; I am the only one living now: the fourth wife had four children born; do not know whether any died or not; two were boys and two were girls: the fifth wife had five children; three of them are dead, two are living: the sixth wife had three children; all of them are dead; the eldest was a boy, the other two were girls: the last four wives were sisters.

"Father went to St. Joseph last spring. When we were coming back he said he could not fight the white men, but would go below and steal horses from them and give them to his children, so that they could be comfortable, and then he would go away off.

"Father also told me that he was getting old, and wanted me to go with him to carry his bundles. He left his wives and other children behind. There were sixteen men and one squaw in the party that went below with us. We had no horses, but walked all the way down to the settlements. Father and I were picking red berries near 'Scattered Lake' at the time he was shot. It was near night. He was hit the first time in the side, just above the hip. His gun and mine were lying on the ground. He took up my gun and fired it first, and then fired his own. He was shot the second time when he was firing his own gun. The ball struck the stock of his gun, and then hit him in the side, near the shoulder. This was the shot that killed him. He told me that he was killed, and asked me for water, which I gave him. He died immediately after. When I heard the first shot fired, I lay down, and the man did not see me before father was killed.

"A short time before father was killed, an Indian

named Hi-u-ka, who married the daughter of my father's second wife, came to him. He had a horse with him—also a gray-colored coat that he had taken from a man that he had killed to the north of where father was killed. He gave the coat to father, telling him he might need it when it rained, as he had no coat with him. Hi-u-ka said he had a horse now, and was going back to the Indian country.

"The Indians that went down with us separated. Eight of them and the squaw went north, the other eight went farther down. I have not seen any of them since after father was killed. I took both guns and the ammunition, and started to go to Devil's Lake, where I expected to find some of my friends. When I got to Beaver Creek I saw the tracks of two Indians, and at Standing Buffalo's village saw where the eight Indians that had gone north had crossed.

"I carried both guns as far as the Cheyenne River, where I saw two men. I was scared, and threw my gun and the ammunition down. After that I traveled only in the night, and as I had no ammunition to kill any thing to eat, I had not strength enough to travel fast. I went on until I arrived near Devil's Lake, when I staid in one place three days, being so weak and hungry that I could go no farther. I had picked up a cartridge near Big Stone Lake, which I still had with me, and loaded father's gun with it, cutting the ball into slugs; with this charge I shot a wolf; ate some of it, which gave me strength to travel, and I went on up the lake until the day I was captured, which was twenty-six days from the day my father was killed."

CHAPTER XX.

THRILLING AND FATAL ADVENTURE OF MESSRS. BRACKETT AND FREEMAN.

On the morning of July 20th, General Sibley, leaving a portion of his forces at Camp Atcheson, near Devil's Lake, pushed on toward the Missouri Couteau with 1400 infantry and 500 cavalry. On the fourth day, two members of the expedition, unsuspicious of danger, strayed away from the column. The exciting adventure which they met with is detailed by Mr. Brackett, the survivor, as follows:

"We left camp on the 24th at the usual time, about five o'clock A.M., the first battalion Minnesota Mounted Rangers in the rear. Lieutenant Ambrose Freeman, Company D, said to me several times that whenever I had a chance to go to the flank, he wanted to go with me. Soon as I had my cattle started, I went to Captain Taylor, and told him if he could spare Captain Freeman, we wanted to go out on the flank a little way. I left the main column about two miles out from camp, struck off to the left, and went on to a range of hills which was estimated to be about five miles from the main column. Saw three scouts out about the same distance. After getting there we struck a parallel course, and supposed we were going in the same direction as the main body. We watered our horses in a lake. Saw two other scouts on the opposite side of the lake. We then went still farther

O

on, over one range of bluffs, probably about three quarters of a mile. We followed along parallel, or perhaps a little to the left of the main body, a distance of three miles.

"Lieutenant Freeman saw three antelope, an old and two young ones. We fired and wounded the old one. She then made off. I had the lieutenant's horse, and he followed her on foot, which took us off our course some way round the bluffs. We got into a section of country by a large lake, and succeeded in killing the antelope near the lake.

"As we were coming down toward the lake, and while the lieutenant was creeping up toward the antelope, I saw some scouts on the opposite side of the lake, the train in sight on the side hill several miles distant. Instead of taking our course back, we had a curiosity to go around the lake to where we saw the scouts. We saw cherry-bushes newly cut and piled up. I set out to tear them down. Lieutenant Freeman persisted in saying they were Indian signs, and Indians were there. We cocked our rifles, and made around the bushes, so as not to put ourselves in a too exposed condition. We then took our course, as we supposed, toward the train, or where the train had passed.

"Between one and two o'clock we discovered three objects a long distance off, between us and the train's course, and making toward the train. This action, as soon as we came near enough to judge, convinced us that they were Indians. Yet we still kept toward them, and they were making preparations to meet us, one leading and the other two riding their horses. We got all ready to give them a trial, they creeping around on one side of the bluff, and we creeping around to meet them. I saw one raise. He had a straw hat on, and I recognized him as one of our scouts. He beckoned us to come toward him. From all the description that I had of him, I supposed him to be 'Chaska;' the other two were full-blooded Sioux. Both had government horses, and armed, one with a Springfield rifle, the other with a carbine. I asked him where General Sibley was. They pointed to a hill, I should judge, three miles distant from where we stood, in the direction where the train passed.

"I saw a large number of men on a bluff, judged to be about two hundred in number, whom I supposed to be General Sibley's men (in camp), looking upon us. We all at once started direct for them. About the time we started we saw what we supposed to be a guard of cavalry start toward us. After we started the scouts turned to a little lake to water their horses; ours being previously watered, we did not go with them. We still saw the cavalry (as we supposed) coming, about fifteen in number.

"I remarked to Lieutenant Freeman that they must have turned back, as they had disappeared and were out of sight. We were soon surprised by seeing fifteen Indians charging upon us with a flag of truce. As we whirled, they fired a volley upon us. I yelled to the scouts that they were Indians. I remarked to Lieutenant Freeman that we had better put for the scouts. When we got within twenty or twenty-five rods of the scouts, we were riding about three rods apart. One Indian rode up to Lieutenant Freeman and put an arrow through his back, on the left side, and at the same time another Indian dismounted and discharged his gun at me. I laid low on my horse's neck, as close as I possibly could, and 'Chaska' stepped up to the top of a knoll and fired once at the Indian who fired at me. As Lieutenant Freeman dropped from his horse, I asked him if he was hurt. He replied, '*I am gone.*' He wished me to cut a piece of string which was around his neck, and supported a part of the antelope which he was carrying. As I cut the string he changed his position more on his side, and rested more up-hill. He asked faintly for water. The scouts had then mounted their horses and left us. The Indians were then all around us, one at the side of the lake. As the scouts ran toward them they fell back. I then took Lieutenant Freeman's rifle and revolver and followed the scouts. Lieutenant Freeman, to all appearance, was dead. The Indian mentioned, seeing the lieutenant's horse, which followed me, left us and broke for the horse. In that way it allowed me to overtake the scouts. He succeeded in catching the horse. Then the whole crowd started after us again. We rode about four miles, when we were surrounded by them again by the side of a little marsh. We all jumped off our horses. The scouts made motions and ran up to meet them, and 'Chaska' motioned for me to jump into the tall rushes on the marsh. I saw nothing more of the scouts. The Indians all rushed down to where the horses were. I cocked my rifle, and lay in the rushes within ten feet of them. They got into a wrangle about the horses. They presently started off, I suppose from fear of being overtaken by our forces, taking a course around the marsh. I lay there about an hour. By accident in putting down the hammer of my rifle, it went off. This was about three P.M. There was a shower. After it cleared off I immediately started a course with the sun at my back, and traveled two hours. I followed this direction two days, stopping in marshes during the night-time. I struck a river at night of the second day. It was clear water, running in a southerly direction, and a quarter of a mile in width.

"Next morning I struck from there due south, and traveled that day until almost night; then took a westerly course, concluding that the trail was not in that direction; traveled a little north of west, and struck General Sibley's trail the afternoon of the third day, about twelve miles from where we camped the night before I left the main column, and made the camp that night. I started next morning for Camp Atcheson, and made it in two days. Arrived here the second night, between eight and nine o'clock, making the distance of the four camps in two days—bareheaded, barefooted, and without a coat. I was obliged to leave my rifle on the last day of my travel, not having sufficient strength to carry it any farther.

"About ten miles before reaching Camp Atcheson I sat down to rest, and had such difficulty in getting under way again that I determined to stop no more, feeling sure that once again down I should never be able to regain my feet unaided. I entered the camp near the camp-fire of a detachment of the 'Pioneers' (Captain Chase's company of the 9th Minnesota Infantry), and fell to the ground, unable to rise again. But, thank God! around that fire were sitting some St. Anthony friends, among whom were Messrs. M'Mullen and Whittier, attached to that company, who kindly picked me up and carried me to my tent.

"I lost my coat, hat, and knife in the fight on the first day. I took Lieutenant Freeman's knife, and with it made moccasins of my boot-legs, my boots so chafing my feet in walking that I could not wear them. These moccasins were constantly getting out of repair, and my knife was as much needed to keep them in order for use as to make them in the first place. But just before reaching the trail of the expedition on the fifth day I lost Lieutenant Freeman's knife. This loss, I felt at the time, decided my fate, if I had much farther to go; but kind Providence was in my favor, for almost the first object that greeted my eyes upon reaching the trail was a knife, old and worn to be sure, but priceless to me. This incident some may deem a mere accident; but let such a one be placed in my situation at that time, and he would feel with me that it was a boon granted by the Great Giver of good. On the third day, about ten miles from the river spoken of, I left Lieutenant Freeman's rifle on the prairie, becoming too weak to carry it longer; besides, it had already been so damaged by rain that I could not use it. I wrote upon it that Lieutenant Freeman had been killed, and named the course I was then pursuing. I brought the pistol into Camp Atcheson.

"While wandering I lived on cherries, roots, birds' eggs, young birds, and frogs, caught by hand, all my ammunition but one cartridge having spoiled by the rain on the first day. That cartridge was one for Smith's breech-loading carbine, and had a gutta-percha case. I had also some water-proof percussion caps in my porte-monnaie. I took one half the powder in the cartridge and a percussion cap, and with the pistol and some dry grass started a nice fire, at which I cooked a young bird, something like a loon, and about the size. This was on the second night. On the fourth I used the remainder of the cartridge in the same way and for a like purpose. The rest of the time I ate my food uncooked, except some hard bread (found at the fourth camp mentioned above), which had been fried and then thrown into the ashes. I have forgotten one sweet morsel (and all were sweet and very palatable to me), viz., some sinews spared by the wolves from a buffalo carcass. As near as I am able to judge, I traveled in the seven days at least two hundred miles. I had ample means for a like journey in civilized localities, but for the first time in my life found gold and silver coin a useless thing. My bootleg moccasins saved me; for a walk of ten miles upon such a prairie, barefooted, would stop all farther progress of any person accustomed to wear covering upon the feet. The exposure at night, caused more particularly by lying in low and wet places in order to hide myself, was more prostrating to me than scarcity of food. The loneliness of the prairies would have been terrible in itself but for the drove of wolves that, after the first day, hovered, in the daytime, at a respectful distance, and in the night howled closely around me, seemingly sure that my failing strength would soon render me an easy prey. But a merciful Providence has spared my life by what seems now, even to myself, almost a miracle."

The body of Lieutenant Freeman was afterward found by members of General Sibley's main force and buried. An arrow had pierced his breast, and the tomahawk and scalping-knife had left bloody traces about his head.* They buried him on the desolate plain, five hundred miles away from the loved wife and children who bemoan his sad and untimely fate.

* Correspondence of the Pioneer and Democrat.

LONE PRAIRIE GRAVE.

CHAPTER XXI.

THE BATTLES ON THE MISSOURI.

THE BATTLE OF THE BIG MOUND.

"ON the 24th of July, about one o'clock, as the expedition under General Sibley was moving along the western base of a great hill or ridge of the Couteau Missouri, scouts who were in the advance returned with the report that the force was in the immediate vicinity of a large camp of Indians. Other scouts came who had seen the Indians, and believed them to be preparing in great numbers for battle; that they were then collecting in the rocky ravines and behind the ridges of the great hill. Soon the Indians were seen on the Big Mound, the highest peak of the hill. The train was turned off to the right a little way, and corraled on a salt lake.

"Details of men were made to throw up intrenchments, so that a small number of men could defend the train and camp while the main force should be engaged elsewhere. The camp was encircled by the several regiments, with the artillery placed at intervals between. The Big Mound was directly east of camp, a mile and a quarter distant; a succession of hills, or the broken side of the big hill, rising from the camp to the Big Mound. There was a ravine directly east of camp which extended nearly to the Big Mound.

"The 6th regiment was placed on the north side

of the corral, its left resting on the lake; the 10th regiment next to the 6th, fronting northeast, and to the left of the ravine; the 7th regiment on the right of the 10th, fronting east and southeast on the ravine; the cavalry on the south side of the camp, with its right flank on the lake.

"These dispositions had hardly been made before the report of fire-arms was heard on the hill directly in front of the 7th regiment. Some of the scouts had gone part way up the hill, and were talking with the Indians. Dr. Weiser, surgeon of the Mounted Rangers, joined them, and shook hands with one or two Indians whom he had probably known at Shakopee. One Indian advanced and shot him through the heart. He fell and died without speaking a word. The scouts fired, and the Indians fell back behind the ridge, returning the fire, one shot taking effect upon scout Solon Stevens, of Mankato. It proved to be but a slight wound in the hip. The ball had first passed through his rubber blanket, which was rolled up on his saddle. An ambulance was promptly sent out, which met the body of Dr. Weiser being brought in on a horse.

"The first battalion of cavalry—Captain Taylor, Wilson, and Anderson's companies—was promptly ordered to the scene of Dr. Weiser's death, where the scouts were skirmishing with the Indians. They found the ground so broken that they dismounted and sent their horses back to camp. Major Bradley, with Captains Stevens and Gilfillan's companies of the 7th, were ordered to the support of the cavalry. The general, with a 6-pounder, advanced to a hill on the left of the ravine, and began to shell the Indians at the head of the ravine and about the Big Mound. Captain Edgerton's company of the 10th supported the 6-pounder.

"The 6th regiment was deployed on the foot-hills in front of its line, to the north and northeast of camp, Captain Banks's company of the 7th on the right of the 6th regiment. Lieutenant Colonel Marshall, with the remaining five companies of the 7th regiment, Captains Kennedy, Williston, Hall, Carter, and Arnold, advanced up the ravine toward the Big Mound, and deployed on the left of the dismounted cavalry and Major Bradley's line.

"The artillery, under the immediate direction of the general, drove the Indians out from the head of the ravine and from about the Big Mound. They fell back to the table-land east of the mound, and into the broken ridges and ravines southward. They had come from that quarter, their camp being formed around the hill about five miles ahead.

"The shelling they received near the Big Mound prevented their getting around to the northward in any considerable numbers. They were massed on the broken ground to the south of the mound.

"The line of the 7th regiment and the three companies of cavalry named advanced steadily and rapidly, pouring a constant fire into the Indians, which reached them before their shorter range guns could have any effect on our troops. The left of the 7th crossed the summit range just to the right of the mound, and, flanking the right of the Indians, swept around to the southward, and pursued them through the ridges and ravines on the east of the range, while Major Bradley, and Captains Taylor and Anderson, pressed them hotly on the west side. Captain Wilson, of the cavalry, crossed to the right of the mound, and pursued some Indians that separated from the main body and retreated more directly eastward.

"The Indians were thus pursued three or four miles, and until they were completely dislodged and driven from the hills to a broad plain southward. They would try to hold ridge after ridge, and to cover themselves in the ravines, but the better weapons of the whites were too much for them. They were sparing of ammunition, and probably not over half had fire-arms. Their number exceeded a thousand warriors.

"As they were precipitately retreating down the ravines, toward the plain, after the last stand, two companies of cavalry, Captain Austin's and Lieutenant Barton's, under the immediate command of Colonel M'Phaill, took the advance and charged the Indians, doing execution. Corporal Hazlep was shot in the shoulder by an Indian he was riding on to. Colonel M'Phaill thrust his sabre through the Indian. It was here that a stroke of lightning killed Private John Murphy, of Company B, and his horse, and stunned another cavalryman. Colonel M'Phaill's grasp was loosened on his sword by the shock. He thought a shell had fallen among them. This momentarily checked the charge and rendered it less effective, the Indians getting out on the plain, where their immense numbers deterred any farther charge until the cavalry could be re-enforced.

"Lieutenant Colonel Marshall had left his line for a moment, and, taking care of Colonel M'Phaill's right flank, charged down the hill with the Rangers. In an effort to cut off some Indians to the right, he got into rather close quarters with some of them. The thunder-stroke checked the cavalrymen that he thought were following him in the dash. He wheeled his horse in time to avoid a single-handed encounter with a dozen warriors.

"While the dismounted companies of cavalry were getting their horses from camp, and Captains Rubles, Davey, and Lieutenant Johnson's companies, that had been on the right of the hill with Major Bradley, were being formed for the pursuit, the Indians had got three or four miles away. Their families had been started ahead, and the warriors were covering the rear of the train. The cavalry pursued, and the 7th regiment followed on. Lieutenant Whipple's section of the battery was sent forward, and Company B, of the 10th, to support it. The cavalry reached the Indians before dark, and made five successive charges on their rear, killing a great number. The battery and the 7th regiment were not up in time to take a hand.

"The Indians fought desperately. One stalwart warrior, with an American flag wrapped around him theatrically, fired twice while the cavalry were within twenty rods charging upon him, his balls taking effect in the overcoat and saddle of Private Green, and rubber blanket of Carlson, of Company F. The Indian got the powder down, but not the ball, for the third load, which he discharged at the breast of Archy M'Nee, of Company F, of course without effect. He then clubbed his gun and struck Carlson, nearly unhorsing him. A dozen carbine balls were put into him, and then he had to be sabred to finish him.

"Gustaf Stark, of Company B, was killed in one of these charges, and Andrew Moore dangerously, if not mortally wounded.

"The cavalry boys took twenty-one scalps in this charge.

"Colonel M'Phaill had told them that it was very barbarous to take scalps, but that he wouldn't believe any man had killed an Indian unless he showed the hair, and enough of it, so that two locks couldn't be taken from the same head.*

"The trail of the Indians was strewed with tons of dried buffalo meat, pemmican, robes, and undressed buffalo skins, besides camp furniture. It was a wild flight, in which they abandoned every thing that impeded them. Much of this stuff they left in camp.

"The 7th regiment, with Company B of the 10th, had reached a point ten or twelve miles from camp, the artillery a point farther advanced, while Colonel M'Phaill was engaged fifteen miles from camp. Darkness came on, and Colonel Marshall ordered a bivouac of his men and Captain Edgerton's company of the 10th. Guards were posted, and the exhausted men had lain down to sleep, when Colonel M'Phaill returned on his way to camp, having received an order not to pursue after dark, and—mistakenly delivered—to return to camp. The general intended to leave it discretionary with Colonel M'Phaill to bivouac or return to camp accordingly as he might have got many miles

* In all Indian wars the whites have taken scalps.

The Massachusetts government paid from fifteen to two hundred pounds for every scalp. Hannah Dustin, her boy, and a nurse, of Haverhill, killed and scalped ten of their Indian captors on an island in the Merrimac, and escaped with a bag full of their bloody trophies. In the Black Hawk war the United States paid the Sioux a reward for every Sauk and Fox scalp taken. This mutilation was not adopted as retaliation, but to obtain the infallible evidence of the death of the murderers.

away or be near to camp. The infantry joined the cavalry and artillery, and marched until daylight the next morning before reaching camp, having been twenty-four hours marching or fighting, and since ten o'clock in the morning without water.

"The general was just ready to leave camp with the other forces, but the exhausted condition of the men and cavalry horses that had been out all night precluded the march that day. This unfortunate mistake delayed the pursuit two days, for it required the next day's march, the 26th, to reach the point of the cavalry fight of the night of the 24th."

THE BATTLE OF DEAD BUFFALO LAKE.

"Camp was moved on the 25th three miles, on to the great hill where a pond of fresh water and grass was found. Murphy's and Stark's bodies were buried at Camp Sibley, below the hill; Dr. Weiser's was buried at Camp Whitney, on the hill.

"The march was resumed on the 26th, and Dead Buffalo Lake reached about noon. The Indians were seen in the distance advancing toward us. It was not known that there was any good camping place within reach that day ahead, and it was decided to go into camp on the lake.

"Lieutenant Whipple's 6-pounders were advanced to a hill half a mile in advance toward the Indians, and the 6th regiment was deployed forward to support the battery and engage the Indians.

"The Indians circled around, got on the high knolls and ridges, and took observations, but seemed indisposed to commence hostilities. The artillery shelled them when they ventured near enough, and the skirmishers gave them shots when they approached any where near the camp.

"Thus some hours passed without the Indians developing their purpose. A large portion of them kept out of sight. Finally, about three o'clock, a mounted force of Indians suddenly dashed in on the north side of the camp, where mules had been turned out to graze, and where teamsters were getting grass.

"They had almost reached them, when Captain Wilson's and Davey's companies of cavalry—the latter under Lieutenant Kidder—putting their horses to the jump, dashed upon the Indians, and so dismayed them that they wheeled their ponies to escape, but not in time to escape the carbine shots, followed by the revolver and sabre, that left a goodly number of the red warriors on the field. Some of the scouts did good service in this charge.

"One wounded Indian tried to escape by seizing his horse's tail; but, unfortunately for him, the pony got a shot in the shoulder. John Platt, of Company L, dashed up to finish the Indian with his revolver, but it didn't go off, and before he could check his horse he was upon the Indian, who had reserved a shot in his gun, which he fired into the thigh and bowels of poor Platt, giving him his death-wound. Joe Campbell, one of the scouts, tried to save Platt, but it was too late. Campbell's shot, fired at the same instant that the Indian fired the fatal shot at Platt, went through the vitals of the savage and finished him. Platt's comrades, exasperated at his mortal wound, tore the Indian's scalp from his head before he was dead.

"A part of the 6th regiment, under Major M'Laren,

had returned to camp, and was on their color line, on the side where the Indians made the dash. They promptly advanced to the support of the cavalry, and took a hand in. Thus the 6th, among the infantry regiments, on this day did the fighting. The cavalry and artillery, in this as in the previous and subsequent engagement, had always their full share of work. The Indians appeared on the south side of the camp, out of range, but made no farther attack."

THE BATTLE OF STONY LAKE.

"The march was resumed on the 27th, and the trail, still marked by robes and other articles, was followed toward the Missouri River.

"After a march of nearly twenty miles, camp was pitched on a small lake half a mile long and twenty rods wide.

"On the morning of the 28th, just as the rear of the train was filing around the south end of the lake, the advance being nearly to the top of a long hill, the Indians suddenly made their appearance in front and on the flanks, rapidly circling around to the rear. They were in immense numbers, seemingly all mounted.

"Major Joe Brown, guide, and some of the scouts, who were in advance, narrowly escaped being captured. The 10th regiment, Colonel Baker, which was in the advance, promptly and gallantly met the attack in front, which was the first demonstration of the Indians. The artillery was quickly brought into play, and the savages drew back to a safe distance. Colonel Crooks,* with the 6th regiment, on the right flank,

* Colonel Crooks is a prompt, first-class officer, who received his

held them at bay and effectually guarded the train, while the cavalry on the left, and the 7th regiment and cavalry in the rear, presented an unassailable line. The Indians got partly under cover of broken ground at the south end of the lake, but were soon dislodged by the fire of Lieutenant Western's section of the battery and a line of skirmishers of the 7th. One shot from an Indian, evidently aimed at Colonel Marshall while he was locating a howitzer, struck the ground at his feet. The most determined effort, however, to make a breach was in front, and was fairly resisted by the 10th regiment, so that it had its day of fighting.

"The Indians, as they came on at first, were heard to say, 'It is too late, it is too late,' evidently having expected to surprise the force in camp. Another Indian answered, 'We must fight for our children.'

"After seeing that the proper dispositions had been made for guarding the train, the general ordered the column to move forward regardless of the Indians. The Indians, seeing the purpose of the whites to press on toward their families, quickly withdrew, the whole demonstration not delaying the march over two hours.

"General Sibley, Major Brown, and others, estimated the number of Indians this day at over *two thousand*. In the battle of Big Mound were all the Lower Indians, the Sissetons, and part of the Yanktonais. In the last day's fight, that of Stony Lake, they had been re-enforced by another camp of Yanktonais, and some Tetons from the west side of the Missouri River. The whites captured a Teton boy who had no gun, and was subsequently released at the Missouri

military education at West Point. His knowledge and experience were of great avail upon the expeditions of 1862 and 1863.

River. This Teton and an old squaw were the only prisoners taken in battle or near a battle. The supplications for life of the wretches when they had fired their last shot were generally met by a sabre-thrust that finished them."

SKIRMISH ON THE MISSOURI.

"No more Indians were encountered until the banks of the Missouri were reached on the morning of the 29th. The Indians had made good use of the night, and got their families and ponies over. Their wagons, to the number of over one hundred, and a remnant of their plunder that had not been strewn along the route of their flight, was left on the east bank of the river. The Indians crowded the bluffs on the west side.

"The 6th regiment, then in the advance, advanced, deployed as skirmishers, through the woods a mile and a half to the river. As they were starting to return, a heavy volley, that came from the high grass on the opposite bank, fell harmless about them or short of them. They stopped a moment to return it, but the distance was too great for effect.

"While Colonel Crooks was at the river, the general sent an order by Lieutenant Beever, aid-de-camp. On his return with an answer, Lieutenant Beever mistook a trail that led down the river, where his body was found next day pierced by three arrows and a ball. He had also wounds from a tomahawk on his head. His horse lay near him. Two pools of blood twenty paces from his body indicated that two of his murderers had paid dearly for his life. On the same trail was found the body of Private Nicholas Miller, of Company K, 6th regiment, who had made the same mistake in taking the trail that Beever had.

"Two days were passed in camp at the mouth of Apple Creek, on the Missouri, opposite Burnt Boot Island, and then the homeward march was resumed. The expedition had but fifteen days' rations, nine or ten of which would be consumed in returning to Camp Atcheson. It would take two or three days to cross the Missouri, so that all the surplus would have been consumed in crossing and recrossing the river.

"The animals were completely worn down. Over twelve miles a day could not be made on the scanty feed they were getting. It would therefore have been useless to go farther. Much had been accomplished. Forty-four bodies of warriors had been found, many more carried off and concealed. The season's supplies of meat and clothing material, and their wagons, were destroyed. The howlings of the squaws that came across the river told the tale of their misery and despair."*

It was hoped that General Sully would have arrived in time to co-operate with General Sibley, but no indications of his whereabouts could then be ascertained.

General Sibley, after the battles, caused the following order to be read on dress parade:

Copy of General Orders No. 51.

"To the Officers and Soldiers of the Expeditionary Force in Camp:

"It is proper for the brigadier general commanding to announce to you that the march to the west and

* The account of these battles, as furnished by Lieutenant Colonel Marshall, is taken from the St. Paul Press.

north is completed, and that to-morrow the column will move homeward, to discharge such other duties connected with the objects of the expedition on the way as may from time to time present themselves.

"In making this announcement, General Sibley expresses also his high gratification that the campaign has been a complete success. The design of the government in chastising the savages, and thereby preventing for the future the raids upon the frontier, has been fully accomplished. You have routed the miscreants who murdered our people last year, banded as they were with the Upper Sioux to the number of nearly 2000 warriors, in three successive engagements, with heavy loss, and driven them in confusion and dismay across the Missouri River, leaving behind them all their provisions, vehicles, and skins designed for clothing, which have been destroyed. Forty-four bodies of warriors have been found, and many others concealed or taken away, according to the custom of these savages, so that it is certain that they have lost in killed and wounded not less than from one hundred and twenty to one hundred and fifty men. All this has been accomplished with the comparatively trifling loss on our part of three killed and as many wounded. You have marched nearly six hundred miles from St. Paul, and the powerful bands of the Dakotas, who have heretofore held undisputed possession of these great prairies, have succumbed to your valor and discipline, and sought safety in flight. The intense heat and drouth have caused much suffering, which you have endured without a murmur. The companies of the 6th, 7th, 9th, and 10th regiments of Minnesota Volunteers, First Minnesota Mounted Rangers, and the sections of the battery, have amply sustained the reputation of the state by their bravery and endurance amid unknown dangers and great hardships. Each has had opportunity to distinguish itself against a foe at least equal in numbers to itself.

"It would be a gratification if these remorseless savages could have been pursued and utterly extirpated, for their crimes and barbarities merited such a full measure of punishment; but men and animals are alike exhausted after so long a march, and a farther pursuit would only be futile and hopeless. The military results of the campaign have been fully accomplished; for the savages have not only been destroyed in great numbers, and their main strength broken, but their prospects for the future are hopeless indeed, for they can hardly escape starvation during the coming winter.

"It is peculiarly gratifying to the brigadier general commanding to know that the tremendous fatigues and manifold dangers of the expedition thus far have entailed so small a loss of life on his command. A less careful policy than that adopted might have effected the destruction of more of the enemy, but that could only have been done by a proportional exposure on our part, and the consequent loss of many more lives, bringing sorrow and mourning to our own homes. Let us therefore return thanks to a merciful God for His manifest interposition in our favor, and for the success attendant upon our efforts to secure peace to the borders of our own state, and of our neighbors and friends in Dakota Territory. And as we proceed on our march toward those most near and dear to us, let us be prepared to discharge other duties which may be imposed upon us during our journey with cheerful and willing hearts.

"To the regimental and company officers of the command the brigadier general commanding tenders his warmest thanks for their co-operation and aid, on every occasion, during the passage of the column through the heart of an unknown region inhabited by a subtle and merciless foe. To the friends and families of our fallen comrades, we have our warmest sympathies to offer in their bereavement.

"General Sibley takes this occasion to express his appreciation of the activity and zeal displayed by the members of his staff, one and all.

"By command of Brigadier General SIBLEY."*

"The point on the Missouri reached by General Sibley was in latitude 46° 42′, longitude 100° 35′, about forty miles by land below Fort Clarke. The distance from Fort Snelling, by the line of march, was made by Colonel Crooks to be 585 miles."†

"The entire list of casualties up to July 31st was as follows:

* Henry H. Sibley was born at Detroit in 1812. In 1834 he commenced his residence at Mendota, at the mouth of the Minnesota River, as an employé of the American Fur Company, where he has ever since resided. He was the first delegate to Congress from the Territory of Minnesota, and the first governor of the state. In person he is tall, portly, and commanding. His attention to whatever he undertakes is systematic and unwearied, and his reputation for honesty and courage unquestioned. Captain Olin acted as his adjutant general during the campaign of 1863. That position was filled in 1862, after Colonel Fowler's resignation, by Major Joseph R. Brown, long a resident in the Indian country, and whose invaluable advice, together with that of Messrs. Riggs and Forbes, General Sibley frequently availed himself of.

† Pioneer and Democrat.

"*Killed.*—Dr. Weiser, of Shakopee, surgeon to the Mounted Rangers; F. J. Holt Beever, aid to General Sibley, with rank of lieutenant; Lieutenant Freeman, of the Mounted Rangers; G. A. Stark, of St. Peter's, of the Rangers; John Murphy, of Waseca, of the Rangers—killed by lightning; John Platt, of Fillmore County, Company L, Mounted Rangers; Nicholas Miller, of the 6th regiment. *Wounded.*—Andrew Moar, of Fillmore County, of the Mounted Rangers; Corporal William B. Hezlep, Company B, 1st Minnesota Mounted Rangers; Sergeant James R. Grady, Company L, 1st Minnesota Mounted Rangers."*

* St. Paul Press.

CHAPTER XXII.

THE FUTURE.

THE hostilities of the Sioux have not yet ended. The Yanktonais and Tetons have suffered but little, and their warriors are numerous and by no means cowed. Neither tribe ever entered into treaties with the government, and are not dependent upon it for support. The Tetons cherish a deadly hatred toward the whites for the massacre of their families several years ago by General Harney's forces, and the Yanktonais have been threatening hostilities ever since the treaties of 1851 and 1852 for the land in Minnesota, in which they rightfully claimed an interest, and for which they received no compensation. The recent battles in which they were engaged will but inflame their resentment, and we shall have, unless vigorous measures are taken against it, a lengthy continuation of the desolating war upon the frontier.

Most of the tribes beyond these are seriously disaffected, and loud in their complaints against the government, as the report made last year to Congress upon Indian Affairs will show. Some of them have been actually engaged in hostilities, and their natural desire for war may induce them to join the others. Pontiac's war lasted six, and the Seminole war seven years. In the spring another expedition should be fitted out to inflict farther chastisement upon all wrong-doers, and enforce security.

In the mean time the frontier should be carefully

guarded with a large force. The Mounted Rangers, whose term of service will soon expire, should be induced to re-enlist, and Major Hatch's* battalion should be increased to a regiment. These are necessary for patrol duty and the speedy relief of any post which might suddenly be attacked, and more especially for the hunting down of small parties of murderers, who, by the celerity and secrecy of their movements, evade the pursuit of infantry.

There is another nation of Indians who are to be feared more than those who are engaged in open war, because the government is not aware of the danger which exists, and are taking no precautions against it. That nation is the Chippeway. They extend from Dakota to the St. Lawrence. The number of their warriors in the United States alone is fully four thousand, and there are nearly as many more in the British Possessions.

The Sioux war has already cost the country over ten millions of dollars, and will cost many millions more before its completion. The scene of military operations against them is a prairie country, where the hiding-places are few and pursuit easy. What will be the expenses of a conflict with the Chippeways, who are mostly located in a wilderness filled with lakes, swamps, and thickets? Ninety thousand square miles of such territory, closely bordered by settlements of the whites, is included in their possessions in Wisconsin and Minnesota.†

* Major Hatch has lived among the Indians many years, and is thoroughly acquainted with their mode of warfare. Fearless, indefatigable, and vigilant, no better commander could be selected.

† The Seminoles, to whose seven years' war one with the Chippe-

This formidable foe, at least so far as the latter states are concerned, are as dissatisfied as the Sioux, from similar causes, and their grievances have been of as long standing. They have often importuned for redress, but in vain. In the spring preceding the Sioux massacre, Hole-in-the-Day visited Washington to expose their grievances; but an audience was so long delayed by those in authority that he returned in disgust, and advised a junction with the Sioux.

This was prevented by their hereditary enmity toward the latter, and the interposition and promises of the Hon. Henry M. Rice, and other whites who had influence with them, and by a solemn treaty that their wrongs should be inquired into by commissioners (who were then appointed) and forthwith redressed. Over a year has elapsed, and no such examination or redress has been authorized by the government.

Last winter a number of the chiefs were taken to Washington, and there, *in the absence of their braves and head men*, a treaty was agreed to for the cession of a part of their lands. The chiefs passed through St. Paul on their return, and were then in a state of beastly intoxication. The Indians were dissatisfied with their action, and put one of them to death.

ways has been likened, were able to bring into the field only 1910 warriors, of whom 250 were their negro slaves, and occupied only 47,000 square miles of territory. The United States sent against them more than 20,000 men, and paid $20,000,000 to militia and volunteers, or to compensate losses incurred by citizens, *exclusive of the expenditures pertaining to the regular army*. Blood-hounds were used to hunt them down; a reward of $200 was given for every Indian killed; 750 Creek Indians were employed to assist the whites; the best generals in the service were placed in command, including General Scott; and yet the United States had to abandon the attempt to remove all the Seminoles from the country, and were forced at last to make a treaty with them.

The very fact of a treaty being made at Washington and not at home is ominous of danger. Recollect the treaties of 1858, which were there made with the Sioux chiefs. From that time they lost all influence with their young men, who believed they had been bribed with *presents.*

The magazine of combustibles which have been accumulating for years is rapidly approaching repletion, and the spark of fire will not be wanting. The Sioux war, when the minds of the people were in such a condition, grew out of the breaking of a few hens' eggs.

What shall be done?

1. Place an adequate force for security upon every reservation, and keep it there. Men can easily be induced to volunteer for such service. It will be cheaper than afterward to employ ten times the number of experienced troops, who are needed elsewhere, after hundreds of people are massacred and their property destroyed.

2. Let the commissioners, who were appointed in good faith by the Indians and the state authorities, with the concurrence of Commissioner Doll, of the Indian Department, for the adjustment of grievances, be empowered to proceed, and let ample reparation be made.

3. Pay the Indians henceforth their dues in full. If robberies are committed by Indians, deduct the value of the article stolen from the annuity *due the culprit,* and not from the general fund of all, and let this not be done on an *ex-parte* statement, but after a full examination, in which the accused shall have an opportunity to be heard.

4. Let the stipulations of the treaties for farming implements, seeds, goods, etc., be fully carried out.

These three last recommendations have been guaranteed to the Indians by solemn treaty.

5. Remove the traders from the reservations, and let the government furnish the Indians with goods; also prohibit all traffic on credit between the whites and Indians by making the contract void. The traders now engaged in the business should be fully remunerated for the loss they will incur, as they embarked in the trade in good faith.

6. Justice and humanity require that, as we have deprived the Indian of his occupation of hunting and the indulgence of the wild habits of centuries, we should make a *genuine attempt* to have him adapt himself to his altered condition. Such an attempt has never yet been *made*, although the treaties contemplate it, and the officials pretend it has been done. A proper code of laws and policy, having in view this end, should be adopted, and their administration intrusted to the *state government*, which should also be made the medium for the disbursement of the goods, etc., due under the treaties. The federal government is never awakened to the corruption, inefficiency, and want of knowledge which pervades the Indian Department until some awful catastrophe shocks the public heart, and then it quickly relapses again into its accustomed lethargy. I recently saw in the Herald an editorial note that serious charges against the department had been handed in for publication, but that the public were too much occupied with more important matters to justify any notice of them.

Let the officer intrusted with the administration of

Indian affairs be responsible to a people whose lives and fortunes are dependent upon the performance of his duties, and whose situation is such as to enable them to know when he does perform them, and we shall have fewer massacres and less sins to answer for as a nation. Penn treated the Indians honestly and fairly, and for nearly a century the history of the commonwealth which he founded was unstained by the bloody records of barbarities which characterize the annals of the other states.

The Chippeways are less warlike than the Sioux, and having been accustomed to live more upon fish, and upon wild rice and corn, than upon the products of the chase, will be the more easily induced to adopt the habit of cultivating the soil; and much of their land is of such a nature as not to be speedily needed by the whites. If the government will take prompt and proper action in the premises, "out of the nettle danger we may pluck the flower safety." The tide of travel which was setting across the continent for the distant Pacific, so suddenly checked, will flow on again with redoubled volume—the buffalo, who has come far within the former bounds of civilization, speed away—the scarred and devastated fields wave once more with the bounteous harvest—the blighted homestead rear its peaceful walls, clad with clambering vines, and vocal with the songs of happy childhood; and the "North Star State," the state of lakes, and streams, and bounteous lands, and healthful, invigorating air, and steel-blue skies, become in the future, as it has been in the past, the resort of the emigrant from every clime.

APPENDIX.

As confirmatory of some of the statements and views contained in the foregoing pages, I append the following Missionary Paper issued by the "Bishop Seabury Mission" of Minnesota in January, 1863.

AN APPEAL FOR THE RED MAN.

By Bishop Whipple, of Minnesota.

There are times when the Christian laborer has the right to ask for the sympathy, the prayers, and the co-operation of all good men; for this reason I ask the calm attention of my fellow-citizens to an appeal in behalf of one of the most wretched races of heathen men on the earth. I do not make this plea simply for a heathen race—I plead for every interest which is dear to my heart. The fair fame of the state, the blessing of God upon the nation, the protection of peaceful citizens from savage violence, the welfare of our children, and the prosperity of the Church of Christ, are bound up in our settlement of this Indian question. It is too late to shrink from responsibility. The fearful issues are upon us, and as we settle them justly or unjustly, we shall receive the blessing or the curse of Almighty God.

It is not a pleasant task to make an appeal where excited public feeling may arouse unkind suspicions and unjust accusations. Few men love more than myself the approval of their fellow-citizens, and none desire more the affection of those among whom they labor. I dare not be silent; I fear less the reproaches of the people than the anger of God.

The nation has heard of the most fearful Indian massacre in history; but those who live remote from the border can have no idea of the awful horrors which have accompanied the desolation of two hundred miles of the fairest country on the earth. Many of these victims of savage ferocity were my friends. They had mingled their voices with mine in prayer; they had given to me such hospitality as can only be found in the log cabin of the frontier. It fills my heart with grief, and blinds my eyes with tears, whenever I think of their nameless graves. It is because I love them, and would save others from their fate, that I ask that the people shall lay the blame of this great crime where it belongs, and rise up with one voice to demand the reform of an atrocious Indian system, which has always garnered for us the same fruit of anguish and blood.

There is not a man in America who ever gave an hour's calm reflection to this subject who does not know that our Indian system is an organized system of robbery, and has been for years a disgrace to the nation. It has left savage men without governmental control; it has looked on unconcerned at every crime against the law of God and man; it has fostered savage life by wasting thousands of dollars in the purchase of paint, beads, scalping-knives, and tomahawks;* it has fostered a system of trade which robbed the thrifty and virtuous to pay the debts of the indolent and vicious; it has squandered the funds for civilization and schools; it has connived at theft; it has winked at murder; and at last, after dragging the savage down to a brutishness unknown to his fathers, it has brought a harvest of blood to our own door.

It was under this Indian system that the fierce, warlike Sioux were fitted and trained to be the actors in this bloody drama; and the same causes are to-day slowly but surely preparing the way for a Chippeway war. There is not to-day an old citizen of Minnesota who will not shrug his shoulders as he speaks of the dishonesty which accompanied the purchase of the lands of the Sioux. It left in savage minds a deep sense of injustice. There followed ten years of savage life, unchecked by law, and uninfluenced by good example. They were taught by white men that lying was no disgrace, adultery no sin, and theft no crime. Their hunting-grounds were gone; the onward march of civilization crowded them on every side. Their only possible hope of being saved from starvation was the fidelity with which a great nation fulfilled its plighted faith, which before God and man it had pledged to its heathen wards. The people here on the border, and the rulers at Washington, know how that faith has been broken. The constant irritations of such a system would in time have secured an Indian massacre. It was hastened and precipitated by the sale of nearly 800,000 acres of land, for which they never received one farthing, for it was all absorbed in claims. Then came the story (and it was true) that half of their annuity money had also been taken

* In the advertisement for Indian supplies during the autumn of the Sioux massacre were 100 doz. scalping-knives, 600 lbs. of beads, 100 doz. butcher-knives, 150 lbs. of paint.

for claims. They waited two months, mad, exasperated, hungry—the agent utterly powerless to undo the wrong committed at Washington—and they resolved on savage vengeance. For every dollar of which they have been defrauded we shall pay ten dollars in the cost of this war. It has been so for fifty years, it will be so again. God's retributive justice always has compelled a people to reap exactly what they have permitted to be sown. In the Chippeway country there was the same wretched policy, and, if possible, tenfold more of wrong. They had seen an innocent woman die by the brutal violence of white men. They knew that fictitious amounts were certified to, and dead men's names placed on the pay-rolls. They saw disease and death holding a carnival in every Indian village, and they knew that much of their sorrow was a cup of degradation which we had given them to drink. They have always been our friends, and, hoping against hope, have waited for the tardy justice of white men. Last fall a crafty leader sought to use these elements of discontent to excite an Indian outbreak, and, had it not been that there was a Christian Indian clergyman, and faithful Indian friends to give us warning, there would have been another devastated border. That Indian clergyman lost his all by his fidelity. His eldest son, then sick, died in consequence of that night journey; another child is lying at the point of death; and his wife is broken-hearted with grief and care. His Indian friends were many of them also sufferers from the anger of their savage people, but they felt overpaid by having saved their white friends from death. The Indian Commissioner, the Secretary of the Interior, the Clerk of the Department, all knew these facts, and pledged these men, in the name of their Great Father, ample reward and protection for their fidelity, and that the leaders in this attempted insurrection should be punished. The Legislature of the state also sent a commission to the Indian country, and they made pledges in a solemn treaty that all past wrongs should be redressed. Has any such examination been made? any effort made to redress these wrongs? The Indian chiefs say that the government has rewarded the wrongdoer,* whom they can prove had made a treaty with Little Crow, and they also say that the reason of this reward is that he knew too much of the past robberies of his own people. They warn us that the government is teaching their young men that they will be losers to follow the advice of good chiefs, and that we will surely secure a bolder outbreak and massacre. They complain that no discrimination is ever made between the good and the bad Indian; that no law punishes

* Hole-in-the-Day.

the one or protects the other; that no efforts are made to redress their wrongs; that no help is offered them to become like white men; that we are crowding them into their graves; and that, however much they desire peace, the time is coming when we shall compel them to a choice of deaths. After months of waiting for the fulfillment of these pledges, these Indians have received at the hands of their agent a treaty, which they are urged to sign at once. The alternative is peaceable or forcible removal. This treaty provides that they shall relinquish all their reservations, many of which are valuable, and receive as payment therefor a tract of country, much of it so poor that it is absolutely valueless. Any white man who has traveled over that country knows that these Indians can not live on that proposed reservation without they are aided far beyond the provisions of this treaty. It has filled the friendly Indians with sorrow, and the bad with anger. A chief who did as much as any man to prevent a Chippeway war said in the council that he thought their Great Father would never have asked Indians to give up their homes, who had lived in peace with the white man, and been so faithful to them. He said that no confidence can be placed in white men's words, for they have again and again made promises which they have broken. He said, "Before you came to us we had plenty and were happy, but since we sold you our land we are growing poorer and poorer every day. If you will take away our annuities, you may do so; we can not leave our country; we love the place where good braves and chiefs closed their eyes; we love our country as much as you love your great city at Washington, named after your great chief; we can not leave it." This feeling that our faith has been broken is common among the Chippeways. During the last summer I visited the Indians at Red Lake. After the services, the head chief came to me and said, "You have spoken good words to us; you are the servant of the Great Spirit. I want you to go and see my people's gardens, and then I will ask your advice." I took the chief's pony, and rode four miles through cornfields, every acre of which was cultivated with the hoe. I ate new corn and new potatoes from these gardens the first week in August. My interpreter counted twenty-nine sacks of last year's corn in one lodge, and we hardly found a lodge without plenty of old corn. On my return the chief said, "You have seen my people; they have plenty; they are not hungry. Our Great Father is about to send a commissioner here to buy our land; I have noticed that whenever Indians sell their lands to their Great Father, they always perish. I should be sorry to have my people become like the Indians at Crow

Wing. Will the bishop tell me all that he has in his head?" Never did my cheeks mantle as they did then with shame. What could I say? If I told him what I knew, no treaty could have been made, and I could not afford to have the government accuse me of preventing the making of an Indian treaty. I simply said, "I am a spiritual chief; I have no right to say one word about treaties; I can advise you what to do when you do sell your land. Select your home, not for its game, but as a place where you can live as white men, by labor. Take your pay, not in paint, beads, and hatchets, but in implements of labor. Try to become like white men; embrace the white man's religion; the Great Spirit will bless you, and you will save your people."

Recently I received a message from an old chief: it was a story he told his young men: "A very nice and pretty bird of all colors came and sang beside our village; a voice said, 'Listen not to him; pay no heed to his song; look not on his colors:' he went away. He came again with finer colors and sweeter songs, and he continued to do so until we heard him, and he led us away to die. The bird is the *big knives*, his songs are his fair words and lying promises, his colors are the paints, the beads, and goods he gives for our country: woe to us, for the day we hear the big knives' words we go to our graves."

Our Indian clergyman writes to me: "Do, dear bishop, do all you can for my dying people; to-day, if we had never seen the white man, we would be a hundred times better off; our only hope is in you; if you fail we shall perish; that the good bishop may yet be the means of doing much good to our oppressed people, in private and public we make our devotions. We have remembered him at the throne of grace, and may he, as our spiritual parent, live many days, and be the means of the salvation of our people." Can I hear the cry of this wretched people and be silent? Can I see these wrongs and not speak out? I should be ashamed of my manhood if I dared to be silent; I should be recreant to my awful trust as shepherd of souls!

I shall be told it is too late to reform. It is never too late to redress wrong. It will cost time, labor, and money. This course of injustice will provoke a Chippeway war, and our people can imagine what that war will be when savage foes have wilderness hiding-places filled with lakes, swamps, and thickets 300 miles long and 300 miles broad. Such a war we tried in Florida. After long years of wasted treasure and precious lives sacrificed, we may hunt them out. But the most expensive justice would be a thousand-fold cheaper. The chiefs among the Chippeways desire peace; they dread a war more than we do. This whole question can be settled whenever good men can say to them your people shall be cared for honestly and faithfully; but mere promises will not answer. On my recent visit they plead with me for hours, and asked me to write their old friend Wabah Manomin (Senator Rice) to come and settle all these questions. But they say truly an unjust treaty will never be approved by the Indians. It must lead to war. The people, who have no interest in the gains of this wicked system, are desirous for such reform; but the agitations, the threats of public speakers, the retaliatory measures offered in the Legislature, are all read by half-bloods on the border, and repeated with exaggeration to Indians, and they are like goads to drive them to madness.

There are questions pressing upon us more grave than the hanging of a few hundred Indian prisoners. They concern a nation's broken faith and the reform of a crying evil. Deeply as our people feel on the question of slavery, they may see here on the border a system which in curses to body and soul, in the loss of manhood, home, and heaven, has worked out a degradation to Red men which slavery never has done for the African race.

For openly asking this reform I have been accused of sympathy with savage crimes. The story was sent out on the wings of the wind that my absence from my diocese was to secure pardon for savage murderers, when the truth was that I visited Washington at the request of the governor to secure protection for our defenseless people, and I delayed my return simply to secure relief for our poor homeless sufferers. I have no desire to condemn individuals. There have been Indian traders and Indian agents who have desired to do their duty, but they were utterly powerless. The blame of the Sioux massacre does not lie at the agent's door. The same system which has destroyed Indian missions has fettered them. I submit to every man the question whether the time has not come for a nation to hear the cry of wrong, if not for the sake of the heathen, for the sake of the memory of our friends whose bones are bleaching on our prairies. I should feel less sad at this history of sorrow if I did not see that in Canada there has never been an Indian massacre or an Indian war. They are not compelled, as we, to remove the Indians or live in terror. They spend a hundredth part in preventing that we spend in suppressing Indian outbreaks. Their missions are prospered and ours are blasted—they live in peace, and we live in perpetual strife.

More than a year ago I felt that we were living over a slumbering volcano; I felt sure that the day was at hand when it would burst forth; I plead with all the earnestness of a man pleading for his home; and I believe, if my prayer had been heard, there would be no widowed wives, nor orphaned children, nor blackened homes from this savage war. Last fall I sent another petition to our chief magistrate signed by all of our Northern Bishops, and many of the first clergy and laity in the nation. It was as follows:

To his Excellency the President of the United States:

SIR,—We respectfully call your attention to the recent Indian outbreak, which has desolated one of the fairest portions of our country, as demanding the careful examination of the government.

The history of our relations with the Indian tribes of North America shows that after they enter into treaty stipulations with the United States a rapid deterioration always takes place. They become degraded, liable to savage outbreaks, often incited to war, until at last the wretched remnant perish from the face of the earth.

It is believed that much of this record has been the result of fundamental errors in the policy of the government, which thwarts its kind intentions toward this hopeless race. We therefore respectfully call your attention to the following suggestions:

First, That it is impolitic for our government to treat a heathen community living within our borders as an independent nation, but that they ought to be regarded as our wards. So far as we know, the English government has never had an Indian war in Canada, while we have seldom passed a year without one.

Second, That it is dangerous to ourselves and to them to leave these Indian tribes without a government, not subject to our own laws, and where every corrupt influence of the border must inevitably foster a spirit of revenge leading to murder and war.

Third, That the solemn responsibility of the care of a heathen race requires that the agent and servants of the government who have them in charge shall be men of eminent fitness, and in no case should such offices be regarded as a reward for political service.

Fourth, That every feeling of honor and of justice demands that the Indian funds which we hold from them as a trust shall be carefully expended under some well-devised system which will encourage their efforts toward civilization.

Fifth, That the present system of Indian trade is mischievous and demoralizing, and ought to be so amended as to protect the Indian, and wholly to prevent the possibility of the sale of the patrimony of the tribe to satisfy individual debts.

Sixth, That it is believed that the history of our dealings with the Indians has been marked by gross acts of injustice and robbery, such as could not be prevented under the present system of management, and that these wrongs have often proved the prolific cause of war and bloodshed. It is due to these helpless Red men that these evils shall be redressed, and without this we can not hope for the blessing of Almighty God in our efforts to secure permanent peace and tranquillity on our western border.

We feel that these results can not be secured without much careful thought, and therefore request you to take such steps as may be necessary to appoint a commission of men of high character, who have no political ends to subserve, to whom may be referred this whole question, in order that they may devise a more perfect system for the administration of Indian affairs, which shall redress these wrongs, preserve the honor of the government, and call down upon us the blessings of God.

H. B. Whipple, Bishop of Minnesota.
T. H. Clark, Bishop of Rhode Island.
Jackson Kemper, Bishop of Wisconsin.
C. S. Hawks, Bishop of Missouri.
George Burgess, Bishop of Maine.
Henry J. Whitehouse, Bishop of Illinois.
Alonzo Potter, Bishop of Pennsylvania.
Carlton Chase, Bishop of New Hampshire.
Alfred Lee, Bishop of Delaware.
Charles P. M'Ilvaine, Bishop of Ohio.
B. B. Smith, Bishop of Kentucky.
Manton Eastburn, Bishop of Massachusetts.
Horatio Potter, Bishop of New York.
G. T. Bedell, Assistant Bishop of Ohio.
S. P. Parker, Rector of St. Paul's Church, Stockton.
Geo. C. Shattuck, Deputy from Massachusetts.
Andrew Oliver, Rec. Immanuel Ch., Bellows Falls, Vt.
J. L. Clark, Rector St. John's Ch., Waterbury, Conn.
M. Schuyler, Rector of Christ Church, St. Louis.
T. Wilcoxon, Missionary in Minnesota.
R. S. Adams, Rector St. Andrew's Ch., Brooklyn, N. Y.
Francis Chase, Rec. St. Andrew's Ch., Hopkinton, N. H.
Alex. Burgess, Rector St. Luke's Ch., Portland, Maine.

John W. Andrews, of Ohio.
Erastus Burr, of Ohio.
Wm. Welsh, of Philadelphia.
Murray Hoffman, of New York.
Isaac Atwater, Ass. Justice Supreme Court, Minn.
Jos. C. Talbot, Missionary Bishop of Northwest.
Wm. Bacon Stevens, Assist. Bishop of Pennsylvania.
Henry W. Lee, Bishop of Diocese of Iowa.
George Upfold, Bishop of Indiana.
Nicholas Hoppin, Rec. Christ Ch., Cambridge, Mass.
John E. Warren, of St. Paul.
E. T. Wilder, Red Wing, Minnesota.
L. Bradish, of New York.
Samuel B. Ruggles, of New York.
Fred. S. Winston, of New York.

I am sick at heart; I fear the words of one of our statesmen to me were true: "Bishop, every word you say of this Indian system is true; the nation knows it. It is useless; you will not be heard. Your faith is only like that of the man that stood on the bank of the river waiting for the water to run by that he might cross over dry shod." All I have to say is, that if a nation trembling on the brink of anarchy and ruin is so dead that it will not hear a plea to redress wrongs which the whole people admit call for reform, God in mercy pity us and our children. H. B. Whipple, Bishop of Minnesota.

Since the bishop prepared the foregoing paper, I have received the following letter from Mr. George Bunga, of Leech Lake. I would state that Mr. Bunga is a mixed blood of African and Chippeway descent, and from my personal knowledge of him for many years past I know him to be entirely reliable in his statements, and from a residence in the country described by him I can bear witness to the truth of them. J. Lloyd Breck.

Leech Lake, January 28th, 1863.

To Rev. J. Lloyd Breck:

Reverend Sir,—Knowing your feelings, and those of the bishop, for the Red men, I thought I would write you and let you know what was going on in Indian matters in this part of the country. Nothing that we could say could prevail on the Red Lake Indians to get them to go to Washington to make a treaty, they had it so firmly in their minds that once they got there they would have to accept of what was offered them. They said they were willing to meet any one at the Grand Forks next summer, and there sell their lands. Most of the annuity chiefs have got back from the agency, where they were called to sign a treaty that had been dictated and left by Judge Usher. They did not sign it. The purport of the treaty was, that all the Mississippi bands would abandon their reserves, and settle on a tract of country lying between this and Cass, and Winnipeg Lakes. The judge must have got the idea from maps, or some person that wanted to have something to say and did not care what he said, or probably some one had an axe of his own to grind, and after ground, would not care what became of the Indians, or the whites that may be living with them. The idea is ridiculous to us who know the country. The most of it is swamps, marshes, or the kind of country that produces the small, black, low pine. There are only a few small lakes, but there is no fish or rice in them. The government land at Cass Lake is nothing but this yellow pine and sand, and the whole of that country is destitute of any kind of game, and even rabbits are but few. It is true, at this lake there is a fair view for them to get along, and their children after them, and in such a kind of country, with one tenth of the money that the government has already spent for them, would induce them, little by little, and would hope to become another people, and their children would be enabled to mingle among the civilized world. I am led to believe why their chances to benefit the Indians, and to agree with the wishes of the government are not acted on, is because that persons are sent, and too often they are men who pay no attention, for the reason they are afraid they would not come within their jurisdiction, and of course would be no benefit to their pockets, and some of them would be against any thing of the kind if it did not suit them. Few persons are so well acquainted with the Chippeways and their former country as myself, for I have lived with almost every band from Sault St. Mary to this, and am well acquainted with all their lakes and rivers, from the Lakes Superior to Michigan, and I honestly say I don't know of a lake or river that abounds in fish as the Red Lake, and Red Lake River, and from thence up the Thieving River. From the first time I became acquainted with these rivers it seemed to me it was designed by the Great Spirit for the home of the Indians. There is every thing to make them content. Plenty of good land (part prairie), and fish right at their doors. The objection I see, that there is not so many maple-trees as could be wished for, but perhaps some could be found in the interior. Reverend sir, it looks to me that we have got to a crisis that has not been known in this country. The Indians are very much dissatisfied, and the whites below won't have the Indians about them any more, and we all feel that something has got to be done. There is some government land, but it is and has always been occupied by these Indians as their sugar-camp. At the time of their treaty of 1855 they were given to understand that they might use it, and the whites would not want it for one hundred years to come. Knowing the country as I do, I am aware that there is not five sugar-camps within two days' travel of this lake that was belonging to the Leech Lake Indians, and if the Lower Indians are moved on their lands, they will have to occupy those sugar-camps, and thence would come the strife among themselves and dissatisfaction against the whites, and perhaps the cause of more trouble. Of late years these Indians have had as hard times for want of food in the summer as they have in the winter; the only difference is the warm weather, and berries and roots. There is not one half of the fish caught now that there was at the time you resided at this lake; in fact, we know that it can't be otherwise when we know that every day there is from three to four hundred nets in the water, and from eight hundred to one thousand Indians living by them. Reverend sir, how can it be expected that Indians can live in such a country as I have described, which I defy any one to say to the contrary. It is to be supposed that they will hear of the kind of country that they are required to settle on, and it is my poor opinion that they will never go unless the soldiers drive and keep them there. Even if they went there they can't get an existence without they rob and plunder the whites, and thence perhaps the beginning of the extermination of these Indians. Pardon me if I say here, that if the government is induced to move and keep these Indians, what will be the cost. I am to be pitied for writing as I do; would it not be more satisfactory to the government, and thousands of dollars cheaper, to move them at once to a suitable country, and where they would be out of the way of the whites?

I wrote to Senator Rice a few days ago, and stated to him about the Red Lake Country, but was not so particular in defining as here, for I don't see how the Indians can be friends to the whites in such a state of affairs. Another question, Who is the person that can straighten out things and make the path smooth? Such a man is now wanted. Of late the Indians have been so mixed up that now they have no confidence in the government or its officers. I presume the bad health of Senator Rice would not allow him to come to this wild country, for I candidly believe he is the only man that can make a removal of the Indians satisfactory to them, for it must be taken into consideration that it is ten times more difficult to move Indians than it is to make a treaty to buy their lands. Senator Rice has this in favor more than any one else that could be sent by the government. Every trader and half-breed, or any person of influence, are his friends, and that is a good deal in removing Indians; and these people have always told them that he was the friend of the Indian, and would do every thing in justice that lay in his power for them. The cry is, I wish Wabe Manomin would come to us once more. They have that respect for him that in their smoking and camp-fires it is seldom but that they speak of him. My sincere wish is that the Indian Department at Washington only knew what a suitable country there was vacant for the permanent home of the Chippeways; it appears to me it would be adopted, for it is of no use to the whites, and it would agree with one of the great wishes of the government by placing the Indian where he would not be in the way of the white population, and, with some care on the part of the government, the ruination of all Indians (fire-water) could be kept from him.

Reverend sir, what I have written is strictly true; and how proud I would be if I saw some person (disinterested, and some sympathy and justice to the Indians), to be here at the opening of the Lakes, say the 25th of April, and see the country that I have here written about; I feel confident that my opinion would be the opinion of all who wished for the existence of the Chippeways some years longer. I write of this country because I know that there is no other part of the former Chippeway country that they can be moved to and live.

Reverend sir, knowing how hard the bishop works for the welfare of the Indian, I beg of you to show him this, my poor opinion as regards the removal of the Indians. I ought to have said, too, that the Otter Tail band was ordered by Judge Usher to come on their reserves at this lake. So they will have to get a share of these sugar-camps; for you are aware that a Chippeway without fish, or the means to make sugar, would be as strange to him as a white man without a shirt. Your unworthy servant, G. BUNGA.

THE END.

GENERAL MARCY'S HAND-BOOK FOR OVERLAND EXPEDITIONS. The Prairie Traveler. A Hand-Book for Overland Emigrants. With Maps, Illustrations, and Itineraries of the Principal Routes between the Mississippi and the Pacific. By Colonel RANDOLPH B. MARCY, U. S. A. *Published by Authority of the War Department.* Small 12mo, Cloth, $1 00.

LOSSING'S FIELD-BOOK OF THE REVOLUTION. Pictorial Field-Book of the Revolution; or, Illustrations by Pen and Pencil of the History, Biography, Scenery, Relics, and Traditions of the War for Independence. By BENSON J. LOSSING. 2 vols. 8vo, Cloth, $10 00; Sheep extra, $11 25.

CREASY'S FIFTEEN DECISIVE BATTLES. The Fifteen Decisive Battles of the World; from Marathon to Waterloo. By E. S. CREASY, A.M. 12mo, Cloth, $1 25.

ALISON'S MILITARY LIFE OF MARLBOROUGH. Military Life of John, Duke of Marlborough. With Maps. 12mo, Cloth, $1 75.

MOTLEY'S DUTCH REPUBLIC. The Rise of the Dutch Republic. A History. By JOHN LOTHROP MOTLEY. With a Portrait of William of Orange. 3 vols. 8vo, Cloth, $7 50.

MOTLEY'S UNITED NETHERLANDS. History of the United Netherlands: from the Death of William the Silent to the Synod of Dort, With a full View of the English-Dutch Struggle against Spain, and of the Origin and Destruction of the Spanish Armada. By JOHN LOTHROP MOTLEY, LL.D., D.C.L., Author of "The Rise of the Dutch Republic." 2 vols. 8vo, Cloth, $5 00.

HARPER & BROTHERS'

LIST OF NEW BOOKS.

☞ *Mailing Notice.—*Harper & Brothers *will send their Books by Mail, postage free (for any distance in the United States under 1500 miles), on receipt of the Price.*

☞ *HARPER'S CATALOGUE may be obtained gratuitously, on application to the Publishers personally, or by letter, inclosing Six Cents in Postage Stamps.*

A HISTORY OF THE INTELLECTUAL DEVELOPMENT OF EUROPE. By John William Draper, Professor of Chemistry and Physiology in the University of New York; Author of a "Treatise on Human Physiology," &c., &c. 8vo, Cloth, $3 50.

MEMOIR OF THE LIFE AND CHARACTER OF THE LATE HON. THEO. FRELINGHUYSEN, LL.D. By Talbot W. Chambers. With Portrait on Steel. 12mo, Cloth, $1 25.

A POINT OF HONOR. A Novel. 8vo, Paper, 25 cents.

LIFE ON A GEORGIAN PLANTATION. Journal of a Residence on a Georgian Plantation in 1838-1839. By Frances Anne Kemble. 12mo, Cloth, $1 25

THE CAPITAL OF THE TYCOON: A Narrative of a Three Years' Residence in Japan. By Sir RUTHERFORD ALCOCK, K.C.B., Her Majesty's Envoy Extraordinary and Minister Plenipotentiary in Japan. With Maps and Engravings. 2 vols. 12mo, Cloth, $3 00.

HARPER'S HAND-BOOK FOR TRAVELLERS IN EUROPE AND THE EAST: being a Guide through France, Belgium, Holland, Germany Austria, Italy, Sicily, Egypt, Syria, Turkey, Greece, Switzerland, Russia, Denmark, Sweden, Spain, and Great Britain and Ireland. By W. PEMBROKE FETRIDGE. With a Map embracing Colored Routes of Travel in the above Countries, and a new Railroad Map. Revised and Enlarged Edition. Large 12mo, Cloth, $3 00; Leather Tucks, $3 50.

ELEANOR'S VICTORY. A Novel. By the Author of "Aurora Floyd." 8vo, Paper, 50 cents.

JOHN MARCHMONT'S LEGACY. A Novel. By the Author of "Aurora Floyd." (*In Press.*)

LIVE IT DOWN. A Story of the Light Lands. By J. C. JEAFFRESON, Author of "Olive Blake's Good Work," "Isabel; the Young Wife and the Old Love," &c. 8vo, Paper, 50 cents.

M'GREGOR'S SYSTEM OF LOGIC. A System of Logic, comprising a Discussion of the various Means of acquiring and retaining Knowledge, and avoiding Error. By P. M'GREGOR, A.M. 12mo, Cloth, $1 00; Sheep, $1 25.

MISS MULOCK'S FAIRY STORIES. The Fairy Book. The best Popular Fairy Stories selected and rendered anew. By the Author of "John Halifax, Gentleman," "Olive," "The Ogilvies," &c., &c. Illustrations. 16mo, Cloth, $1 00.

ST. OLAVE'S. A Novel. 8vo, Paper, 50 cents.

A FIRST FRIENDSHIP. A Tale. 8vo, Paper, 25 cents.

KNAPP'S FRENCH READING-BOOK. CHRESTOMATHIE FRANÇAISE; Containing I. Selections from the best French Writers, with Copious References to the Author's French Grammar. II. The Master-Pieces of Molière, Racine, Boileau, and Voltaire; with Explanatory Notes, a Glossary of Idiomatic Phrases, and a Vocabulary. By William J. Knapp, A.M., Professor of Modern Languages and Literature in Madison University, N. Y. 12mo, Cloth, $1 25.

HOOKER'S NATURAL PHILOSOPHY. Science for the School and Family. Part I. Natural Philosophy. By Worthington Hooker, M.D., Professor of the Theory and Practice of Medicine in Yale College, Author of "Child's Book of Nature," "Natural History," "First Book in Chemistry," &c. Illustrated by nearly 300 Engravings. 12mo, Cloth, $1 25.

CHRONICLES OF CARLINGFORD. A Novel. By Mrs. Oliphant, Author of "The Life of Edward Irving," "The Last of the Mortimers," "The Days of My Life," "The Laird of Norlaw," "The House on the Moor," &c. 8vo, Paper, 75 cents; Cloth, $1 00.

KINGLAKE'S CRIMEAN WAR. The Invasion of the Crimea: its Origin, and an Account of its Progress down to the Death of Lord Raglan. By ALEXANDER WILLIAM KINGLAKE. With Maps and Plans. 2 vols. 12mo, Cloth. (*Vol. I., Price* $1 50, *just ready.*)

THE BOYHOOD OF MARTIN LUTHER; or, the Sufferings of the Heroic Little Beggar-Boy, who afterward became the Great German Reformer. By HENRY MAYHEW, Author of "Young Benjamin Franklin," "The Peasant-Boy Philosopher, or the Life of Ferguson the Astronomer;" "The Wonders of Science, or Young Humphrey Davy," &c. With Illustrations. Small 12mo, Cloth gilt. (*In Press.*)

SYLVIA'S LOVERS. A Novel. By Mrs. GASKELL, Author of "Mary Barton," "Cranford," "My Lady Ludlow," "North and South," "The Moorland Cottage," "Right at Last," &c. 8vo, Paper, 50 cents.

A DARK NIGHT'S WORK. A Tale. By Mrs. GASKELL, Author of "Sylvia's Lovers," "Mary Barton," &c. 8vo, Paper, 25 cents.

GENERAL BUTTERFIELD'S CAMP AND OUTPOST DUTY. Camp and Outpost Duty for Infantry. With Standing Orders, Extracts from the Revised Regulations for the Army, Rules for Health, Maxims for Soldiers, and Duties of Officers. By DANIEL BUTTERFIELD, Major-Gen. Vols., U. S. A. *Approved by the War Department.* 18mo, Flexible Cloth, 60 cents.

www.ingramcontent.com/pod-product-compliance
Lightning Source LLC
LaVergne TN
LVHW010147110826
845151LV00002B/443

* 9 7 8 1 4 2 5 5 3 7 0 4 3 *